Behavior
Modification
in
Clinical Psychology

Century Psychology Series

Kenneth MacCorquodale
Gardner Lindzey
Kenneth E. Clark

Editors

Contributors

DONALD M. BAER, *University of Kansas*
JUDITH ELBERT FAVELL, *University of Kansas*
FREDERICK H. KANFER, *University of Cincinnati*
LEONARD KRASNER, *State University of New York (Stony Brook)*
MALCOLM KUSHNER *(Miami, Florida)*
OGDEN R. LINDSLEY, *University of Kansas*
JACK L. MICHAEL, *Western Michigan University*
CHARLES NEURINGER, *University of Kansas*
GERALD R. PATTERSON, *Oregon Research Institute*
JOHN B. REID, *University of Wisconsin*
ROGER E. ULRICH, *Western Michigan University*
MONTROSE M. WOLF, *University of Kansas*

Behavior Modification in Clinical Psychology

edited by

CHARLES NEURINGER
University of Kansas

JACK L. MICHAEL
Western Michigan University

Appleton-Century-Crofts

Educational Division

New York Meredith Corporation

To my parents
C. N.

Preface

This volume is the outgrowth of the proceedings of the Ninth Annual Institute for Research in Clinical Psychology, sponsored by the University of Kansas, Department of Psychology. The Institute was held at the University of Kansas campus on April 3rd to 5th, 1967. These institutes were initiated by M. Erik Wright of the University of Kansas Psychology Department in the late 1950s. Their focus has been on new developments in research and theory in clinical psychology. The ninth of these institutes concerned the role and place of behavior modification techniques in clinical psychology.

If one uses numbers of journal articles, presentations at professional meetings, books, and the organization of a new APA division as criteria of impact, then behavior modification techniques have, in the span of only a few short years, made an impressive impact on clinical psychological thinking and practice. There can be little doubt as to the success of these techniques in clinical practice. By focusing on modification of specific behavior, the behavior modifier has been able to teach the retarded to care for themselves, to extinguish maladaptive neurotic behavior, to develop verbal tools for the seemingly mute, etc. The papers in this volume reflect the width and depth of the behavior modifier's involvement with the areas of concern for clinical psychology. Attempted solutions to problems having to do with preschool socialization, control of neurotic and psychotic symptoms, psychological and physical rehabilitation of the handicapped, neuropsychiatric ward management, control of human aggression, family interaction "dynamics," and self-regulatory behavior are presented in the following pages. Of special interest and concern to the reader should be Dr. Lindsley's use of Behavior Modification analysis techniques to describe what went on during the Institute, and Dr. Baer's discussion (in the Appendix) of the ethics involved in the use of punishment to shape behavior.

It is our hope that this book will be useful to all clinical psychologists, and especially to those who are not fully acquainted with behavior modification techniques. The papers in this volume will also be of great use to ancillary mental health workers by acquainting them with this particular kind of current psychological practice.

The editors wish to express their gratification to M. Erik Wright for his valuable counseling and assistance in setting up the Institute. To Gerda Brouhard goes a great deal of appreciation for her careful handling of the myriad number of details attending the smooth operation of the Institute. We would also like to thank Donald M. Baer for his general help and advice to the Institute. To Sandra Bunce and Gerda Brouhard goes our gratification for their careful and interested typing of the many manuscripts making up this book. The editors would also like to express their appreciation to Jack K. Burton of Appleton-Century-Crofts for his patience and interest in this volume.

C. N.
J. L. M.

Contents

1: Behavior Modification as the Clinical Psychologist Views It

CHARLES NEURINGER

An increasing number of clinical psychologists have become intrigued with the techniques utilized by Behavior Modification psychologists. Their interest primarily centers around the changes effected among patients and clients by the procedures of Behavior Modification. At the same time an equally large number of clinical psychologists are also distrustful of the Behavior Modifiers because of a series of conceptions they hold about the Behavior Modification movement. The Behavior Modifiers are thought to lack "sympathy" and "feeling" for patients and clients; they are scornful of psychodynamic "depth" explorations of behavior and try to equate human behavior with the responses given by rats in an animal laboratory. However, the belief that most antagonizes the clinical psychologist is the conviction that the Behavior Modifier is as such the precursor of totalitarian thought control.

Some of the above characterizations are the result of breakdowns in communication. Lapses in communication between Behavior Modifiers and the more traditional clinical psychologists have led many members of each group to dichotomize their differences to such an extent that amelioration and rappochement have become somewhat difficult. Dichotomized positions tend to take on with the passage of time an inflexible character, a condition which makes future psychological movement even more difficult. It is hoped that this paper will lead to more moderate stances, and hopefully to mutual acceptance.

Behavior Modifiers have been industrious in spreading their message, but they have sometimes done this with an evangelical belligerence, the main effect of which has been to antagonize other psychologists. How-

The author wishes to express his appreciation and gratitude to Franklin C. Shontz, Anthony J. Smith and Barbara G. Smith, for their time spent in reading this manuscript, and especially for their many valuable suggestions.

1

ever, behind much of the polemical fervor there is much of importance to clinical psychology. One should not be put off by this fervor since the history of psychology tells us that the early Freudians, Gestaltists, and Watsonians were in their day also somewhat overenthusiastic.

Even critics will agree that Behavior Modifiers have, in the span of only a few short years, made an impressive impact on clinical psychological practice and technique. By focusing on the modification of specific behaviors these psychologists have been able to teach the severely mentally retarded to care for themselves; to extinguish self-destructive behavior in autistic and schizophrenic children as well as help them communicate with other children and adults; to relieve various functional speech disorders; to put an end to mutism; and to deal with a variety of motor and ideational symptoms such as fetishisms, tics, smoking, alcoholism, suicidal thoughts, and depressive ruminations. In some instances, the Behavior Modifiers have changed the character of the mental hospital ward through the use of token economy programs, have modified behaviors of whole families, have developed physical rehabilitation techniques, and have been able to extinguish successfully a whole host of maladaptive neurotic and psychotic behaviors. As is often found in psychology, the Behavior Modifier has succeeded where others using the more traditional techniques of clinical psychology have failed. The papers in this volume bear witness to the vast scope of Behavior Modification techniques.

Because many of the Behavior Modifier's accomplishments have been with patients who were thought to be intractable, unmanageable, and hopeless, they have given impetus to a new enthusiasm and optimism in clinical psychology. This new optimism can best be observed in our present day graduate students. These students are less conservative than their clinical psychology university professors, and the students' enthusiasm is only now "leaking up" to their mentors. Why has the Behavior Modification movement been successful? The answer to this question is related to its achievements. When a Behavior Modifier succeeds in getting a mute autistic child to speak, after the child has been silent for seven years (part of which time was spent fruitlessly in psychoanalysis) there is bound to be a positive emotional reaction on the part of the observer.

The efficacy of the Behavior Modification approach lies in its pragmatic and concrete approach to behavior. The history of clinical psychology's therapeutic endeavors is strewn with highly abstract theories and concepts. Psychologists have been trained to think in terms of "gaining insight," "strengthening the ego," "liberating the libido," "interpreting the defenses," "building stress tolerance," "accepting the self as is." Because these concepts appear reasonable and are enmeshed in highly logical theories, they have taken on an aura of face validity. Their logic has been very seductive, and through constant verbal repetition among psychologists they have taken on "truth" status. The mutually agreeing verbal reinforcement given by one psychologist to another psychologist, when discussing these concepts, must be very powerful since the paucity of experimental confirmation does very little to extinguish the behavior.

Aside from their general resistance to being experimentally demonstrated, these conceptualizations have not proved to be readily useful in the teaching of psychotherapy. This is due to the theory's lack of specification as to what particular concrete behaviors are associated with "insight," "ego strength," "libido," "frustration tolerance," "defense mechanisms," "the Self." The Behavior Modifiers, by focusing on changing specific and concretely identifiable behaviors, such as head bangs, nail bites, number of words, or number of bed wets, have been able to change crippling and debilitating behavior to that which is socially acceptable and adaptive.

Clinical psychologists should, for one very important reason, closely examine the Behavior Modification movement. The therapeutic procedures and techniques that Behavior Modifiers utilize come from the Experimental Psychological Laboratory. They did not arise as ancillary developments from medicine. For this reason also, Behavior Modification should have great appeal to all psychologists. Since its procedures with humans are based on controlled research, it represents that much called for rapprochment between experimental and clinical psychology. Here we find a way of dealing with human problems that has been extrapolated from experimental psychology. It has been a fond (and loudly repeated) wish on the part of clinical psychologists that experimental psychologists do something to help them in dealing with patients and clients. They may now be confronted with a response to the wish.

Behavior Modification is a purely psychological approach and as such eschews the medical model of "disease" and "healing." In fact some Behavior Modifiers would like to get rid of terms like "pathology," "deviant," "cure," "neurotic," and replace them with "training," "educational procedures," "problem solving." The medical model and settings that determine the procedures and conceptualizations of many clinical psychologists, have, the Behavior Modifiers point out, inhibited psychology's usefulness, and kept it from broadening and expanding its approaches and techniques because it has shifted the emphasis toward etiology and away from dealing with the directly observable behavior. Recent reports from training conferences in clinical psychology and numerous *American Psychologist* articles written by psychologists, many of whom are not Behavior Modifiers, seem to echo the sentiment about the confining character of the medical model.

The Behavior Modification method can be utilized in a wide variety of settings aside from hospitals and clinics. As can be seen from reading the chapters in this volume, it has been utilized in such places as classrooms, homes, children's camps, therapists' offices, and playgrounds, since its application is not contingent upon the approval of psychiatric jurisprudence. A psychiatrist wishing to use the method would have to learn from, and be supervised by, a psychologist. Since the technique can be taught to many persons, Behavior Modification allows for a broadening of the base of people that can help such patients. The Behavior Modifier stands ready to train nurses, hospital aids, volunteers, Grey Ladies, parents, physicians, teachers, social workers, secretaries, psychiatrists, playmates, or siblings in the methods used in Behavior Modification.

This nonexclusiveness on the part of the Behavior Modifier seems to have upset a few clinical psychologists. Some clinical psychologists feel that there is a mystique about psychotherapy, that there is an elusive and undefinable quality that must be possessed in order to become a good psychotherapist. This feeling of being the guardian of an evanescent and impalpable, omniscience-giving knowledge about how to do psychotherapy is bolstered by having spent a requisite number of years in graduate school, negotiating an internship, and perhaps even a personal psychotherapy, and finally completing a dissertation. It is no wonder that these clinical psychologists become hostile to the Behavior Modifier who is training janitors and hospital aides to shape behavior and thus effect cures.

Uneasiness on the part of the clinical psychologist may also be engendered by the models that the Behavior Modifier has adopted. Some Behavior Modifiers have adopted an educational or "training" model. Since many of the basic laboratory techniques that the Behavior Modifier uses are allied to learning theory, he tends to use a trainer-pupil paradigm. He teaches or trains another person to do so-and-so. There is no mystery about the training—it is straightforward. Another model that is even more unpalatable to the clinical psychologist is that of behavior engineering. Here the paradigm is that of a psychologist arranging and ordering circumstances so that an individual is forced to react in such-and-such a way. It is this latter model which has given rise to cries of "thought control." As in the educational model, the specification of the procedures are straightforward.

Both these models have one thing in common. They both have the same implications for the conceptualization of human difficulties. Both models, since they reject the medical model, remove the stigma of pathology from the unhappiness that has motivated the person to be trained or engineered. Only the client's concrete-observable symptom is dealt with. Whether one conceptualizes the Behavior Modification technique as teaching or engineering, it is not "cure" but the elimination or shaping of particular, specific, concrete behavior that is central to the Behavior Modifier's activities.

It is of interest to note that clinical psychology and Behavior Modification share the same basic methodology—that of the case study. Both work with single individuals. The Behavior Modifier is ideographic in his approach both in the laboratory and in clinical practice. He avoids pooled statistical research designs in favor of the single organism approach, be it pigeons in the laboratory or human beings in the clinic. The Behavior Modifier argues that research designed to yield results in terms of means and standard deviations obscures functional relationships, and is probabilistic ignorance substituted for precision. Such research designs are not, he argues, helpful in making predictions about specific individuals. Clinical psychologists have often concurred about the usefulness of nomothetic methods in clinical psychology.

The Behavior Modifier's case study approach is different from that generally used by clinical psychologists. Although they work with a single individual and inquire into the reinforcement history, they also make careful, precise and quantifiable observations of rates of various behaviors until a stable base rate for these behaviors is established. Then they intervene with a program that attaches certain reinforcement contingencies to the behavior. Then they resume their careful observations of the behavior in order to evaluate the efficacy of the program. What has just been described is the case study method but with greater precision and quantification than is generally found in clinical psychology. The case study method has for a long time ranked low in the prestige hierarchy of psychological methods. The Behavior Modifier, through the use of his laboratory derived techniques, has legitimized the case study.

There are no hard and fast rules for developing programs to modify behavior. Many of the programs described in this volume reflect the variety, and even creative artistry, that these psychologists have used in their modification of behavior. If one program does not achieve the desired goal, another one is tried out. The Behavior Modifiers have been accused of being engineers. This accusation has a highly emotional value judgment flavor. Many Behavior Modifiers would not deny the engineering characterization since they consider themselves to be behavioral engineers who use laboratory derived psychological principles to help individuals achieve new levels of competence.

There are two particular issues that have done much to hinder communication between Behavior Modifiers and clinical psychologists which need to be examined. They are (1) the symptom treatment emphasis in Behavior Modification, and (2) the ethical issues attendant on behavior control techniques.

Behavior Modifiers have de-emphasized etiology. They admit that organisms have complex reinforcement histories and that these have been instrumental in producing the current behavior. They further assert that these histories cannot be changed and that it is the current behavior that is causing the difficulty. It is not as important to know why an autistic child smashes his head against a wall 80 to 100 times a day as it is to stop the behavior. The Behavior Modifiers argue that it is the current behavior that is making people miserable, and that current behavior needs to be changed. The Behavior Modifier is, then, according to the traditionally trained clinical psychologist, dealing only with the symptoms and not with the real causes of behavior. The Behavior Modifier usually responds to this by saying that the "real" causes (if they exist) cannot any longer be handled and one can only deal with current behavior. They also feel that trying to work with "depth" or "real" causes has for the most part proved to be a fruitless procedure for clinical psychologists. The Behavior Modifier equates cause and effect to reinforcement histories and current rates of behavior emission. They feel that to speculate about unobservable and unknowable mediational processes is unscientific and that the reinforcement paradigm is a more economical explanatory tool.

The Behavior Modifier feels that current behavior has been shaped lawfully by the principles of reinforcement and extinction. These concepts are also used to explain maladaptive behavior. Bed-wetting in a child is a behavior that brings attention. The mother will notice and talk to the child. In a family where children receive very little attention from the mother, even admonishments may be powerful reinforcers maintaining the behavior. An arm-biting, self-destructive child is comforted by an aide or nurse, while other children displaying less violent symptoms receive perfunctory attention from overworked hospital staffs. In this volume the reader can find a vast number of illustrations of the Behavior Modifier's views as to the maintenance consequences of symptoms. Their conceptualization is very much like the psychoanalytic concept of symptom secondary gain.

The clinical psychologist can argue that symptom elimination is only temporary; another symptom will develop because the underlying reasons for symptom formation have not been eliminated. To this, the Behavior Modifier replies that many of his studies have indicated that symptom migration does not occur. They also point out that when a substitute symptom (or, to be more explicit, another behavior) arises, then that symptom can also be treated. Treating any number of symptoms is still more economical than long drawn-out therapy, and more humane than allowing the person to suffer. In addition, they also assert that the chance for new symptoms to develop is diminished by the treatment of the major maladaptive behavior because the symptom relief frees the client from a great many unfortunate side effects (tension, anxiety, guilt, etc.). The person is now freed from the symptom, less tense and therefore open to new experiences. Often, by using this technique, the Behavior Modification removes the conditions leading to new symptom formation.

The Behavior Modifier will even go further and argue that in many instances the symptom is the problem and not that "pathology" gives rise to symptoms. In these cases, they feel that when the symptom is eliminated, the person is released from agony and the social deterrents that have been engendered by it. When violent head twitching has been programmed out, the person feels better and is thus able now to meet people without embarrassment. Previously, people shied away from him. His head twitching made him lonely and ashamed of himself. In the same way, the extinction of hitting-other-children behavior makes it possible for a child to make new friends. Symptom removal, aside from diminishing unwanted side effects, makes the individual less repulsive to others. This, in turn, now gives others the chance to approach the individual and even become sources of positive reinforcement. The symptom removal does more than just remove the symptom; it is the occasion for the acquisition of new socially acceptable behavior. This is one of the goals of Behavior Modification. It is done by either extinguishing unwanted behavior by the cessation of reinforcement of the behavior or by having it followed by aversive consequences. If a new response is to be developed (a procedure which the traditional clinical psychologist is loath to do) this is done by attaching new reinforcing consequences to the behavior to be shaped. In order to accomplish this, the Behavior Modifier has to control the patient's environment. He needs to arrange consequences and reinforcers; he needs to engineer the situation in such a way to achieve his goals. And the necessity of these prerequisites have led to ethical questions concerning the control of another person's behavior.

The phrase "controlling of another person's behavior" has taken on very negative connotations. It implies "thought control," "brainwashing," and totalitarian political states, all of which are repellent to Americans. It is unfortunate, but in the minds of many, the Behavior Modifier has become more identified with the negative connotation (brainwashing) than with the positive implications (symptom relief) of control. The aversion is heightened further because the Behavior Modification techniques seem to be very powerful tools that are used successfully and often.

The Behavior Modifier feels that control cannot be avoided or eliminated. Everybody is under the control of other people (e.g., parents, teachers, employers, wives, siblings, professors, platoon sergeants). A person can never be completely controlled by another person because there are too many competing sources of control, and because the controlee also can exert influence over others.

The Behavior Modifier admits that he tries to control behavior. Often he assumes the controlling position at the request of the controlee, as when a client seeks out a therapist for help. The Behavior Modifier also notes that it is very difficult to control completely. The controlee already has a reinforcement history that is affecting his behavior. In addition there are others in the environment (e.g., wife, boss) that are also shaping behavior. Finally, the patient himself can to some measure control the behavior of the Behavior Modifier.

The Behavior Modifier does believe in control. However, the Behavior Modifier feels that he is exerting certain kinds of control for the good of the patient. The ethical permission to do this is based on his value system that says his technique provides a release from suffering either by eliminating a crippling symptom or by building in a new behavior that will make a person more competent. He feels that the end results are diametrically opposed to the implications of "brainwashing." Once the behavior is changed (either through symptom elimination or building in increased competence), the person is now *free* to explore his world further; he is *free* to consider new possibilities. Behavior modification opens up to the patient a whole new world of possible reinforcements that were previously closed off to him because of the presence of the symptom or symptoms. Every psychologist operates on the basis of value systems and the value system of Behavior Modification is as justifiable as any found in psychology.

It is unfair that the Behavior Modifier has been singled out by being placed in the position of being accountable for his values. He is often characterized as a psychologist with no, or at best reprehensible, values. All psychologists exert control (perhaps while denying it). One has only to remember the discussions occurring during the early 1950s among psychotherapists, in private and in print, about whether patients should be influenced by the therapist to accept society's values. There was much pointing out that this was a serious problem because the psychotherapist was such a powerful model. Certainly those therapists appreciated the power they had over their clients. Behavior Modifiers have been attacked because they have acknowledged the obvious and publicly stated their goals.

Another ethical consideration that needs to be commented upon is the very serious one concerning the Behavior Modifier's use of aversive stimuli (i.e., the utilization of pain to modify behavior). The utilization of pain to achieve certain purposes is very distasteful to psychologists. Even the Behavior Modifiers are split on the issue of the need for aversive stimuli for Behavior Modification. One has to weigh the amount of pain inflicted during behavior modification against the pain that is endured because of the presence of the symptom. Is it better for a child to literally bite off his fingers than to stop finger-biting with three or four electric shocks?[1]

It is hoped that these observations have contributed towards clarification of the Behavior Modification movement's procedures and orientations. It would be a serious mistake to ignore the methods of behavior modification since they can make a valuable contribution to psychology. The methods used by Behavior Modifiers are effective, often even more effective than standard procedures used in clinical psychology. The Behavior Modifiers have supplied clinical psychology with a new set of techniques to add to the armamentarium of procedures in clinical psychology, techniques that even the cognitively oriented psychologists can utilize when symptom relief is of crucial importance. The Behavior Modifiers have also reminded the clinician that they are "total" psychologists. They have implored the clinical psychologist to get involved in the laboratory, to experiment, to innovate and use knowledge thus gained in the realm of human behavior. These exhortations may lead to an eventual obliteration of the professional distinctions between "clinical" and "experimental" psychology. That may be, in the end, the Behavior Modifier's greatest contribution to clinical psychology.

NOTE

1. There are many facets to the problem of the place of aversive techniques in Behavior Modification. The issues have nowhere been more incisively examined than by Donald M. Baer. His discussion of these issues at the Institute can be found in the appendix to this volume.

2: Recent Examples of Behavior Modification in Preschool Settings

DONALD M. BAER
MONTROSE M. WOLF

A good deal of modern behavior therapy is based on the principles of reinforcement and the technology of operant conditioning. The studies to be described in this discussion are from a program examining those principles by using that technology in the life setting of the preschool. In the process, a type of behavior therapy emerges, one which seems capable of remediating a wide range of behavior problems discernible in preschool children, and of preventing the probable development of other future behavior problems by forestalling what at the time appears to be an undesirable line of development.

For purposes of application, the basic principle of reinforcement may be stated in this way: To control the consequences of another's behavior is to control that behavior. If this principle is to be applied to the free behavior of children in a preschool setting, it requires an analysis of the possible stimulus consequences of child behavior in that setting. Straightforward observation suggests immediately that two classes of stimulus consequences are very prominent in that environment: social

Part of this chapter was incorporated into a paper entitled *Extinction: Some Complexities of a Nonprocedure*, by Donald M. Baer, presented at the biennial meeting of the Society for Research in Child Development, New York, 1967.

Another part was incorporated into a paper entitled *The Entry Into Natural Communities of Reinforcement*, by Donald M. Baer and Montrose M. Wolf, presented at the annual meeting of the American Psychological Association, Washington, 1967.

The authors are grateful to the United States Public Health Service, National Institute of Mental Health, for research grants MH 02208 and MH 11768, which supported much of the research reported here. In addition great appreciation is due Miss Carolyn Thomson, head teacher of the preschool group in which the Foxwell and Coats Master's theses were performed, for her active participation in the design and execution of those studies, and for her guidance in the training of these assistant teachers.

stimulation from the teachers, and from the other children. Given a staff who are aware of the implications of reinforcement theory and are open to an experimental evaluation of their own conduct as preschool teachers, it is immediately possible to achieve an application of this principle. For the past several years, exactly such an experimental program has been pursued in a continuing series of studies conducted first in collaboration with the staff of the University of Washington Preschool, and now with the staff of the University of Kansas Preschool Laboratories. These studies attempt to analyze the function of social stimuli in the preschool setting; they concentrate on teacher-supplied social stimuli. Almost without exception over the past 6 years, these experiments have shown that quite ordinary forms of social responsiveness in the preschool teacher function as positive social reinforcers for the children in her group. By controlling the timing of this stimulation, that is, its contingency with the behaviors of children in the group, it has proven possible to change those behaviors quickly and extensively (Baer & Wolf, 1968). The behavior chosen for study invariably has been one which offends the values of preschool teachers: too little of a desirable behavior, too much of an undesirable behavior, or some other failure of a child to exploit the special opportunities which the teachers believe their preschool environment offers almost uniquely.

A common characteristic of these studies has been the experimental use of social reinforcement contingencies. This has meant that first an operant level of the child's behavior has been observed, quantitatively measured, and found stable over time. This serves three functions: it confirms that there is indeed a problem which might well be remediated; it suggests that the problem is not about to solve itself in the natural course of preschool events (as many such behavior problems do); and it provides a baseline against which to compare the effects of future operations. Then, a new and specially designed set of contingencies involving the child's behavior and the teacher's responsiveness to that behavior is applied. A desirable behavior, previously too weak for satisfaction, now is attended to whenever it occurs; simultaneously, any undesirable behaviors, previously too strong for toleration, now are not attended to at all. These new contingencies continue until the expected change in the child's behavior has made an obvious appearance (or until it is clear that these contingencies are not going to produce the planned result, in which case a new set is designed and tried, until the looked-for change in the child's behavior is produced). At that point, the experimental contingencies are either discontinued or reversed, to see if the change apparently produced by them in fact does depend on them, both historically and currently. Almost invariably, the new behavior change does extinguish. In such studies, the reinforcing stimulus usually does not disappear from the environment during extinction, as it may in an animal laboratory demonstration of extinction. Instead, the teacher's responsiveness simply shifts from one contingency to another. Given a short demonstration of the effectiveness of this kind of extinction, these studies invariably go on to a reinstatement of the experimental contingencies, and a continuation of them coupled with a gradual adjustment of their intrinsic reinforcement schedules, to produce a sufficiently large and durable behavior change for teacher satisfaction.

Judgments about such behavior changes require precise estimates of their magnitude. The technique used in these studies was continuous daily time sampling, in 10-second blocks of the entire preschool session. The observers hired for this purpose made a check for every 10-second block of the day during which the behavior in question occurred, and another check for every 10-second block during which the child was attended to by a teacher. A 2½-hour session in preschool becomes 900 successive blocks. Scanning these blocks makes the distribution of the child's behaviors and the teacher's reinforcement or extinction of them apparent to the eye. The critical blocks can be added for a daily summary, a convenient one being the proportion of these blocks during which the behavior in question occurred. A daily progress chart of this score allows frequent judgments of developing success or failure.

It is important that a teacher not undertake these projects without an observer. The teacher's daily estimates of the child's behavior have often been incorrect, not only in magnitude of change but in direction.

The actual technique of contingent social reinforcement is very readily described, and quite easily made a part of the preschool teacher's repertoire. It is, in fact, a use of her own behavior in just the form she ordinarily uses when she responds to the children in her group. A good deal of "normal" activity could be summarized as two response classes: turning toward children, and turning away from children. When they turn toward a child, teachers may then emit a wide range of further behaviors: they may look at him closely, or at what he is doing; they may smile and nod, or raise their eyebrows, or frown; they may touch him, and even take him onto their lap; and they may speak to him in a wide range of messages, conveying interest, approval, inquiry, or reflection of his own behavior. Call that—any or all of that—the *social responsiveness* of the teacher. It is a class of stimuli which almost invariably has positive reinforcing function for the preschool child; in the rare cases when it has little or no such function, it can be given some. Thus, when a teacher turns toward a child, she is dispensing a highly probable social reinforcer at that moment, and any response which occurred immediately prior will benefit from that reinforcement. Similarly, when a teacher turns away from a child, that stimulus is being withdrawn from the child's environment, and is no longer acting to reinforce a behavior. A teacher may reinforce a behavior, then, by turning toward it in her usual way; when the behavior ceases, or is replaced by an undesirable behavior, the teacher may keep the effects of her reinforcement consistent simply by turning away. The teacher turns away not in anger, disapproval, or spite; she simply turns away, as she does many times from every child during a normal session.

For the teacher, then, her techniques of reinforcement are simple: (1) what she turns toward will increase; (2) what she does not turn toward, or turns away from, will not increase; (3) if previously she often had turned toward a behavior, now if she no longer does, the behavior will decrease.

Thus, it is simply the timing of the teacher's normal professional behavior which constitutes her technique of reinforcement or extinction, not ordinarily the content of it. As a result, the teacher must learn to time her response to fall into contingency with the behavior of her children, but she need not learn a new set of behaviors to make up her performance. This is probably due to the training of preschool teachers, which selectively reinforces very positive components of their social responsiveness, and to the self-selection of girls with strong affection for children.

Using just such techniques and experimental designs, it has proven possible to make quick and important changes in a wide range of preschool child behaviors. During the past 4 years, an experimental analysis of the teacher's potential for social reinforcement has been approached while making desirable changes in behavior problems of the following types:

lack of social interaction with other children,
interaction with only a single other child,
lack of vigorous physical activity,
poor verbal behavior,
hyperactivity,
excessive dependence on adults,
regressive crawling,
fear of heights,
excessive crying,
noncooperative behavior,
rejection of adults.

Four relatively recent studies will be summarized as examples of this program, and as analyses of other variables involved in such a program. All deal with the problem of developing social interaction with other children, and indeed, this is one of the more frequent problems noted in preschool children. It is not a surprising problem: many preschoolers have had little prior history with children of their own age when they first come to preschool. But, exactly because preschool is a place where groups of age mates are brought together for play and learning, preschool teachers consider a persistent failure in social development especially disappointing. Social development is one of the kinds of development for which the preschool setting is uniquely appropriate, and it is indeed ironic if the opportunity is wasted throughout the 2-year preschool program.

The first study (Hart, Reynolds, Baer, Brawley, & Harris, 1968) dealt with noncooperative behavior, which appeared to be a possible precursor of very undesirable future social development. In this case, the child presenting the problem was a 5-year-old girl whose behavior was characterized by a great deal of nonsocial tricycle riding, sand box play, swinging, cooking of imaginary meals, and play with animal toys. Her contacts with other children were frequent enough, but quite brief. However, most of these interactions consisted of taunts, refusals to play when invited, claims of her own superiority ("I can do that better than you, so there"), rambling accounts of violent accidents, and generally obscene language (sometimes referred to by preschool teachers as "bathroom talk"). Thus, her brevity of social contact seemed quite understandable, especially in a preschool peopled mainly by the gentle children of the university faculty. The child's typical pattern of interaction with the teachers consisted of dawdling through routines, apparently to delay the next activity planned, and also included extremely frequent "accidental" upsetting of paints and other materials which the teachers might be setting up. This led them to characterize her by that quietly disappointed term, "noncooperative." Consequently, they decided to shape cooperation in her, as a favor to all concerned.

In the process, they examined a frequently encountered hypothesis advanced in explanation of such behavior in children, namely, that these children are acting out the effects of too little love and attention from adults. It was clear to the teachers that this child's behaviors were effective in driving away not only the other children, but the teachers as well, on many occasions. Perhaps, indeed, the teachers had fallen into a trap which was intensifying the child's undesirable behavior.

Consequently, they proceeded to collect baselines of cooperative and other related behaviors of the child, and of their own interaction with the child. Ten days of observation indicated that the child spent about 50 percent of each day in proximity with other children (meaning within 3 feet of them indoors, or 6 feet outdoors). Despite this frequent proximity, however, the child spent only about 2 percent of her day in cooperative play with these children. The teachers, it was found, interacted with this girl about 20 percent of the day, not all of it pleasant. The teachers therefore set up a period of intense social reinforcement, offered not for cooperative play but free of any response requirement at all: the teachers took turns standing near the girl, attending closely to her activities, offering her materials, and smiling and laughing with

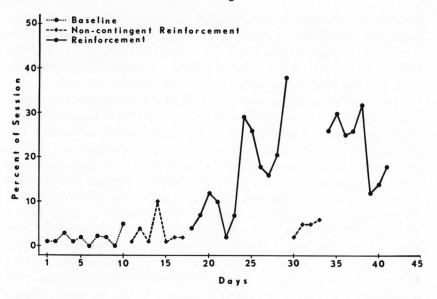

FIGURE 2.1

her in a happy and admiring manner. The results of 7 days of this non-contingent extravagance of social reinforcement were straightforward: the child's cooperative play changed not at all, despite the fact that the other children of the group were greatly attracted to the scene, offering the child nearly double the chance to interact with them cooperatively. These 7 days having produced no useful change, the teachers then began their planned reinforcement of cooperative behavior. They defined cooperative behavior in four easily observed categories, subdivided into nine classes of very specific activities, with which a team of observers achieved reliabilities of 92 percent and better. Contingent social reinforcement, used in amounts less than half that given during the noncontingent period, increased the child's cooperative play from its usual 2 percent to a high of 40 percent in the course of 12 days of reinforcement. At that point, in the interests of certainty, the teachers discontinued contingent reinforcement in favor of noncontingent. In the course of 4 days, they lost virtually all of the cooperative behavior they had gained during the reinforcement period of the study, the child showing about a 5 percent average of cooperative play over that period of time. Naturally, the study concluded with a return to the contingent use of social reinforcement, a recovery of desirable levels of cooperative play, and a gradual reduction of the teacher's role in maintaining that behavior. These data are displayed in Figure 2.1.

One point for emphasis in this context is that the extinction of a category of behavior was accomplished not by nondelivery of the reinforcing stimulus, but by noncontingent delivery of the reinforcing stimulus. There is indeed an effective mode of nonreinforcement involving merely the removal of a contingency between response and reinforcement, but not the removal of the reinforcing stimulus as well.

Noncontingent reinforcement as a method of extinction has certain characteristics which may make it the method of choice for some experimental designs, especially for those designs in which an adult offers reinforcers to a child. In such situations, it is not uncommon to hypothesize that a generalized relationship between child and adult comes into existence, and that this relationship, hypothetical as it may be, is capable of producing many widespread changes in the child's behavior. In particular, it is often enough suggested that if one wished to create such a relationship between an adult and a child, a very effective way to start would be for the adult to offer the child reinforcers. However, the logic of such hypotheses seems to suggest that the relationship may be aided by these reinforcers, but that it is something above and beyond the mere contingency between these reinforcers and the child's response. When a reinforcing experimenter builds up a desirable response in a child, apparently by reinforcement, it may not be very illuminating for this hypothesis when the experimenter discontinues reinforcement and subsequently observes a loss of the new behavior. Perhaps the behavior depended on the reinforcement (which is now absent); but, it may be argued, perhaps the behavior really depended on the relationship between child and experimenter, which, in the absence of the previous tangible signs of its inception, is now suffering some decay. That is, to discontinue reinforcement is often to discontinue most of the experimenter, seen as a source of stimuli for the child. Noncontingent reinforcement solves part of that problem: it keeps the experimenter just as busy with the child as ever; it maintains him as a source of reinforcers; but it destroys the contingencies between the response in question and those reinforcers. If the response depends on the general relationship between experimenter and child, it should survive rather well under noncontingent reinforcement, but if it depends on the reinforcement contingency as such, it should show the effects of extinction.

A different way of stating the same point would be to emphasize the discriminative properties of reinforcement. Reinforcers are stimuli, after all; the fact that they have reinforcing function does not mean that they can have no other function. Often enough, it is found, reinforcers have a discriminative or cue function, as well as a reinforcing function. A situation in which reinforcement suddenly ceases is thus a situation in which a potentially radical stimulus change has occurred. Decrement in response may sometimes be better explained by this sudden change in the general stimulus setting, than in the weakening of a response through discontinuation of its stimulus consequences. Noncontingent reinforcement makes for a minimal change in the total stimulus environment: the reinforcing stimuli are still there, and they may be presented at much the same rate as before. Thus, whatever discriminative properties of the situation the reinforcers may contribute to are not much changed, when their presentation shifts from systematic contingency with a particular response to random contingencies with any responses.

The next studies should be considered as a pair. They are both quite simple examples of increasing social interaction with other children, but together they make a point about the role of extinction in such behavior modification. The first study (Foxwell, 1966) involved a 3-year-old girl with very strong adult-oriented behaviors. She tagged along after teachers, spoke to them almost exclusively, played only at activities which teachers were conducting or watching closely, and became more thorough in this pattern as the weeks of the preschool program went by. Observation indicated that the girl indeed spent only about 3 percent of the typical preschool session in interaction with other children, but that by contrast she spent nearly 20 percent of her time interacting with the teachers. That description holding true quite stably over 9 days of observation, and probably over the preceding 8 weeks of the school program, social reinforcement of child interaction was begun. At the same time, extinction of adult interaction was instituted. Thus, the teachers attended to the girl only when she played with other children, but virtually every time that she did; when she attempted to interact with the teachers, they turned away, often with a friendly but brief excuse, but nevertheless ceasing to provide social stimulation for adult-oriented behavior.

During the first 6 days of this new condition, changes in child-oriented interactions were slight, and due primarily to an auxiliary technique used by the teachers, called "priming." In order to provoke some child interaction to reinforce, the teachers prompted other children to approach the girl, perhaps with an attractive doll or other piece of play equipment. If an interaction ensued between the children, the distant but alert teacher immediately moved in to admire both children, thus reinforcing the girl for her behavior involving the other child. This prompting of such child interactions naturally increased the amount of that interaction observed each day, but did not immediately produce very lengthy or complex social behavior in the girl.

During this same period of time, the child was increasingly following teachers about the preschool, asking for materials or to help them in their activities. These requests were met with friendly but very brief explanations, when necessary, to the effect that the teacher was "busy," or had to go somewhere else or do something obviously not suitable for the child, whereupon the teacher indeed left on her errand. This clearly made the child quite sad, on one day bringing her close to tears. How-

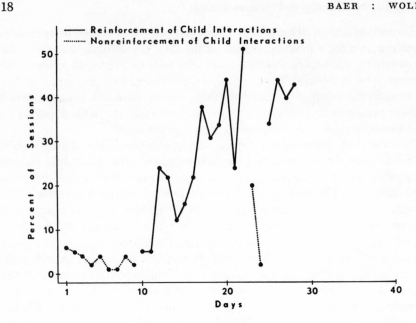

FIGURE 2.2

ever, by the seventh day of this condition of simultaneous reinforcement for the child interactions and extinction of adult interactions, there was a marked decrease in adult-oriented behavior, whereupon child-oriented behavior quite suddenly increased in both frequency and typical length of interactions. Six more days of reinforcement with no further priming produced a very high rate of child interaction, averaging in the last half of this period some 40 percent of the time available. Adult-oriented interaction decreased at the same time to a quite stable 5 percent of the typical session.

Two days of reversal of these contingencies were programmed, to make it quite clear that the changes observed were in fact dependent upon the teachers' experimental practices. In the course of these 2 days, the child's behavior correspondingly reversed itself: child interactions fell, on the first day to 20 percent, on the second day to 2 percent; meanwhile, adult interaction averaged 35 percent of the sessions. The necessity of the teachers' experimental contingencies in maintaining the desired behavior now being clear, they were resumed at that point. Over the next 4 days, the teachers produced child interactions averaging near 50 percent of each session. Then, they began a quite gradual reduction of their practices. They reinforced fewer and fewer of the girl's interactions with other children, reducing the schedule of reinforcement but not altering the nature of the contingency: positive reinforcement for child interaction. As this went on, the quality of the child's play with other children increased, such that she derived a correspondingly growing amount of social reinforcement from the other children. As this was seen, the teachers withdrew more quickly, and found that they could eventually forget the case as such. The child was now firmly in the reinforcing hands of her peer group. She had developed a repertoire of behavior, rather new for her, which produced stimulus consequences from other children of a reinforcing kind. The other children represented a stable and dependable source of such reinforcement for anyone who would play with them well, and thus it was clear that this behavior should indeed be maintained in the preschool setting. Later observations, 5, 6, and 7 weeks after the 2-day reversal period, showed the child's degree and quality of social interaction remaining quite high, despite the fact that the teachers were planning no special contingencies for her at all. Figure 2.2 shows this development of the child's behavior.

The second case (Coats, 1967) was strikingly similar, except in one essential of procedure. The child in this study was a girl, again one who showed very sophisticated adult-oriented behaviors but very little child-oriented interaction. She attracted the attention of the teachers at first because she showed very little involvement in the activities of the pre-school, and quite often explained to the teachers that these activities were incorrect, in that they involved fantasy and other elements of make-believe which, she had been told at home, were simply not to be credited. Subsequent observation demonstrated to the teachers an almost complete lack of skills in this child for dealing with children other than verbal disdain for their play, and thus suggested strongly that the girl was becoming the class prude at the age of 4.

In her case, very similar techniques of reinforcement were applied, but without the simultaneous use of extinction for adult-oriented be-haviors. The teachers thus continued to respond to behavior aimed at them by the child just as they always had, which was intermittently. However, they undertook to reinforce virtually every instance of child-oriented behavior that occurred. Thus, differential reinforcement of child interaction was accomplished, in this case as in the last example. In the previous case, reinforcement for one often-primed behavior had been coupled with extinction for a second behavior; in this case, intensive reinforcement for one often-primed behavior was coupled with modest reinforcement for a second behavior never primed as such.

The results were qualitatively the same in both cases. That is, in this study, too, systematic reinforcement of child interaction produced a marked increase in that behavior class. Discontinuation of such intensive reinforcement of child interaction for a brief period thoroughly disrupted it, shortly after it had developed to desirable levels, but resumption of its intensive reinforcement quickly returned it to a quite good level of quantity and quality. Teacher reinforcement was again withdrawn in a gradual manner, and this child, like the other, fell increasingly under

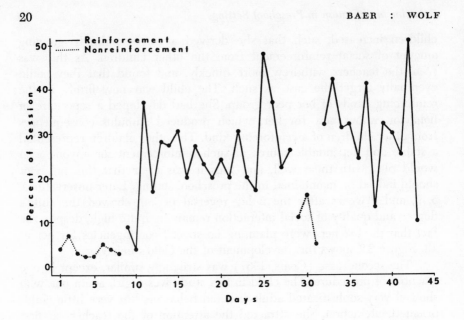

FIGURE 2.3

the control of the social reinforcement from her peer group, to which she had been introduced by this experimental technique. That peer group being a stable source of reinforcement for social behavior directed toward it, the behavior would be expected to persist without teacher intervention, once thoroughly inserted into that setting—and it did. Figure 2.3 illustrates the course of this study; it should be compared to Figure 2.2.

The qualitative similarity of these two studies can serve as evidence that differential reinforcement is all that is required for at least some behavior modification problems in a preschool setting. Differential reinforcement need not pit extinction against reinforcement; it can match much reinforcement against less, just as reasonably. Whether or not the latter combination will prove as effective as the former in all cases remains to be seen. However, it is a technique which is sometimes easier for teachers to use than one involving complete extinction for what is, after all, a rather pleasant form of behavior: social interaction with the teacher alone. Consequently, this technique is being pursued in further studies, to see if indeed it will prove practical often enough for value. If so, it would seem the more desirable of the two methods, especially where the problem in hand is the development of better repertoires in children.

The fourth study (Ingram, 1967) was again an application of social reinforcement to develop social interaction in a child who seemed to lack such skills. This study, however, went beyond that by now routine assignment: it began an experimental analysis of the priming technique used incidentally in almost all of the previous studies. In addition to that, it undertook to examine the growing independence of the child's social skills from teacher reinforcement, as they developed under initial teacher reinforcement but then met increasing peer reinforcement.

This child was a boy, 4 years of age, showing a very low rate of skillful social interaction with either children or adults. For some weeks in preschool, he remained very quiet and detached from the organized activities of the group. He would, however, follow teachers about, staring at them intently for long periods of time. When they encouraged him to play, he would follow their suggestion; but when they turned away, satisfied that he was at last engaged in some constructive activity, he would pack up his materials and follow along behind them, setting up shop momentarily wherever they might stop. Eight days of observation showed that fully 30 percent of his average preschool session was devoted to staring intently at teachers or other children at play, but doing little else. Other categories of social interaction, such as following the lead of others in some activity, saying the same things that others said, sharing materials and toys, conversing or laughing with others, or cooperating in the building of a structure, the conduct of a game, or a role-playing activity such as playing store, averaged a mere 3 percent of his day at preschool. Yet other preschoolers, skilled and happy in social interactions in this setting, would average only about 10 percent of a session simply staring at others, and would spend close to 30 percent of their time in one or another of the categories of social interaction just described.

Following 8 days of such observation, it was clear that this was a stable picture of the child's behavior, and several months of preschool already having passed, it seemed unlikely that this pattern of behavior would correct itself without more systematic intervention by the teachers. It was decided to examine the effects simply of priming other children to play with the boy. That meant that teachers would suggest to other children that they approach him, perhaps with a toy, perhaps with an idea for joint play. These suggestions were made to other children out of the boy's hearing, so that it would not seem to the boy that teachers were in fact attending to his isolated behavior. Ten days of this priming of others to approach the child and play produced a small and stable effect: his interactions with children rose from their usual 3 percent average to a new level of about 7 percent of each session. No sign of a developing increase above that average appeared. Consequently, the teachers tried a different technique of priming: they suggested directly to the boy that he approach some other child, with a toy, some materials, or a play idea. Typically, the child did as suggested. But, just as typically, the play that

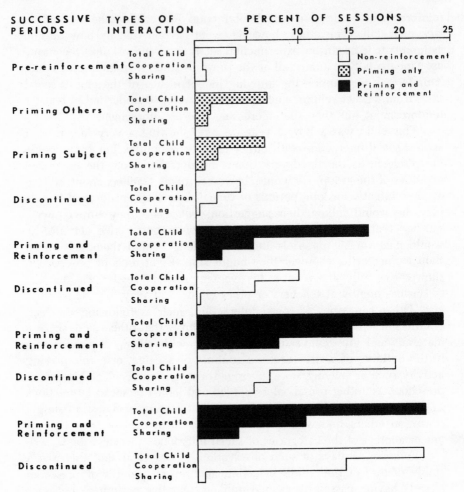

FIGURE 2.4

was thus created would be brief and unlikely to be renewed without further teacher intervention. Total interaction with other children remained at its stable level of 7 percent during 8 days of this condition. During these 18 days of priming, the teachers had averaged 25 such primes each day. Figure 2.4 summarizes these data (and also shows the outcome of further procedures to be described).

It seemed clear that priming alone would not produce the extensive development desired. Priming had more than doubled the child's rate of interacting with other children, from 3 percent to 7 percent. Nevertheless, this doubling apparently was supported almost entirely by the teachers' efforts. To see if indeed the 7 percent rate of child interaction depended on the teachers, the priming technique was discontinued for 5 days. In the course of these 5 days, the boy's rate of child interaction dropped to an average of 4 percent, similar to the 3 percent level he had displayed prior to the 18 days of priming. Thus, it seemed clear that priming effects alone were neither large enough for value, nor durable.

The teachers had of course been watching the child closely during these periods. They had noted repeatedly that he did not seem to know anything about playing with other children: he had no repertoire of ready responses that had any positive stimulus value for the other children. Occasionally, he would emit a suitable response in answer to another child's bid to play, but since it would occur perhaps 30 seconds later than appropriate, his audience had often left by then. Consequently, a combination of double-priming and minimal social reinforcement was designed and applied. The teachers primed other children to approach the boy with some suggestion for play; as this occurred, the teacher would "drop in" and prompt the boy to reply; if necessary, the teacher would put words in his mouth or materials in his hands, and push him gently into the interaction that had just been invited. The shaping of behavior in this setting became very nearly literal. The reinforcement was minimal, in that the teacher, having put one suitable response into the boy for the occasion, then would leave, to see if with at least a start, the child could maintain the interaction himself.

To some extent, he could. Over a period of 9 days of double-priming and minimal reinforcement, the boy achieved an average level of child interaction approximating 17 percent of each session. His previous level with simple priming had been 7 percent; thus, the new technique had more than doubled the level of child interaction. However, the teachers were spending no more time with the boy than previously, and so the difference represented a result of at least some of his own efforts in maintaining the interactions which the teachers had started and lightly reinforced. The quality of this interaction had developed as well: sharing and cooperation showed considerable gains, sharing behavior rising from its usual 1 percent level to a new average of 4 percent, and cooperation growing from a typical 2 percent level to a near 7 percent figure.

Then, for 4 days, the teachers discontinued their priming and minimal reinforcement technique, to see if the child would maintain his new level of interacting with children. To some extent, he did; to a greater extent, he did not. Over the 4 days, he showed an average of 10 percent of each session spent interacting with other children, entirely on his own initiative, or theirs, but without teacher support. His early levels of child interaction were about 3 or 4 percent; this level was 10 percent, and showed no signs of deteriorating further. The teachers noted that he was indeed using some new behaviors in dealing with other children, and was at least responding to their bids much more promptly than he had previously in the study. This represented progress, but not enough for satisfaction.

Consequently, double-priming was resumed, this time with intensive social reinforcement of any interaction that resulted. The teachers' techniques, in sequence, were these: another child was primed to approach the boy; as he did so, the boy was primed to respond; if he did, the teachers displayed delight over the interaction; they then gently faded away from the interaction, but returned soon, if it were still going on, to express more delight and appreciation. They continued "dropping in" in this manner as long as the interaction went on, but attempted to do so more and more minimally, and less and less frequently. Five days of this priming and intensive reinforcement produced child interaction averaging 24 percent of each session. The quality of this interaction was measurably superior to that seen previously, in that cooperation in structured activities rose to a new high, averaging 15 percent of the typical session.

Again, teacher intervention was discontinued to see if the child's new attainments would survive without such intervention. This time, they did to a considerable extent: without teacher support for 4 days, the boy nevertheless averaged 19 percent child interaction throughout these days. That was judged quite good, but not quite good enough, especially since the rate of cooperative interactions was cut in half, to a mere 7 percent of the typical session. Therefore, priming and reinforcement were resumed. Six days produced an average of 23 percent. That average was attained almost immediately, and appeared quite stable; it was very close to the interaction level accomplished during the preceding reinforcement period, and was considered a desirable level for this boy, considering that cooperative interactions had again achieved an average level of 15 percent of each session.

Once again, the independence of these developments from teacher reinforcement was probed. For 7 days, the teachers discontinued their systematic intervention into these behaviors. This time, their withdrawal had no measurable effect at all: total child interactions averaged 22 percent of each session, and cooperative interactions maintained their previous 15 percent level. In effect, this child's overall rate of social interaction with other children was no longer readily available for teacher control.

What has emerged from this study is a picture of the effectiveness of priming and reinforcement techniques, separately and in combination. It seems that behavior cannot live by priming alone. What has also emerged is an account of the growing independence of changes in social behavior from the teacher-supplied reinforcement which initially creates them. A preschool is intrinsically a community of reinforcement contingencies which will support social behavior oriented toward children, once it has made its appearance. Thus, these studies are in large part simply techniques of introducing a child to that community, of developing social skills which will come into contact with the reinforcement practices of the community, and then of letting those skills prosper in that community without further—now unnecessary—teacher intervention.

A final point is appropriate in this setting. The program of research in behavior modification exemplified by these four studies is relatively new to the field of preschool education. However, it must be emphasized that the materials of this research are not new at all. These are not behavior changes brought about by stimuli newly imported into the preschool. These stimuli have always been there, and, observation shows, often are used in a contingent manner. Too often, these contingencies are the kind which promote undesirable behavior, and undo desirable behavior. The preschool teacher consequently has no real choice in acting as a Behavior Modifier: she is armed with a very potent weapon, and she cannot help but use it. Thus, she must learn to use it well. In this context, that means choosing her contingency with a child's behavior. If she tries not to choose any such contingency, ordinary human nature may trap her into attending to and thereby strengthening very undesirable behavior in her children. It is not easy to ignore a child who is always alone, or who dawdles, sucks his thumb, cries, fights, or destroys things. The preschool teacher is a natural dispenser of social reinforcement contingencies; she must become a student of her own behavior in doing so, since that behavior, these studies show, can be extremely potent in changing the behavior of the children who come to her school.

REFERENCES

Baer, D. M. & Wolf, M. M. The reinforcement contingency in preschool and remedial education. In R. D. Hess & R. M. Bear (Eds.), *Early education: Current theory, research and practice.* Chicago: Aldine, 1968.

Coats, Betty Ann. The effect of social reinforcement on low verbal interaction in a nursery school child. Unpublished Master's thesis, University of Kansas, 1967.

Foxwell, Helen R. The development of social responsiveness to other children in a preschool child through experimental use of social reinforcement. Unpublished Master's thesis, University of Kansas, 1966.

Hart, B. M., Reynolds, N. J., Baer, D. M., Brawley, E. R., & Harris, F. R. Effects of contingent and noncontingent social reinforcement on the cooperative behavior of a preschool child. *Journal of Applied Behavior Analysis,* 1968, 1, 73-76.

Ingram, Ellen M. Discriminative and reinforcing functions in the experimental development of social behavior in a preschool child. Unpublished Master's thesis, University of Kansas, 1967.

3: Faradic Aversive Controls in Clinical Practice

MALCOLM KUSHNER

The past decade and more particularly the last five years have seen an increasing interest in and application of the behavior modification efforts which have collectively become known as Behavior Therapy. In part this grew out of a recognition that one of the core problems of contemporary psychotherapy was that it did not have at its disposal a basic fund of knowledge from which it could develop a comprehensive, solid framework to understand deviant behavior, much as general medicine relies upon biochemistry and physiology, or engineering depends upon physics for its basic concepts and working principles. As a result, our theory has too frequently been generated from subjective speculations and "insights," unamenable to testing or controlled observation and too often derived from abnormal behavior and then extrapolated to explain normal behavior. No wonder then that in the realm of psychotherapy, as opposed to the organic approaches, the last 50 years have seen relatively few significant gains commensurate with the efforts which have been made.

Psychology, however, does have a respectable array of "hard" information which can be profitably put to use in understanding and dealing with behavioral disorders. This information, dealing essentially with the acquisition, modification, extinction, etc., of normal behavior, and often referred to as Learning Theory, has been derived in the laboratory under carefully controlled conditions utilizing organisms down the phylogenetic scale. These findings have been replicated, modified, and extended by others, finally culminating in hypotheses and principles which themselves

The author wishes to acknowledge the contributions of Jack Sandler and Ed Malagodi in reviewing this paper and making helpful suggestions during its formulation.

generate further inquiry and experimentation. While the amount of data is modest as compared to some other disciplines, nevertheless there is a body of knowledge in psychology which has ready application to the kinds of problems which clinicians are called upon to resolve. It has been the growing recognition of the relevancy and transferability of this research derived material to deviant behavior that has given the impetus to this recent activity.

It is ironic that it has taken over 40 years for the clinical community to pick up again where Jones (1924) and Watson and Rayner (1920) had first pointed the way with their work with phobias. This early promising beginning of the application of learning principles to behavior disorders was displaced in this country in part by the more "dynamic" and spectacular schools of psychoanalysis which first began to make their impact felt at that time. Likely of equal importance was the absence of clinical psychology as we know it today with the result that the efforts of Watson and his students remained, for the most part, within the academic setting and did not filter down to the practicing clinicians who were almost exclusively physicians. The growing disenchantment with psychoanalytically oriented theory and technique as well as the critiques of Eysenck (1952, 1959), the work of Wolpe (1958), and the invaluable investigations of clinically interested research psychologists have now brought the wheel full circle.

Until recently the treatment of behavior disorders by means of aversion therapy has been regarded with skepticism. No doubt this is in part a reaction to earlier ineffective, often brutal conditions imposed on the emotionally disturbed. In addition, the psychoanalytic emphasis on the presumed relationship between neurosis and early trauma further reinforced this position. Solomon (1964) has pointed out how certain persistent legends among learning theorists have also contributed to such views. Of even more importance were the apparently contradictory findings in the punishment literature. Whereas positively reinforcing agents are usually readily identifiable and reliably exhibit the effect of increasing response probability, a host of studies has appeared which do not demonstrate the obverse of this principle (Church, 1963; Martin, 1963; Sandler, 1964; Solomon, 1964). Thus, noxious events have often failed to decrease response occurrence and, on occasion, have increased response rates, revealing the effects of positive reinforcement. A current survey of the literature, however, indicates an increasing use of aversive techniques (Rachman & Teasdale, 1969). This state of affairs has been paralleled, and in part encouraged, by new attention given to the concept of punishment, since it is in this framework that aversion therapy may be best understood (Azrin & Holz, 1966; Campbell & Church, 1967; Church, 1963; Kushner & Sandler, 1966; Solomon, 1964). Although the research literature in this area now offers considerable guidelines for practical application, more work is needed specifically dealing with humans and in the context of clinical situations.

In this paper I will discuss the techniques and conditions under which faradic aversive controls may be utilized by the service-oriented clinician. These operations will be presented primarily within an operant framework. The emphasis upon aversive procedures is meant in no way to diminish the importance of other approaches and principles involved in modifying behavior but will merely attempt to place these techniques in their proper context in the armamentarium of the behavior therapist.

It must be recognized from the outset that although there are situations in which aversive procedures are synonymous with punishment, there are many instances—and perhaps in clinical situations they are in the majority—when aversive techniques are not punishing per se. If we accept the definition of Azrin and Holz (1966, p. 381) that "punishment is a reduction of the future probability of a specific response as a result of the immediate delivery of a stimulus for that response" then in such situations aversive stimuli may be considered to be punishers. However, when we consider negative reinforcement procedures such as escape or avoidance training whose purpose is to increase the frequency of desirable responses by means of escape from or avoidance of the aversive stimulus then such is not the case. In general then, whereas punishment makes use of aversive stimuli, all situations in which aversive techniques are utilized may not be considered to be punishing.

Since the essential purpose of aversive and/or punishment procedures is either to reduce or increase the frequency of behavior the stimulus chosen to efficiently produce this change is of great importance. As outlined by Azrin and Holz (1966) the ideal punishing stimulus has definite properties which allow for an accurate appraisal of this procedure. We may include aversive stimuli in this context: 1. The physical dimensions should be specific and precise allowing for accurate measurement. The use of discrete units permits ready replication and reliable measurement. 2. The actual contact the stimulus makes with the subject should be constant. As they point out, the stimulus may be highly specified at its source but vary considerably in its impact on the subject. 3. The subject should not be able to escape the stimulation unless this is built into the procedure, as with avoidance or escape contingencies. Inasmuch as punishment achieves its effect through an increase in the amount of stimulation acting on the organism, variations beyond the therapist's control weaken his efforts and make measurement haphazard at best. An example of this will be discussed later in the section on clinical applications. 4. There should be no undue skeletal reactions to the stimulus. If the stimulus disrupts or reduces ongoing behavior because the elicited gross bodily responses are incompatible with the punished response then we are not sure whether the stimulus itself is effectively aversive. 5. Finally, the stimulus should be able to be varied widely so as to yield no effect at the lowest ranges and complete response reduction at the higher ranges. It is obvious that without such variation the full range of its effectiveness cannot be evaluated.

Various noxious stimuli have been used clinically including chemical agents such as apomorphine and emetine which produce nausea and vomiting, electric shock, curare-like drugs to inhibit breathing, blasts of air, and white noise. Other conditions which involve the removal of positive reinforcement are time-out and response cost which may be classified as aversive states and have been used effectively in this context.

Barker (1965), Franks (1958), Rachman (1965), and others have discussed the advantages and disadvantages of the various forms of aversive stimulation and agree on the overall desirability and advantages of electric shock. Some of the important features include the ease and relative simplicity of operation. The stimulus may be activated either automatically via programming or by the therapist. Technicians or quasi-professional personnel can be readily trained to operate the equipment in distinct contrast to the highly skilled medical team which must be in attendance when drugs are used.

Safety is another important clinical feature. First, aside from serious heart conditions, there are practically no medical contraindications to the use of mild electric shock. The possible serious side effects such as might occur with drugs are absent. By the same token, frequent repetition is practical without concern for physical debilitation and the occurrence of severe stress reactions. Of course the safety factors within the apparatus, particularly if line current is being used, must be assured. Battery powered units eliminate this problem.

The irregular lag between administration and activation of drugs also is a limiting factor. Faradic stimulation impinges upon the subject immediately upon activation and, within limits, its effects are highly uniform. In contrast, drug effects vary considerably from subject to subject and even within the same subject from trial to trial. As such, electric shock permits much better control and accurate presentation of CS-UCS and response-shock temporal sequences.

Concomitant with better control there is the capacity to deliver a stimulus of specifiable intensity for a given period of time at any chosen moment. As can be readily seen, partial reinforcement is an easy option using this type of stimulus whereas it is much more cumbersome with chemical stimuli. Measurement of both input as well as patient responsiveness, e.g., response latency, as well as replication of procedures, is accurate and easily accomplished using faradic stimulation. Adaptations necessary to account for individual differences between patients are also much easier to effect with electric shock than with drugs or other stimuli.

Another significant advantage is the broad range of applicability of electric shock. It may be used with a wide variety of disorders in many contexts ranging from such simple problems as nail-biting to sexual perversions, which when treated by standard methods are ordinarily refractory to change. It is also relatively more simple to utilize a socially conditioned punisher such as the word "no" paired with shock than with many other stimuli. Finally, and of the utmost importance, because of its range electric shock can produce whatever degree of response suppression desired.

It is readily obvious that aversive stimuli such as air blasts, hand slapping, and verbalizations, do not meet enough of the criteria specified by Azrin and Holz (1966) nor approach the advantages outlined above for electric shock, although under specific conditions they may be effective. White noise most closely approximates electric shock in overall desirability in a number of areas such as possessing discrete physical dimensions, limiting excessive skeletal responses, variation over a wide range, simplicity of operation, safety (care must be given to limiting duration at the higher exposure levels), and good control. There are limitations, however, in portability, degree of noxiousness, narrow range of effectiveness, expense of the apparatus, and limited studies reporting its use. Further use of this modality, however, appears promising and is recommended for use under the appropriate circumstances.

Mention should be made regarding the disadvantages of electric shock. Much of the criticism may be directed to the undesirable aspects of aversive or punishing situations in general rather than to electric shock per se. Azrin and Holz (1966) comment upon the aggression resulting from punishment and differentiate between operant aggression and elicited aggression (Ulrich & Azrin, 1962). The former is described as aggression directed against the punishing stimulus or person and the latter as aggression directed toward others and therefore not instrumental in reducing the aversive state of affairs. In the latter, one might therefore consider the possibility of some kind of an attack upon noninvolved innocent individuals resulting from the use of painful aversive procedures. This is similar to the concept of displacement utilized by clinicians. In response to their cautions as well as similar comments of Rachman (1965) it should be pointed out that the experimental evidence for this elicited aggression is primarily derived from paired animal studies which are not directly analogous to the type of controls operating in treatment situations. Although the dentist causes pain, discomfort, and apprehension, his patient recognizes the context in which it is taking place and appreciates that the end results are to his advantage. The same may be said for the use of aversive techniques in the behavioral disorders. It is doubtful whether any elicited aggression resulting from aversive conditioning is of substance enough to be seriously disruptive socially. Except for one instance, this writer has not observed any aggressive behavior of sufficient intensity, of either variety, which contraindicated the utilization of faradic aversive techniques. In the one exception, a paranoid schizophrenic in partial remission, the operant aggression was apparent enough at the initial treatment session to warrant a judicious change of approach. This might be instructive with regard to the type of patient for whom aversive procedures of this type are contraindicated. It is my feeling that under most circumstances this consideration may be minimized although certainly this is an area to which clinicians must be attentive as well as one in which more experimental work is needed (Risley, 1968).

Another criticism noted by Azrin and Holz (1966), the possibility of driving the patient away from the treatment situation, is likely of more frequent occurrence. We have found that one test of the patient's motivation is his determination to endure the discomfort and pain attendant with these procedures. This comment is not intended to invoke the old excuse of blaming the patient for therapeutic failures since I agree with Feldman (1966) that failure is more often a result of the therapist's failure to use the proper technique or reflects inadequate stimulus control. However, in special cases such as patients being forced to undergo treatment by the courts, or because of pressure from parents or spouse, the likelihood of escape from the treatment situation increases. This observation is usually made very early in treatment, however, and is of help in evaluating the situation and planning the subsequent treatment program. Some patients are seriously traumatized by the mere thought of electric shock and, as Beech (1960) points out, the increased anxiety level aroused by this procedure may interfere with effective conditioned avoidance responses requiring either a change of the aversive technique or of approach. Turner and Solomon (1962) concluded from their studies of human traumatic avoidance learning that for highly anxious patients most rapid learning may be achieved by starting with a short CS-UCS interval and then lengthening it. Initially the UCS intensity is high and is gradually reduced in order to produce latency escape responses. This approach may be one way of overcoming this limitation.

Finally, as pointed out by Feldman (1966) and Rachman (1965), relapse is a frequent occurrence when aversive procedures in general are used. As both reviewers indicate, the best way to counter this problem—and perhaps this is the heart of the issue—is to use techniques which the research literature supports as being most efficacious from the standpoint of response acquisition and resistance to extinction. It is felt that electric shock, for the reasons outlined above, is a modality particularly suited to these ends.

What then are the significant variables related to the effective administration of aversive procedures? Here, too, the punishment literature is of much relevance to this question. There is good agreement (Azrin, Holz & Hake, 1963; Brethower & Reynolds, 1962; Masserman, 1946; Miller, 1960) that the most effective suppression of responses occurs when the aversive stimulus is presented suddenly and at full intensity, thus making the initial onset of the punishment of great importance. Too frequently shock is presented in a gradually increasing fashion which permits habituation and continuation of the undesirable behavior under stimulus intensities far above those which would otherwise be effective. This presents the clinician with the problem of rapidly arriving at a distinctly aversive intensity while, at the same time, not traumatizing the patient to the degree that he will refuse to return. Unfortunately, at this time we know too little about the range of effectiveness of this modality with regard to the problem of individual differences. However, with some experience, this problem usually can be minimized. It is also worthwhile to note that a sudden significant increase in shock intensity above the level being used will also result in a substantial suppression effect. Thus, as Azrin and Holz (1966) point out, all studies using electric shock have found that the greater the shock intensity the greater is the response suppression and that at high intensities suppression is practically complete (Appel, 1963; Azrin, 1959; Azrin, Holz & Hake, 1963; Brethower & Reynolds, 1962; Dinsmoor, 1952; Estes, 1944).

The point in time at which the aversive stimulus is to be presented is a significant variable to be considered. For the best maintenance of response reduction punishment should be presented immediately following the behavior to be suppressed. Although some studies indicated that immediate punishment was no more effective than nonimmediate punishment during the first hour (Azrin, 1956; Estes, 1944; Hunt & Brady, 1955) the responses recovered significantly during nonimmediate punishment. Immediate punishment therefore is recommended.

How frequently should shock be delivered, or what schedule of punishment is most effective, are other practical questions. Studies indicate that continuous punishment, particularly under high intensities of shock, results in the greatest response reduction and is superior to intermittent punishment (Azrin, Holz & Hake, 1963; Sandler, Davidson & Malagodi, 1966; Zimmerman & Ferster, 1963). Generalizing from the instrumental avoidance literature (Humphrey, 1939; Lewis, 1960; Lovibond, 1963a), however, where the purpose is to increase the frequency of response, it has been found that intermittent stimulation will lead to increased resistance to extinction. Here again the distinction between punishment and aversion techniques in general must be kept in mind by the therapist.

A further factor to be considered when considering the problem of relapse is Eysenck's (1963) suggestion of the use of booster sessions as a means of maintaining the desired behavior. This, too, is an area which requires more careful scrutiny and controlled studies.

A point of major significance that must be recognized and that may account for apparently contradictory results when using aversive techniques is that the effectiveness of these procedures is critically influenced by reinforcement in different ways and for maximum effectiveness the therapist should be familiar with the manner in which the response he wishes to reduce has been maintained. Unfortunately, however, this information is not always available in clinical situations.

Azrin and Holz (1966) point out that when the subject is provided with an alternative response to receive reinforcement there will be a greater suppression of the punished response than where only one response is available (Herman & Azrin, 1964; Holz, Azrin & Ayllon, 1963; Risley, 1968). This should prompt the therapist to attempt to provide alternate sources of gratification for the patient such as more appropriate sexual objects, better attention gaining mechanisms, etc.

Providing an escape contingency also results in greater suppression of the punished response, or stating this another way, provides increased resistance to the extinction of the escape response (Azrin, Hake, Holz, & Hutchinson, 1965). The same may be said for avoidance contingencies. With this approach both response suppression and resistance to extinction are high (Solomon & Wynn, 1953; Turner & Solomon, 1962). In support of these findings the most successful clinical work with humans, particularly that dealing with more complex behavior, has utilized instrumental techniques with escape or avoidance contingencies as a prominent feature (Feldman & MacCulloch, 1965; Kushner, 1965).

Feldman and MacCulloch (1965) have briefly listed those variables found to contribute to increased resistance to extinction in instrumental avoidance situations: 1. Learning trials should be distributed rather than massed. 2. There should be contiguity of stimulus and response, particularly at onset. 3. Shock should be introduced at a level unpleasant for the subject rather than gradually increased. 4. Partial reinforcement should be used in conjunction with instrumental techniques. 5. Reinforcement should be variable both in ratio and interval schedules. 6. Delaying a proportion of the patient's attempts to avoid should lead to greater resistance to extinction than immediate reinforcement. 7. Vary the conditions of training to approximate real life situations in order to minimize the generalization decrement.

A word of caution should be noted here. Utilizing punishment within an escape or avoidance paradigm is quite different from punishing behavior that is being maintained or reinforced by escape or avoidance. In the latter case punishment often results in an increase, at least initially, in the frequency of the punished response, especially if the aversive stimulus has the same physical characteristics as that used to establish and maintain the escape or avoidance response (Appel, 1960; Brown, Martin & Morrow, 1964; Migler, 1963; Sandler, Davidson, Greene & Holzschuh, 1966; Sidman, Herrnstein & Conrad, 1957). Under these circumstances electric shock is a much better stimulus than social disapproval, for example, inasmuch as it is very unlikely that such a stimulus has been used to maintain escape or avoidance behavior, whereas social disapproval frequently is used in this manner.

Gwinn (1949) demonstrated that the punishment of acts motivated by fear tend to increase the strength of those acts so that aversion therapy with neurotic symptoms of this type may result in increased rather than reduced behavior. This confirms the observation of Beech (1960) that high anxiety states preclude effective conditioning procedures. This entire area, along with the question of personality variables as they affect specific treatment procedures, requires much closer attention. The suggestions of Turner and Solomon (1962) mentioned earlier concerning the conditioning of highly emotional patients may counter this problem and should be tried more in clinical situations. Eysenck and Rachman (1965) indicate that the judicious use of stimulant drugs contributes considerably toward enhancing conditioning effects although with already highly anxious patients this approach could conceivably increase the anxiety level.

There is another significant situation in which efforts to reduce certain behaviors via punishment paradoxically results in response intensity. If the therapist overlooks the possibility of the punishing stimulus acquiring discriminative reinforcement properties (Ayllon & Azrin, 1966; Holz & Azrin, 1961; Sandler, 1964) he can unwittingly reinforce rather than suppress the unwanted behavior. Conversely, mild stimuli may result in substantial response reduction if they are differentially associated with periods of no reinforcement. Care must also be given to the consideration whether reductive responses may be the function of the discriminative properties of the stimulus rather than its aversive characteristics. This entire area has been too frequently overlooked by researchers and clinicians alike.

Before going on to the case material, a few comments should be made regarding some of the common characteristics of faradic aversive conditioning. The clinical evidence confirms the research findings (Azrin, 1959; Dinsmoor, 1952) of rapidity of response reduction. This is observed almost invariably during the initial treatment session and is so reliable that its presence may be used as a guideline of therapeutic effectiveness. This writer has found that failure to get significant response reduction by at least the third session is a mark of either poor technique or inappropriate procedure.

Frequently, during the early stages of aversive treatment, there is a brief increase in the behavior, either motor or ideational, following termination of punishment. This is consistent with what Azrin and Holz (1966) term the "punishment contrast effect" and it occurs particularly when the stimulus intensity is not maximally optimum. Frequently, patients need reassurance that this is an expected occurrence and will diminish. Further punishment reduces this effect, as noted experimentally by Azrin (1960) and Estes (1944). Along these lines, it must be pointed out that this high recovery level occurs only with continuous low or moderate aversive stimulation whereas a partial schedule of stimulation results in gradual recovery (Azrin, Holz & Hake, 1963; Estes, 1944). At high intensities, however, continuous punishment is more effective than partial punishment both with regard to extent of suppression as well as duration.

In general, we have discussed some of the salient features of aversive conditioning focusing upon the advantages of electrical stimulation as an effective modality, and presenting the pertinent variables which contribute either to enhance or reduce the frequency of certain behaviors. Emphasis has been placed upon the research literature for this information and an effort was made to identify as well as differentiate between aversive procedures in general and punishment and escape-avoidance paradigms as distinctly separate approaches.

At this time I would like to present examples of the clinical application of the above-mentioned material conducted in both an institutional as well as private practice setting. One of the first problems confronting the clinician is to ask himself, "How shall I attempt to deal with this particular patient?" and more specifically, "What can I do to modify or eliminate the disturbing behavior which the the patient is presenting?" Our choice of approach is less influenced by the diagnosis or personality characteristics of the patient, i.e., whether extroverted or introverted, hysteric or dysthmic, etc. (Eysenck & Rachman, 1965), and is more determined by the specific behavior to be dealt with. For purposes of this discussion the question posed should be whether this particular behavior is best approached using a faradic aversive technique, or some other learning-oriented method. The best choice can be made only after one has as thorough an understanding of all the ramifications of the behavior in question as possible. This includes, if available, the reinforcement history of the behavior including present reinforcers; whether the behavior is chronic and longstanding and therefore likely to be primarily habitual in nature; or if this is not the case, what current problems are reflected in the behavior.

Where the behavior to be modified is chronic, habitual, and essentially functionally autonomous, simply modifying or eliminating the behavior should allow the patient to carry on effectively with the resources at his disposal. We have found this to be the case. An example of this might be nonorganic enuresis which responds so well to conditioning (Lovibond, 1963b). Too frequently the disturbance seen in both the enuretic and his family is a result of all the circumstances arising from the condition rather than a cause of it. Once the enuresis is eliminated the entire outlook and attitude of patient and family markedly improve.

In those cases where the disturbing behavior reflects ongoing problems removal or modification of the behavior is not contraindicated although some alternate or more appropriate response must also be introduced to help the patient deal more effectively with the problem area. An example here might be a case of sexual perversion where the treatment consisted both of suppressing the inappropriate sexual behavior and then developing appropriate heterosexual responses. This will be described in more detail shortly. The sexual perversions, voyeurism, fetishism, exhibitionism, and homosexuality are particularly responsive to aversive conditioning and in most cases appropriate heterosexual responses must also be shaped in addition to suppressing the inappropriate sexual behavior.

Another important consideration determining the use of aversive procedures is the degree of anxiety manifested by the patient. As was indicated in the earlier material, there is evidence that the effectiveness of conditioning procedures is limited by high anxiety levels (Beech, 1960). We have found that with certain problems such as hysterical symptoms, which frequently are readily modified by aversive conditioning procedures, a high anxiety level does result in a poorer prognosis utilizing this approach. Systematic desensitization offers much better results in such situations. The hysterical conditions accompanied by low anxiety states or the classical *la belle indifférence*, however, are readily modified via aversive conditioning.

With problems having obsessive-compulsive characteristics or psychomotor components of various types we have observed similar results. Where the manifest anxiety level is high, anxiety reducing techniques such as desensitization are effective; in those situations where this is not the case, aversive conditioning may be employed. Frequently it is found necessary to utilize the two approaches concurrently to deal most effectively with both the motor and autonomic components of the difficulty (Eysenck, 1960; Walton & Mather, 1963).

Inasmuch as the considerations discussed above require not only a thorough knowledge of the broad field of behavior therapy but considerable information about the patient and his disorder, it can therefore be appreciated that a thorough history and, when appropriate, psychometric evaluation, must be had. There are far too many temptations to immediately begin pushing buttons, with the likelihood of undue consequences resulting, without first understanding fully the problem at hand and considering other possible approaches to be used.

As Wolpe and Lazarus (1966) indicate, with problems presenting extreme conditions and debilitation reactions, attention must first be directed to as rapid an amelioration of the disturbing behavior as possible. Likewise, attention is usually focused upon the behavior most disturbing to the patient. The treatment program must remain flexible and be determined by the characteristics of each individual case as opposed to following a routinized, predetermined approach which ignores the nature of the problem.

Finally, a brief word regarding the therapist-patient relationship, or rapport. Whereas in many situations operant techniques may become automated and rely upon refinements of apparatus which distanciate the patient from the therapist, one must not lose sight of the fact that the subject is an individual in distress seeking help. We have found consistently, particularly where aversive techniques are used, that the interest and support offered by the therapist, while not the critical factor in the treatment, does play a highly important role in enabling the patient to persevere, thus enabling him to fully benefit from the treatment program. Aversion therapy is most definitely not a cookbook, button pressing procedure, which unfortunately many utilize as such.

In general then, the aversive conditioning program has proven most applicable and successful with problems of a compulsive, habitual nature and need not be restricted to motor behavior alone but is also effective with ideational, ruminative or obsessive behavior as well. The problems successfully dealt with include sexual perversions of many types, tics, conversion reactions, smoking, suicidal ruminations, jealousy reactions, thumb-sucking, nail-biting, intractable sneezing, compulsive hand-biting, and food fads. This wide range of application effectively demonstrates the facility of this approach.

CASE PRESENTATIONS

Case 1. Following is a case of fetishism in a 33-year-old man (Kushner, 1965). The fetish involved women's panties which the patient took from clothes lines or bought in stores and which he then put on and masturbated. He was similarly aroused by pictures of women wearing panties or scanty attire and masturbated to these fantasies. He was impotent in normal heterosexual relationships. The problem was approximately 21 years in duration. This behavior began when he was about 12, when he became sexually aroused watching girls slide down a sliding board with their panties exposed. At about the same period he began to masturbate and quickly associated the feelings he experienced with those sensations he had while observing the girls with exposed panties. Very quickly his fantasies during masturbation centered about the girls and their panties and because of the powerful reinforcing effects of orgasm this association became habitual. This explanation for the development of such a condition is certainly more parsimonious and in keeping with what we know about the acquisition of behavior than the "dynamic" explanations involving symbolism, castration fears, etc.

It was decided to utilize an aversive conditioning procedure by presenting to the patient the fetishistic object, appropriate pictures and ideational stimuli followed by a brief, uncomfortable electric shock. The rationale for the treatment and the above explanation of his problem was given the patient and at the third session the conditioning began. It was recognized beforehand that careful discriminations would have to be made between the fetishistic stimuli and more acceptable sexual behavior lest we condition the patient aversively to normal sexual stimuli.

The patient was seen three times per week for approximately 20 to 30 minutes each session. Four to six different stimuli were presented each session, for a total of twelve stimulus presentations. The patient was instructed to tolerate the shock until he wished it to be terminated and then to signal this by saying "stop" and simultaneously turning the panties or pictures aside. He was shocked during each stimulus presentation. Discussion was limited as much as possible to the patient's response to the shock and his reaction to the fetish between visits. No efforts were made to deal with the patient's problems from the conventional "dynamic" point of view.

After 41 shock sessions representing a total of 492 trials, extending over 14 weeks of treatment, the conditioning was halted since the patient reported no longer being troubled by his former impulses. Changes in the frequency of the fetishistic attraction were reported as early as the second shock session and progressed gradually with increases and decreases in the degree to which the patient was troubled. One month after the cessation of the conditioning the patient reported recovery of the fetishistic impulse but in a weakened form. He was prepared for this in advance and two reinforcement or "booster" sessions were administered with prompt disappearance of the impulses.

At this point in the treatment program, the patient's impotence was dealt with utilizing a form of the desensitization approach. Briefly, in this case, the patient's sexual difficulties were conceptualized as arising from a high anxiety state which he associated with this activity. In order to reduce the anxiety the patient was instructed to engage in sex play and stimulation with his partner but was told that under no circumstances was he to engage in intercourse. This immediately acted to reduce anxiety since it precluded failure. It was assumed that in such a continued program the anxiety level would diminish and ultimately normal sexual responsiveness would occur. Only when he experienced a strong desire for intercourse and a strong erection was the patient instructed to "let himself go" disregarding efforts for trying to prolong the act or any concern for pleasing his partner. Success would be readily achieved if instructions were followed and would enable further development of satisfactory coital expression. The patient was able to achieve this goal in short order.

Approximately 3 months following the cessation of the conditioning sessions the patient had to appear in court for two driving offenses, one of which could result in his incarceration. He was naturally anxious and apprehensive and reported fetishistic thoughts once more although he claimed that he could readily dismiss them from his mind. One more conditioning session was given. The court hearing was resolved in his favor and an 18 month follow-up revealed the patient to be free of the fetish, married, a new father, and experiencing a normal sexual life.

This was the first such case undertaken by the writer and a number of features to further enhance the treatment effectiveness could be considered at this time. These include more trials per session, a higher intensity shock (because of apparatus limitations it was only moderate in intensity for this patient—3.5 ma.), institution of an avoidance contingency, and partial reinforcement midway in the program. While the need to provide the patient with an appropriate sexual goal was a necessary aspect of the overall treatment program this might have been done concurrently with the aversive procedures as demonstrated by Feldman and MacCulloch (1965). The sexual perversions, formerly considered intractable and refractory to change, now appear to be effectively treated by means of the behavior therapies of the type described (Franks, 1966).

Case 2. A case that received very widespread attention was that of a 17-year-old girl who had been vigorously and rapidly sneezing for 6 months with no relief. She had been thoroughly examined from neurological, endocrinological, allergic, urologic, and psychiatric viewpoints; had been exposed to a wide variety of medication; had undergone hypnosis and sleep therapy, and was in psychotherapy—all to no avail. When the patient was first seen, baseline data revealed a sneeze rate of one per 40 seconds. Observation revealed features of the sneezing which had operant properties supporting the decision to utilize an avoidance paradigm with electric shock as the aversive stimulus.

The treatment consisted of placing a microphone around her neck which was connected to a voice key and shock source. Electrodes were placed onto her fingertips via rubber finger tips such as used by clerks. Sneezing activated the sound relay which in turn triggered the shock of approximately 3.5 ma. intensity. Shock therefore was contingent upon

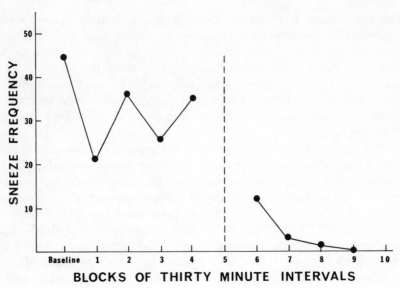

FIGURE 3.1   *Decline in sneeze frequency when paired with con-*
            tingent shock.

sneezing. The patient could avoid the shock by not sneezing. Counters
recorded the shock or sneeze frequency. Responses were recorded in
30-minute intervals. Time between these intervals was not constant due
to the varied requirements of the situation; average time between intervals was approximately 10 minutes. As can be seen in Figure 3.1 the
sneeze rate did not initially decline in the manner expected. This failure
prompted closer observation of the patient (She was not always in direct
view of the therapist.) resulting in the discovery that the fingertip electrodes were not making good contact. Between blocks 3 and 4 the patient
was found holding the electrodes complaining that they kept coming off.
Midway between blocks 4 and 5 again the electrodes came off, forcing
a stop to the procedure while they were taped to her fingers. Block 5
therefore was aborted as indicated by the broken line and block 6 was
begun once the electrodes were taped on. As can be seen, there was a
substantial drop in sneeze rate at this point. Following block 7 the
electrodes were removed from her fingertips and taped to her arm resulting in a further reduction and finally complete cessation of sneezing.

This case is another instance in which the aversive procedure was
only the first phase in the total treatment program. The patient's sneezing
behavior was being maintained by reinforcers in the environment which
made efforts to provide alternate, more appropriate, behavior mandatory.

This effort is now in process. As of this report, 13 months have passed without relapse. A fuller description of this highly interesting case is now in preparation (Kushner, 1968).

Case 3. This case demonstrates the application of an escape-avoidance paradigm to a case of hysterical anesthesia[1] and how these techniques may at times be incidentally utilized for diagnostic as well as therapeutic purposes. A 39-year-old male patient had been involved in an accident in which an elevator dropped suddenly about 4 feet. Although he walked away from the scene he complained of an ache in his back and within 24 hours was admitted to the hospital claiming that he had no feeling in his lower body from the point of an old incision just below the navel downward. He did not respond to pin pricks or other tactual stimulation in this area. Physical examination revealed no apparent neurological impairment and electromyograms indicated normal muscle potentials. He was confined to a wheel chair since he could not walk without grasping wall, or rails for support. After approximately 1 week in the hospital the patient was referred to psychology service from neurosurgery for diagnosis to rule out conversion reaction and for treatment.

Initial interview revealed the *la belle indifference* of the classic conversion reaction as well as a history of brief, transitory amnesic episodes and a current situation dynamically consistent with the need for escape from life pressures. Rather than give the standard test battery of Rorschach, TAT, etc., it was decided to attempt a conditioning approach to resolve the diagnostic question as well as to simultaneously effect a form of treatment.

At first he was connected to a portable shock generator and a simple classical or Pavlovian approach was attempted in which the anesthetic areas were stimulated by the tip of a pencil point followed by shock to the fingertips. Although he reacted to the shock delivered to his normal fingertips, a simple classical conditioned avoidance response was not obtained. The electrodes were then moved to the unfeeling areas in order to observe the degree, if any, of responsiveness to a 5 ma. shock to those areas. He did not respond and so a variation of the conditioning technique was utilized.

The patient was seated behind a one-way mirror connected to two shock sources. One set of electrodes was attached to his fingertips and another pair of electrodes was attached to an elastic band which was placed around the various anesthetized sites and moved from site to site in a systematic manner. He was also given a push button to hold in his other hand. The program was to present a shock to the anesthetized area which the patient could terminate by depressing the push button, thus acknowledging sensation in that area. If the button was not depressed within 3 seconds a more severe shock was delivered to the fingertips.

If the button was depressed both the initial shock was terminated or escaped and the fingertip shock avoided. This technique is known as an escape-avoidance paradigm.

In the initial session the patient was not told of the various contingencies but merely told to signal the awareness of sensation by depressing the button. In this manner a baseline measure of the awareness of sensation in the various anesthesized areas was determined. If he failed to respond during the initial session, shock was not delivered to his fingertips. Twenty trials per site were presented before moving to the next site. During this baseline session the patient depressed the button indicating awareness on only 8 out of 100 trials. On a small area of his left ankle where he acknowledged mild sensation the patient depressed all 20 times.

The next procedure following the baseline measurements was similar except that shock to the fingertips was now introduced contingent upon the patient not acknowledging sensation to the affected sites. During the first two shock-contingent sessions the patient did not indicate awareness of sensation to any significant degree.

The third session was terminated when the patient threw up, effectively stopping the procedure. Although this was certainly a good example of escape behavior, it was not of the type desired. Nevertheless it was felt that a breakthrough had been accomplished.

Next morning, on the final session, the patient depressed the button signalling awareness of sensation on each presentation of shock and on every site stimulated. Inasmuch as it was evident that the patient now acknowledged awareness of sensation in the formerly unfeeling areas he was told that he could now get out of his wheel chair and walk. He did so, at first haltingly but soon efficiently, and walked back to his ward. As a result of this procedure a diagnosis of conversion reaction was far less equivocal than a similar one derived from an interpretation of a test battery. There was no opportunity to follow up this case.

Case 4. This case deals with a problem of self-destructive behavior in a 7-year-old severely retarded child who was nonverbal, lacked bladder and bowel control, and who functioned at about a 2-year-old level. The behavior consisted of hand-biting which was severe enough to cause bleeding and resulted in many infections. The nursing personnel resorted to either the application of elbow splints to prevent his placing his hands in his mouth or placing boxing gloves on his hands. The child also tried to hide his hands from himself by sitting on them or holding onto the nurse's hand. Although he initially cried out in fear when his hands were free, he nevertheless bit them after he cried in pain. This child's hand-biting began at home but become highly intensified when he was hospitalized and placed in a room with another child who suffered from a rare congenital condition which among other things results in very severe com-

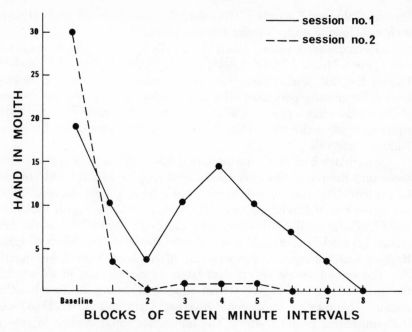

FIGURE 3.2   *Decline in hand-biting behavior when paired with contingent shock.*

pulsive biting of any part of the body, thus requiring continuous restraints.

Discussion with the nursing personnel revealed they felt considerable concern for the child but they also indicated a strong impression that he was little more than a vegetable that could not effectively communicate or learn, and showed skepticism of our ability to shape any of his behavior. Observation also indicated that the nurses' usual response to the crying that resulted from hand-biting was to become very solicitous, pick up the child and, in general, pay him considerable attention. Discussion of the reinforcing properties of this behavior on the child's hand-biting together with the suggestion that they refrain from this was met with obvious resistance.

It was apparent that efforts to extinguish the hand-biting behavior by nonattention would not likely succeed because the nursing personnel were not convinced of the efficacy of the approach and hence likely would not consistently follow through. Another contraindication to this approach was the time necessary before extinction would take place. This is a relatively slow process. In the meanwhile the biting would cause considerable distress, exposing the child to pain and infection. It was therefore decided to use an aversive conditioning approach in which an electric shock would be delivered contingent upon hand-biting. Lovass,

Freitag, Gold, and Kassorla (1965) describe the successful application of such a technique under similar circumstances.

Electrodes were placed about the child's thigh and shock was made contingent with hand-biting. Efforts to hide his hands were also shocked. During the first session there was considerable crying, frantic looking around for nursing personnel who were excluded, and constant moving about on the chair upon which he was seated. He made only one brief effort to remove the electrodes. Responses were recorded in blocks of 7-minute intervals.

After block 2 when the biting rate declined his mother was asked to come into the room. She was encouraged to pick him up and comfort him briefly. The ensuing rise in rate and relatively slow decrease likely are a result of this reinforcement. Beginning with the fourth block the word "no" was used concomitant with the shock. At the end of the first session his mother again held him and used the word "no" when he made hesitant and self-restrained movements of his hand toward his mouth.

The second session was 2 days later. As can be seen in Figure 3.2, the baseline rate was higher at that time than during the first baseline session. This may be an example of what Azrin and Holz (1966) call the punishment contrast effect. The immediate rapid decline in rate is notable. In contrast to the first session, the child sat quietly, uttered only a momentary soft cry when shock was delivered and, in general, was very composed. During the latter part of this session various nurses were asked to come in and observe his behavior. They were also instructed to use the word "no" when they noticed any movement of hand toward mouth and in turn told him "good boy" when he put his hand away. They were also instructed to ignore any subsequent hand-biting and resulting crying. At this time they were very much impressed with the rapid change in the child's biting behavior and were much more ready to follow through on a broader program for the child.

Although circumstances prevented the writer from continuing this case—others versed in behavioral methods did so—it nevertheless is instructive in several ways. First, the general problem of self-destructive behavior requires rapid, effective elimination of the behavior via aversive conditioning which the slower extinction process cannot usually accomplish, because of the danger to the patient. Second, since shaping the behavior of house staff and other important personnel is frequently more difficult than shaping the behavior of patients, a relatively quick, effective technique such as aversive conditioning provides rapid results. This in turn usually influences those personnel to cooperate more actively in a broad spectrum treatment program.

Case 5. In the following case ideational processes are dealt with, an area too frequently overlooked in favor of motor behavior. A 48-year-old male reported depressive symptomatology characterized by persistent, daily suicidal ruminations. There was also a history of several suicidal gestures. The patient's suicidal ruminations focused upon six different, but well integrated, acting-out images, which were regarded as being possibly amenable to reduction by means of aversive conditioning (Kushner & Sandler, 1966).

The patient was seen for 20 sessions, 15 to 20 trials per session, for a total of 350 trials. At each trial the therapist introduced one of the ideational cues which was followed by shock when the patient signalled that he had a clear image of the suicidal thought. An intermittent punishment schedule was introduced beginning with the fourth session. After the twelfth session the patient reported no longer being troubled by daytime ruminations, although one particular image frequently persisted upon awakening. The treatment was continued for three additional sessions, at which he indicated that an older, favorite brother had died, and that he would be absent for a week during the funeral and mourning period. He returned at the scheduled time and reported no suicidal ruminations during his absence. The punishment program was terminated after five more sessions (20th session). Although the patient continued to be mildly depressed, suicidal urges were no longer present except for an occasional transitory thought upon awakening in the morning. Initial follow-up 3 months later revealed no recurrence of the former problem. Contact with the patient after another 2-month period indicated that he could call up the suicidal imagery when he tried but that they still did not intrude upon him as in the past. He was, however, still mildly to moderately depressed. Thus, he was for the most part free of the formerly severe, persistent, and potentially dangerous suicidal ruminations for a period of approximately 6½ months.

The writer has had similar results with another such case including a remission of the depressive symptomatology. These findings may suggest that the effect of EST on depression is the product of punishment avoidance. Further inquiry in this direction may prove fruitful. Successful suppression of jealousy ruminations and other obsessive material in the same manner suggest that aversive procedures may play an important role in eliminating obsessive ruminative behavior (Kushner, 1967). The process involves both a distraction as described by Taylor (1963) in his "thought stopping" procedure as well as a conditioned suppression reaction.

The preceding cases were illustrative of rather severe reactions. Behavior of equal persistence but of little seriousness is thumb-sucking and nail-biting. Even in the most stubbornly resistive cases these behaviors are readily eliminated by requiring the patient to reproduce the appropriate actions and then shocking them contingent upon those acts. This technique has been successful with children as young as 5 and most frequently in as few as one to three sessions. In one instance, one trial sufficed. Parents are advised to supplement this treatment by applying a commercially obtained bitter preparation on the thumb or fingertips which acts as an additional aversive stimulus should there be a momentary lapse. Recurrence of the habit pattern has not been the rule.

A number of additional procedures may be utilized with aversive techniques which offer considerable flexibility and enable the patient to "treat" himself. The first such procedure is called anxiety relief after Wolpe (Wolpe & Lazarus, 1966). Following his suggestions we have initiated a program to attempt to alleviate anxiety states which do not respond to the usual relaxation or desensitization efforts. The rationale for this approach is based upon the recognition that anxiety generated by the administration of an electric shock is reduced or eliminated upon termination of the shock. A stimulus preceding or contiguous with shock termination should then become associated with the experience of relief.

A microphone connected to a voice key is placed around the patient's neck. A tape is programmed to deliver an uncomfortable shock to the fingertips on a random schedule. Shock is terminated when the patient speaks the word "relax" into the microphone which activates the voice key and shuts off the shock. When necessary patients may be placed in the treatment room in the absence of the therapist and be "treated" for 30-minute periods unattended. A timer automatically shuts down the apparatus and the patient may then remove the electrodes and microphone and report to the therapist. Ideally the patient is ultimately able to implicitly use the word "relax" in order to bring on a state of anxiety reduction. We have had both successes and failures with this technique and are now addressing ourselves to a more systematic study of the variables involved, i.e., patient characteristics, parameters of shock intensity, frequency of sessions, etc. Psychophysiological measures such as the electromyogram, galvanic skin response, and electrocardiogram are useful dependent variables in such studies.

Another form of "self-treatment" arose from a research program on alcoholism. In one phase of the study the subjects were to shock themselves contingent upon the presentation of certain stimuli associated with their drinking. For treatment purposes this phase of the research program is utilized. Patients sit behind a one-way mirror connected to fingertip electrodes and hold a switch which they can depress to deliver a shock, again contingent upon responding to instructions programmed on a continuous tape recording and delivered via a squawk box arrangement. If the switch is not depressed within a fixed period of time the shock is automatically delivered. Patients almost invariably shock themselves without too much hesitation. The outcome of such a procedure has not yet been determined but it is anticipated that better control will be obtained when the subject acts to punish his own response as opposed to passively receiving punishment from the therapist. The self-shock technique as well as the self-treatment procedure has considerable possibilities.

Another very useful and flexible approach is the remote activation procedure effective with *in vivo* situations. In this procedure the patient carries a small radio receiver into which is built a battery powered shock unit. The observer stands off at a distance with a walkie talkie type transmitter and delivers the shock at the appropriate moment. Of course care must be taken to accurately delineate the behavior to be punished so as to avoid accidental contingencies confounding the treatment. We have successfully utilized this technique with problems such as longstanding inappropriate mannerisms in a chronic schizophrenic patient as well as with a case of blepharospasm—a usually intractable spasmodic contraction of the eyelids. As an aside, the manneristic patient was switched to tokens or positive reinforcement as soon as a breakthrough was made in reducing the frequency of the undesirable behavior.

We have provided similar portable devices for patients to take home and apply whenever disturbing impulses occurred. This has proved very helpful in that it provides an opportunity to deal effectively with the spontaneous promptings and impulses not ordinarily amenable to intervention by the therapist. Wolpe (1965) has reported the similar use of such a device in the treatment of drug addiction. Feldman's (1966) objections that self-treating patients will tend to use a low level of shock which has the danger of becoming associated with a well reinforced event and thus acting as a positive reinforcer is effectively answered by presetting the intensity level internally so that the patient cannot control it.

A very promising adaptation of the portable device to suppress cigarette smoking has been developed by Whaley (1966) when he was at Coral Gables. He constructed a unit consisting of an electronic pack worn on the belt which contains a shock generator and variable interval timer. This is connected to a commercial cigarette case carried in the pocket. A small normally closed microswitch mounted on the inside of the case activated the timer upon opening the case. A strong shock is then delivered to the forearm on the average of 1½ minutes after the case is opened and usually while the subject is smoking.

Results have been very encouraging. Hospital personnel who have been long-term habitual smokers have stopped smoking relatively quickly and have not relapsed. Follow-up of 13 months without relapse is typical. Of interest is the observation that the few outpatient psychiatric patients who have used the apparatus were not able to tolerate the tension produced by the method and gave up. These findings are preliminary to a more intensive study to be started shortly with a more compact, modified unit which will be, in its entirety, slightly larger than a kingsize package of cigarettes.

In this last section an attempt was made to demonstrate the application of various aversion therapy procedures to a broad range of behavioral disorders. The practice of behavior therapy in general as well as aversive procedures in particular is not to be looked upon as a short cut to the development of clinical skills. Rather, this promising conceptualization and approach to behavioral problems must be considered to be an additional essential skill to be added to those already associated with clinical psychology. The clinician must never lose sight of the fact that he is an essential part of a process involving a complex interaction with people in distress.

NOTE

1. A report of this case study is now being prepared by D. Whaley, P. Knowles, and myself.

REFERENCES

Appel, J. B. Some schedules involving aversive control. *Journal of the Experimental Analysis of Behavior,* 1960, 3, 349-359.

Appel, J. B. Punishment and shock intensity. *Science,* 1963, 141, 528-529.

Ayllon, T., & Azrin, N. H. Punishment as a discriminative stimulus and conditioned reinforcer with humans. *Journal of the Experimental Analysis of Behavior,* 1966, 9, 411-419.

Azrin, N. H. Effects of punishment intensity during variable-interval reinforcement. *Journal of the Experimental Analysis of Behavior,* 1960, 3, 123-142.

Azrin, N. H. Effects of two intermittent schedules of immediate and non-immediate punishment. *Journal of Psychology,* 1956, 42, 3-21.

Azrin, N. H. Punishment and recovery during fixed-ratio performance. *Journal of the Experimental Analysis of Behavior,* 1959, 2, 301-305.

Azrin, N. H., & Holz, W. C. Punishment. In W. Honig (Ed.), *Operant behavior:* ment. *Journal of the Experimental Analysis of Behavior,* 1960, 3, 123-142.

Azrin, N. H., Hake, D. F., Holz, W. C., & Hutchinson, R. R. Motivational aspects of escape from punishment. *Journal of the Experimental Analysis of Behavior,* 1965, 8, 31-44.

Azrin, N. H. & Holz, W. C. Punishment. In W. Honig (Ed.), *Operant behavior: Areas of research and application.* New York: Appleton-Century-Crofts, 1966.

Azrin, N. H., Holz, W. C. & Hake, D. Fixed-ratio punishment. *Journal of the Experimental Analysis of Behavior,* 1963, 6, 141-148.

Barker, J. C. Behavior therapy for transvestism: A comparison of pharmacological and electrical aversion techniques. *British Journal of Psychiatry,* 1965, 111, 268-276.

Beech, H. R. The symptomatic treatment of writer's cramp. In H. J. Eysenck (Ed.), *Behavior therapy and the neuroses.* New York: Pergamon Press, 1960.

Brethower, D. M. & Reynolds, G. S. A facilitative effect of punishment on unpunished behavior. *Journal of the Experimental Analysis of Behavior*, 1962, 5, 191-199.

Brown, J. S., Martin, R. C., & Marrow, M. W. Self-punitive behavior in the rat: Facilitative effects of punishment on resistance to extinction. *Journal of Comparative and Physiological Psychology*, 1964, 57, 127-133.

Campbell, B. A., & Church, R. M. *Punishment and aversive behavior*. New York: Appleton-Century-Crofts, 1967.

Church, R. M. The varied effects of punishment. *Psychological Review*, 1963, 70, 369-402.

Dinsmoor, J. A. A discrimination based on punishment. *Quarterly Journal of Experimental Psychology*, 1952, 4, 27-45.

Estes, W. K. An experimental study of punishment. *Psychological Monographs*, 1944, 57 (Whole No. 263).

Eysenck, H. J. The effects of psychotherapy. *Journal of Consulting Psychology*, 1952, 16, 319-324.

Eysenck, H. J. Learning theory and behavior therapy. *Journal of Mental Science*, 1959, 105, 61-75.

Eysenck, H. J. (Ed.) *Behavior therapy and the neuroses*. New York: Pergamon Press, 1960.

Eysenck, H. J. Behavior therapy, extinction and relapse in neurosis. *British Journal of Psychiatry*, 1963, 109, 12-18.

Eysenck, H. J. & Rachman, S. *The causes and cures of neurosis*. San Diego: Robert R. Knapp, 1965.

Feldman, M. P. Aversion therapy for sexual deviations: A critical review. *Psychological Bulletin*, 1966, 65, 2, 65-79.

Feldman, M. P. & MacCulloch, M. J. The application of anticipatory avoidance learning to the treatment of homosexuality. I. Theory, technique and preliminary results. *Behavior Research and Therapy*, 1965, 2, 165-183.

Franks, C. M. Alcohol, alcoholism and conditioning. *Journal of Mental Science*, 1958, 104, 14-33.

Franks, C. M. Conditioning and conditioned aversion therapy in the treatment of the alcoholic. *The International Journal of the Addict.* 1966, 1, 61-98.

Gwinn, G. T. The effects of punishment on acts motivated by fear. *Journal of Experimental Psychology*, 1949, 39, 260-269.

Herman, R. Z. & Azrin, N. H. Punishment by noise in an alternative response situation. *Journal of the Experimental Analysis of Behavior*, 1964, 7, 185-188.

Holz, W. C., & Azrin, N. H. Discriminative properties of punishment. *Journal of the Experimental Analysis of Behavior*, 1961, 4, 225-252.

Holz, W. C., Azrin, N. H., & Ayllon, T. Elimination of behavior of mental patients by response-produced extinction. *Journal of the Experimental Analysis of Behavior*, 1963, 6, 407-412.

Humphreys, L. G. The effect of random alternation of reinforcement on the acquisition and extinction of conditioned eyelid reactions. *Journal of Experimental Psychology*, 1939, 25, 141-158.

Hunt, H. F., & Brady, J. V. Some effects of punishment and intercurrent anxiety on a simple operant. *Journal of Comparative and Physiological Psychology,* 1955, 48, 305-310.

Jones, M. C. A laboratory study of fear: The case of Peter. *Pedagogical Seminar,* 1924, 31, 308-315.

Kushner, M. The operant control of intractable sneezing. In C. D. Spielberger, R. Fox, & B. Masterton (Eds.), *Contributions to general psychology.* New York: Ronald Press, 1968.

Kushner, M. The reduction of a long standing fetish by means of aversive conditioning. In L. Ulmann & L. Krasner (Eds.), *Case studies in behavior modification.* New York: Holt, Rinehart & Winston, 1965.

Kushner, M. The disruption of ruminative ideation. Paper read at the 2nd Annual Institute in Man's Adjustment in a Complex Environment, The Behavior Therapies. V. A. Hospital, Brecksville, Ohio, May 11-12, 1967.

Kushner, M., & Sandler, J. Aversion therapy and the concept of punishment. *Behavior Research and Therapy,* 1966, 4, 179-186.

Lewis, D. J. Partial reinforcement: A selective review of the literature since 1950. *Psychological Bulletin,* 1960, 57, 1-29.

Lovass, O. I., Freitag, G., Gold, V. J., & Kassorla, I. C. Experimental studies in childhood schizophrenia; Analysis of self-destructive behavior. *Journal of Experimental Child Psychology,* 1965, 2, 67-84.

Lovibond, S. H. Intermittent reinforcement in behavior therapy. *Behavior Research and Therapy,* 1963, 1, 127-132. (a)

Lovibond, S. H. The mechanism of conditioning treatment of enuresis. *Behavior Research and Therapy,* 1963, 1, 1-18. (b)

Martin, B. Reward and punishment associated with the same goal response: A factor in the learning of motives. *Psychological Bulletin,* 1963, 60, 401-451.

Masserman, J. H. *Principles of dynamic psychiatry.* Philadelphia: Saunders, 1946.

Migler, B. Experimental self-punishment and superstitious escape behavior. *Journal of the Experimental Analysis of Behavior,* 1963, 6, 371-385.

Miller, N. E. Learning resistance to pain and fear effects over learning, exposure, and rewarded exposure in context. *Journal of Experimental Psychology,* 1960, 60, 137-145.

Rachman, S. Aversion therapy: Chemical or electrical? *Behavior Research and Therapy,* 1965, 2, 289-300.

Rachman, S., & Teasdale, J. *Aversion therapy and behavior disorders—An analysis.* Coral Gables, Fla.: University of Miami Press, 1969.

Risley, T. R. The effects and side effects of punishing the autistic behaviors of a deviant child. *Journal of Applied Behavior Analysis,* 1968, 1, 21-34.

Sandler, J. Some aspects of self-aversive stimulation in the hooded rat. *Journal of the Experimental Analysis of Behavior,* 1964, 7, 409-414.

Sandler, J., Davidson, R. S., Greene, W. E., & Holzschuh, R. D. The effects of punishment intensity on instrumental avoidance behavior. *Journal of Comparative and Physiological Psychology,* 1966, 61, 212-216.

Sandler, J., Davidson, R., & Malagodi, E. Durable maintenance of behavior during concurrent avoidance and punished-extinction conditioning. *Psychonomic Science,* 1966, 6, 105-106.

Sidman, M., Herrnstein, R. J., & Conrad, D. J. Maintenance of avoidance behavior by unavoidable shocks. *Journal of Comparative and Physiological
Psychology*, 1957, 50, 553-557.

Solomon, R. C. & Wynne, L. C. Traumatic avoidance learning: Acquisition in
normal dogs. *Psychological Monographs*, 1953, 67, 4 (Whole No. 354).

Solomon, R. L. Punishment. *American Psychologist*, 1964, 19, 239-253.

Taylor, J. G. A behavioral interpretation of obsessive-compulsive neuroses.
Behavior Research and Therapy, 1963, 1, 237.

Turner, L. H. & Solomon, R. C. Human traumatic avoidance learning: Theory
and experiments on the operant-respondent distinction and failures to learn.
Psychological Monographs, 1962, 76, 40 (Whole No. 559).

Ulrich, R. E. & Azrin, N. H. Reflexive fighting in response to aversive stimulation. *Journal of the Experimental Analysis of Behavior*, 1962, 5, 511-520.

Walton, D. & Mather, M. D. The application of learning principles to the treatment of obsessive compulsive states. *Behavior Research and Therapy*, 1963,
1, 163-174.

Watson, J. B. & Rayner, R. Conditioned emotional reactions. *Journal of Experimental Psychology*, 1920, 3, 1-14.

Whaley, D. Automatic punishment of cigarette smoking by a portable electronic
device. Unpublished report, 1966.

Wolpe, J. *Psychotherapy by reciprocal inhibition*. Stanford: Stanford University
Press, 1958.

Wolpe, J. Conditioned inhibition of craving in drug addiction: A pilot experiment. *Behavior Research and Therapy*, 1965, 2, 285-288.

Wolpe, J. & Lazarus, A. A. *Behavior therapy techniques: A guide for treatment
of the neuroses*. New York: Pergamon Press, 1966.

Zimmerman, J. & Ferster, C. B. Intermittent punishment of S△ responding in
matching-to-sample. *Journal of the Experimental Analysis of Behavior*,
1963, 6, 349-356.

4: Rehabilitation

JACK L. MICHAEL

The evolution of cultural practices which foster the survival of disabled individuals has been accompanied by an interest in rendering such individuals as independent and socially useful as possible. In the United States the professionalization of this interest is largely due to the economic support and intellectual leadership of the Federal-State Rehabilitation Programs and the primary concern of these programs has been the potentially employable person of labor-force age. For this reason, the field of rehabilitation can best be described as a collection of medical, behavioral, and social technologies developed to deal with this original client population, and the subsequent extension of some of these technologies to other populations, such as the permanently disabled child, the mentally retarded, the emotionally disturbed or mentally ill, the incarcerated criminal, the aged, and recently, the culturally disadvantaged. In spite of this broad extension, however, most workers who would characterize themselves as being involved in rehabilitation, particularly psychologists in rehabilitation, would be likely to show some general orienting attitudes that are residual from the efforts to deal with the original client, the recently disabled adult. The present paper, therefore, will be primarily concerned with the relevance of behavior modification to the rehabilitation of the individual of labor-force age who becomes disabled as a result of injury or illness.

The principle disability conditions in this category are amputations, due to accidents, war, and diseases such as cancer; the crippling conditions collectively referred to as arthritis and rheumatism; cardiovascular

My interest in the field of rehabilitation and many of the ideas contained in this paper are the direct result of my association with Professor Lee Meyerson, and this acknowledgment can only be a partial indication of my deep appreciation for his intellectual stimulation and guidance.

diseases in the forms of hypertension, heart attacks, and cerebrovascular accidents resulting in partial paralysis; other forms of paralysis due to injury or disease of the central or peripheral nervous system; language disorders resulting largely from cerebrovascular accidents, externally produced injuries, and neurological diseases; facial disfigurement; auditory disability and visual disability occurring in adulthood as a result of injury or disease. There are, of course, many disability conditions other than these major categories, but these will serve to characterize the client population.

After considering the relevance of behavior modification to the rehabilitation of the recently disabled adult a brief extension will be made to the "habilitation" of the disabled child, the mentally retarded, and the culturally disadvantaged. Rehabilitation of the mental hospital patient will *not* be considered in this chapter, since this is the area where behavior modification methods are best known, and also the area where "rehabilitation" psychology is least distinguishable from traditional clinical psychology.

THE ROLE OF PSYCHOLOGY IN REHABILITATION

The task of restoring the physically disabled to more effective function can be roughly divided into two phases: preserving and supplementing residual physical function by prosthetic devices and special training; and reestablishing employability by vocational training and guidance. For the first phase, which is commonly called "medical" rehabilitation the relevant technologies and professions are the medical specialties concerned with the various kinds of injury and illness, especially physical medicine; the medically related areas of nursing, physical therapy, occupational therapy, audiology, speech therapy; and the engineering areas concerned with prosthetic appliances. The technologies most relevant to the second phase, "vocational" rehabilitation, are essentially those of the occupational specialist and vocational counselor; and also those of the educator, particularly in the sense of vocational training.

The psychologist became a member of the rehabilitation team because many decisions seem to require a knowledge of the client's abilities, particularly his intelligence, and his emotional and motivational characteristics. In addition to assessing these various characteristics by means of tests and interviews and making this information available to the other rehabilitation workers, the psychologist sometimes becomes involved in supportive counseling and psychotherapy. In other words, the psychologist generally performs the same functions that he performs in the outpatient mental hygiene clinic, or in the mental hospital: testing, counseling, and psychotherapy.

As will be seen from what follows, the behavior modification approach implies a much more important role for the psychologist. Most of the activities of medical and vocational rehabilitation involve and, in fact, require the control of behavior—the behavior of the client, of the treatment staff, and of the client's friends and family—and as the expert in this area the psychologist should be closely involved in all of these activities. Rather than providing information about the client which is then used by someone else, he should be the primary authority in the arrangement of the environment so as to produce, maintain, or eliminate behavior. It may turn out that the psychologist doesn't know enough about behavior to accomplish all of these goals, but even in that case, there is no other specialty to which an appeal can be made.

BEHAVIOR MODIFICATION

By considering many instances of the expression's usage, one is led to describe "behavior modification" in terms of a substantive component, a methodological component, and their *direct* application to the *control* of human behavior (as contrasted with an *inferential* application to the *explanation* of human behavior).

The substantive component consists primarily of a few basic functional relations, and a few derived or more complex relations that have been developed from the study of lower animal behavior and particularly from the work of B. F. Skinner and his associates. Specifically, considerable use is made of the *operant-respondent* distinction, with the identification of *consequence manipulation* as the critical operation relevant to the control of operant behavior. In addition to the fact that some behavior can be increased in frequency by providing certain consequences (*reinforcers*) and decreased by providing others (*punishers*) there are only three other basic qualitative relationships which play an important role in behavior modification. The strengthening effect of reinforcement and the weakening effect of punishment are both temporary in the sense that they are reversed when behavior occurs and is no longer followed by the consequence. In the case of reinforcement, this procedure and its result are referred to as *extinction;* there is no special term for the similar temporariness of the punishment effect. Furthermore, the behavioral changes produced by consequences are somewhat specific to the "ambient" stimulus conditions existing at the moment of occurrence of the consequence. There is, thus, a natural form of *stimulus control* in that the effect of a consequence can be seen at its maximum value when the stimulus conditions resemble most closely those that existed at the moment of occurrence of the consequence. On the other hand, this form of control is only partial, and considerable generalization of the behavioral change occurs to different stimulus conditions (the phenomenon of stimulus generalization). Finally, there is the fact that stimuli present during reinforcement become capable, to some extent, of acting as reinforcers or punishers themselves, that is, they become *conditioned reinforcers* or *conditioned punishers*.

Besides these basic relationships between environmental changes and behavioral changes one need mention only a few more complex relations or techniques to essentially cover the substantive component of behavior modification. When reinforcement is not given for every response the relationship is referred to as *intermittent reinforcement*. There are many kinds of intermittent reinforcement: some involve the requirement that a specified number of similar responses occur before reinforcement; some the requirement that a period of time pass before a response can be reinforced; and there are an unlimited number of other more complex relationships. These complex contingencies, or *reinforcement schedules* produce complex patterns of behavior, and although relatively little use has as yet been made of this information in behavior modification, it will undoubtedly become more useful as behavior modifiers attack more intricate problems. The technique of reinforcing successive approximations to a desired form of behavior, or *shaping*, has been of considerable use, and the analogous procedure for developing control by complex stimuli, *stimulus fading*, is being increasingly applied.

The fact that the current variety of behavior modification owes much more to the approach of B. F. Skinner and his associates than to the several other approaches within the experimental psychology of learning is probably understandable in terms of the methodological contributions of those who have been primarily interested in operant conditioning. A number of phrases have been developed to refer to this methodology, "individual organism research" and the "experimental analysis of behavior" being the most common. Distrust of behavioral principles which can be described only in terms of group averages, and an interest in complex reinforcement contingencies which require many hours of exposure before stable effects can be seen are probably the main factors leading to the development of this methodology which emphasizes the use of a single organism as an experimental subject. The methodology involves considerable reliance on frequency of response in a free-responding situation as the principle dependent variable, and usually makes use of prolonged exposure to a baseline condition, followed by exposure to the experimental condition, then return to baseline, when possible, and so on.[1]

For many kinds of experimental questions this is an extremely valuable and convenient methodology, and for questions involving the long-term effects of complex reinforcement contingencies it is probably the only effective methodology. From the point of view of behavior modification the development of this methodology has had several very important results. In the first place, it is extremely appropriate to what is probably the most common experimental situation involving abnormal behavior: a person with some unique form of abnormal behavior who is subjected to some form of relatively prolonged treatment which is hoped will alter the abnormal behavior. Methodologies involving comparisons of groups are often impossible to use because of the uniqueness of the form of abnormality, and even if several similar patients could be found, these methodologies are prohibitive in terms of time and effort because of the prolonged observation period and prolonged treatment required. The availability of a ready-made technology for recording observations, describing the data in graphic form, and drawing conclusions about its reliability (even though the technology was developed within the animal laboratory) makes the clinical situation one that is subject to the kind of research that is most relevant to truly clinical questions (i.e., those involving the modification of abnormal behavior rather than general issues of typology or personality theory).

Secondly, the individual organism research methodology is the methodology of a group of highly productive experimental psychologists, who publish their research findings in a journal whose publication policies include strong preference for this methodology. This means that the clinician, whose research status had always been in some question, could publish research in a form that had the approval of an important segment of the field of experimental psychology. A number of the early behavior modification papers were published in that journal, *The Journal for the Experimental Analysis of Behavior*. Recently, the organization that published this experimental journal has begun the publication of a journal devoted completely to behavior modification, *The Journal of Applied Behavior Analysis*.

A third effect of this methodological development within the experimental psychology of animal learning was the increasing availability of animal researchers who could become interested in human behavior problems and whose animal laboratory training was quite relevant to research on these problems. The techniques and concepts of the operant conditioning laboratory are readily applicable to the control of behavior in the ward for the chronic psychotic patient, the institution for the severely retarded, and for that matter to the classroom for normal children.

In addition to its procedural contributions, individual organism research has been responsible for the development of a good deal of mechanical and electronic apparatus for the study of lower animal behavior, and this apparatus has proved quite useful in the study of humans.

Beside the substantive and methodological components and probably because of the latter the present behavior modification movement differs considerably from previous "learning theory" approaches to psychotherapy. Learning theory has long been used as a way of interpreting psychodynamic processes and concepts and as a way of justifying or describing the activities of the clinical psychologist, whose activities however, were almost never developed in learning theory contexts. The present behavior modifiers are primarily involved in the direct application of their substantive and methodological tools to the change or control of some form of human behavior, not simply to the explanation of its existence or present features. Such explanation is often given, but it is clearly secondary in importance to manipulation.

One side effect of this concern for direct manipulation has been an emphasis on operant as opposed to respondent processes. There is little question that for many of our smooth muscle and glandular responses unconditioned stimuli can be identified and stimulus pairing can be utilized to bring such responses under the control of previously ineffective stimuli. In other words, there is little question that respondent operations and processes are relevant to human behavior. As it turns out, however, the psychologist is seldom able to characterize his goal for a particular client as the direct alteration of some respondent behavior. There are some exceptions, with toilet training and certain aspects of sexual behavior being probably the clearest examples of respondent involvement, but even in these cases, a good deal of the psychologist's concern is with the operant components of the problem behavior. It was at one time quite common to speak of anxiety as a respondent process and to characterize a good deal of neurotic behavior as resulting from the "conditioning" of anxiety to certain situations. This way of talking about abnormal behavior is still fairly widespread, but such respondent components as may constitute "anxiety" are seldom the behavior of primary interest to the psychologist nor are such respondent components dealt with directly. The main concern of the psychologist as well as the patient is usually the operant behavior which is supposedly interfered with by the anxiety, or the operant behaviors which occur to protect the patient against the effects of the anxiety, or which are related in some even more intricate way to the anxiety. With the development of a powerful technology for controlling operant behavior by the manipulation of its consequences, the concern for anxiety seems to be giving way to an interest in the more direct control of the operant behaviors which actually are at issue.

In any case, behavior modifiers often ignore respondent processes—the current approach is sometimes simply called an operant approach to clinical psychology—but this is usually not out of disrespect for the relevance of respondents to human behavior, but simply because our respondent behaviors do not make the kind of contact with our environment that gets us in trouble.

REHABILITATION OF THE RECENTLY DISABLED ADULT

The defining characteristic of a disability as opposed to a temporary illness is the long-term or permanent change in the individual's life situation. The operant components of this change can be characterized rather generally as an altered pattern of behavioral consequences the dominant feature of which is deterioration. Many reinforcement opportunities are no longer available, and there are a number of new punishment[2] contingencies that result from the disability.

Outstanding of the former are the reinforcers that are interfered with by disability-produced restrictions on physical activity, especially when this involves the individual's livelihood or his main forms of recreation. Significant among new forms of punishment is the pain that often accompanies a disability condition. Another that is seldom appreciated by the nondisabled individual is the widely prevalent social disapproval of a disabled individual. For the nondisabled reader who finds this last notion not in keeping with his own experience, Wright's (1960) convincing description of the many forms of discrimination experienced by the disabled will function as an eye opener. There is no question that many positive attitudes toward the disabled are expressed publicly, but these are far outweighed by a generally negative view. The practical disadvantages of most forms of disability are obvious to everyone, although often exaggerated, and knowledge of these disadvantages creates a relatively strong negative attitude, even if this is accompanied by expressions of tolerance, sympathy, and "understanding." The point can be easily made by considering the general behavior of relatives and friends of a girl who has expressed some interest in marrying a physically disabled individual, for example a man who is confined to a wheel chair. Many parents' "understanding" attitude toward the disabled does not extend to support for their daughter's intention to marry such an individual.

But after all, lost reinforcers and new forms of punishment are a part of life, and we are all exposed to misfortune. Loved ones die; professional opportunities don't materialize, or are missed entirely; strong needs develop which cannot be satisfied. A serious physical disability, however, although not unique among misfortunes, involves several behavioral features which must be kept in mind as we attempt to understand the disability condition. In the first place, the ordinary adult's social and verbal history is sufficiently well developed that he can be affected emotionally by his own and others' descriptions of his future somewhat as he will be affected by the future itself. Although never blind before, his experiences with visual sources of pleasure, his efforts to get around in the dark, his knowledge of the life of blind individuals are all such that he is fully capable of reacting to his own immediate blindness in a manner somewhat appropriate to the future loss of reinforcers that he will experience. The human is capable of a great deal more sadness than the lower animal for just this reason. The dog whose master dies experiences the disadvantages of this change somewhat gradually. The devastating irreversibility of the change only gradually unfolds and the organism can adapt to the gradually changing situation. The human, on the other hand, because of his verbal skills can react to the situation all at once, as soon as the verbal stimuli are appropriate. Furthermore, he can react to it over and over again as he and others provide further stimuli related to the irreversible change, and this reaction, like the immediate reaction to the loss of a reinforcer or to some form of punishment, consists of negative emotional conditions plus his operant repertoire of escape and avoidance behaviors.

A second important feature of a serious physical disability is that it affects a wide range of the individual's life activities. An amputation, for example, will have implications for his vocation, his recreational activities, his social relations—including sex, and many other aspects of his life.

A third feature of a serious physical disability is that it often (but not always) leaves the individual identifiable as a less fortunate or disadvantaged person. Not only is he less fortunate than others but everyone can plainly see the nature of his misfortune.

A fourth and final distinguishing characteristic of a serious disability relates to the widespread negative attitude toward the disabled. Many nondisabled individuals have this negative attitude which usually involves a well-developed verbal repertoire regarding disability. The normal individual has often expressed pity, sympathy, and other forms of negativity toward some disabled person (not to his face) and had this behavior reinforced by agreement from other normal individuals. For example, it is common for normal individuals to express to each other the view that they would "rather be dead than confined to a wheel chair the rest of their lives." This repertoire often extends to all aspects of illness and dependency to the point that many nondisabled individuals talk about the disadvantages of a disability in terms much more severe than are actually warranted. Now when such an individual becomes disabled himself, this well-developed verbal repertoire is invoked but with respect to his own situation. He finds himself with a strong tendency to say unpleasant, perhaps devastating things about his own condition of disability and the emotional effect of "hearing" these things about himself is not attenuated because he is, himself, the speaker.

These four features of a serious disability often combine to produce an emotional catastrophe. The ordinary tasks of rehabilitation can be made very difficult by this overwhelming emotional condition. Many reinforcers which would ordinarily be quite useful are essentially ineffective, and many punishers are equally useless since the individual is already in such a bad state that nothing makes it worse. It is not clear at the present time, and perhaps will always depend to some extent on the individual case, whether it is better to work directly with this emotional state by explicit manipulation of counteremotional variables of some sort (possibly even drugs), or whether one should simply use whatever reinforcers and punishers are effective and allow the emotional effects to subside with time. As will be mentioned below, however, much of the emotional behavior probably has operant components that prolong its effect and it is especially important that these not be maintained by social contacts within the rehabilitation setting.

Behavior Management in the Hospital Setting

When an individual is hospitalized immediately after an injury or during the acute phases of an illness, he is subjected to an environment that differs in a number of ways from his ordinary environment, but there are two changes in particular which are often responsible for future difficulty in the case of the individual with a permanent disability. In the first place, the individual who has been injured or who is seriously ill is the recipient of a good deal of attention and sympathy contingent upon behavior on his part, usually verbal, indicating discontent, discomfort, pain, sadness, etc. Most of us have a well-developed repertoire of sympathetic and helpful behavior toward the friend or relative who is in trouble. In addition, the patient-staff ratio at most hospitals is such that the staff can only attend to those patients who are in trouble and thus various forms of care depend upon some request for care on the part of the patient. It has been shown under a number of circumstances that attention, interest, or approval by one person can function as a strong reinforcer for various kinds of behavior on the part of another person. It is also quite clear that this effect does not require that either individual be "aware" of the relationship between behavior and approval (Ayllon & Haughton, 1964; Harris, Wolf, & Baer, 1964; Meyerson, Kerr & Michael, 1967; Krasner, 1958). The result is simply that the individual's supplicative repertoire is greatly strengthened.

Another feature of the hospital environment is also related to the high patient-staff ratio and the general difficulties of caring for a number of people who are ill or injured. The patient is usually forced to adopt a point of view of practically unquestioning obedience regarding his own welfare. He is not encouraged to do things for himself since his efforts to aid in his own treatment are not necessarily reliable. The patient is usually quite uninformed regarding the medical aspects of his treatment and attempts to explain them to him take valuable time and are frequently misunderstood. So he is not encouraged even to "understand" the purpose and anticipated effects of the various features of his treatment, but only to do as he is told. This authoritarian pattern is thought to be a convenient one for the staff and prevails in most hospitals with the result that the individual's repertoire of independent or self-initiated behavior is extinguished or punished and a pattern of passive dependency is strongly rewarded.

In the case of an individual who recovers completely from whatever the cause of his hospitalization, this strengthened supplicative behavior and the increased dependency do not usually pose a serious problem for future adjustment. As an individual recovers from a broken leg, for example, he gradually assumes the responsibilities and begins to receive the reinforcers appropriate to his previous uninjured condition. The individuals in his environment, having some familiarity with broken legs and recovery therefrom, make increasing demands and require increasing independence. Furthermore, the injured individual's previous repertoire regarding independence is appropriate to his increasingly effective physical condition. He doesn't really have to learn a new way of life, but just assume his old.

On the other hand, an individual with a permanent disability, after he is no longer receiving intense care, continues usually for a long period to receive further treatment, either in a rehabilitation ward at a hospital, at a rehabilitation center as an outpatient, or in his own home. His supplicative behavior and his dependency continue to receive support for a much longer period than the individual with a temporary illness or injury. Furthermore, he usually must adjust to a new way of life for which a good deal of his previous independent behavior is no longer appropriate. And as mentioned earlier, this new way of life often involves a considerable worsening in terms of reinforcers and punishers, a condition which predisposes the social environment to support supplicative and dependency behavior, even when no further treatment of any kind is occurring.

Although it is not difficult to recognize these two sources of undesirable behavior change in the client, it is much harder to prevent them. About all one can hope for in the case of the increased dependency is that an awareness of the problem on the part of rehabilitation personnel will result in their attempting more systematically to undo the effect as soon as the patient comes under their care. A change in ordinary hospital practices is a form of cultural evolution about which the rehabilitation worker can do relatively little.

To avoid the dramatic strengthening of the patient's supplicative behavior that is sometimes seen is also quite difficult. The hospital setting is one where ordinary activities and reinforcers are unavailable and as a result there is a great deal of boredom. Such an environment predisposes the patient to be reinforced by attention and interest beyond what he would be in a more demanding and more reinforcing environment. His permanent disability, furthermore, predisposes others to be unusually sympathetic about his future difficulties and present discomforts. A pattern of verbal behavior in which the injured individual expresses discouragement about the future by characterizing it in most unfavorable terms and the other individuals in his environment reassure him by characterizing it more favorably is a very common form of social "ping pong" played by the disabled and his friends and relatives. The "popularity" of this game is not only due to the strengthening effect on the patient's supplicative behavior; the sympathizer is also strongly reinforced for his behavior because it often temporarily terminates the depressive behavior of the patient by diverting him to other topics.

A far better approach to such discouraging remarks, of course, would be to say nothing and appear somewhat "lost in thought," but to show special interest and attention when any constructive or encouraging behaviors occur. To obtain this kind of deliberate social manipulation by nurses, aides, physicians, relatives, and friends of the patient requires a good deal of supervision, however. Ayllon & Haughton (1964) and Fordyce, Fowler, Lehmann, & Delateur (1968) instructed the supervised such reactions on the part of nurses and aides with considerable success, but the natural behavior of people in the helping profession and in the medical profession does not occur in this way. Within our culture, and it has probably been a desirable cultural development, it is considered particularly unethical to dispense approval, affection, attention and interest in a deliberate manner. "Machiavellian" is a derogatory adjective referring to this type of control. One is expected to show interest only when one is, in fact, interested; to approve only sincerely; and so on. To behave otherwise is described in more modern terms as "being a phoney." The evidence seems quite clear, however, that even well-intentioned and sincere, realistic, concern for another person's difficulties may have the harmful effect of strengthening his unproductive behavior toward these difficulties. And in the same vein, simulated disinterest (while "crying on the inside") coupled with simulated interest when skillfully utilized *can* produce and maintain highly productive problem solving behavior.

One final aspect of behavior management in the hospital concerns the general trend toward starting some of the educational aspects of rehabilitation while the patient is still receiving relatively intense care. At the present time much of this takes the form of counseling with the goal of eliminating some of the emotional reactions to the disability and also providing information that will be needed in later adjustment. From a behavioral point of view much of this "educational" activity suffers because there are no relevant consequences related to the client's behavior. If it is really thought important that the client acquire some information (for example, about employment opportunities, living conditions, or recreational activities for individuals with his disability) the responsibilities of the educator go considerably beyond simply "telling" the client about these aspects of his future. His educational environment should be programmed in such a way that he is presented with stimulus materials and required to behave toward these materials, which behavior is then differentially consequated depending upon its appropriateness (effective forms of consequation will be described in the following section). The rehabilitation counselor who is dealing with the patient still receiving hospital care must function like all other educators who are attempting to develop a repertoire. This will be discussed in detail below, but briefly he should maximize the probability that the initial stages of the repertoire will occur by proper arrangement of stimulus materials, consequate the repertoire as it develops, sample frequently (give tests, in other words) to see that the repertoire is developing, and when it is not, provide remedial training of some sort. As the college professor quickly finds out, simply telling people things and being sure that they "understand" these things as you tell them is not a particularly effective way to change anyone's behavior.

Special Rehabilitation Training

A good deal of rehabilitation is a form of educational management. In order to perform the ordinary activities of daily living the disabled person must acquire new skills. Some of this acquisition involves new verbal stimulus control as in much of our formal education. Quite a bit, however, consists in learning new sensory-motor skills as in athletic training, where muscle strengthening plays a critical role in the acquisition. The areas of physical therapy, occupation therapy,[3] speech therapy, and others are largely devoted to the development of these new skills. From a behavioral point of view, educational management can be broken into two main activities. One is the analysis of the skill into its components and the arrangement of these components into an efficient sequence. The other is the management of the differential consequation that must occur for correct versus incorrect, or for good versus poor performances. A carefully arranged sequence of skill components intricately linked to reinforcement contingencies is a *program of instruction*, and although "programmed instruction" has most commonly referred to the development of verbal stimulus control the term is considerably broader in implication (Skinner, 1968, p. 65-79). Programming in this broader sense consists in reinforcing an organism for behavior that he is already capable of and in fact performs at a reasonably high rate for the available reinforcer, and then gradually altering the task requirement so that new behavior develops without any prolonged period of unreinforced responding.

Although much of present rehabilitation training implicitly involves one or more features of programmed instruction, there are two advantages to the explicit and deliberate application of programming technology. In the first place the behaviorally oriented programmer generally devotes a great deal of his time and effort to breaking the task into components sufficiently small that the gradually changing reinforcement contingencies will not result in any prolonged period of "trial and error" or unreinforced behavior. Without an explicit recognition of the value of this form of gradualness the ordinary instructor or rehabilitation specialist is likely to stop too soon in his task analysis. It should be possible, by careful design of the physical environment (pulley systems to support part of the individual's weight, braces and props to restrict and limit certain kinds of movements), and by gradual alteration of controlling stimuli (starting with artifically gross and obvious cues and gradually fading them out and leaving behavior under the control of the subtle cues appropriate to the realistic situation) to insure the practically errorless generation of a new repertoire. Further refinements in the program can then be directed toward increasing the speed of acquisition.

It is beyond the scope of the present work to present the details of programming technology, but a good deal has been written in this area and a good deal of experimentation and program development has taken place. As a result it is quite likely that something of use and relevance to every rehabilitation task can be found in the programming literature. The reference cited above by Skinner is a very interesting and readable introduction to the concepts underlying the programming movement. Another major reference in this area is Glaser (1965).

The second advantage of explicitly conceptualizing rehabilitation training as a form of programmed instruction (in the broad sense of this term) is the increased likelihood of appropriate concern for the adequacy of the reinforcer and the reinforcement procedure. From a behavioral point of view an individual who is learning must receive some sort of reinforcement for his efforts.

There are, of course, a number of circumstances where the educational manager does not have to arrange the specific reinforcers because the individual comes equipped with an interest in some long-range goal and with the capacity to be reinforced by signs of approach toward this goal. For example, a person who would be highly reinforced by being able to drive a car need not be given specific reinforcement in the sub-activities of driving. It is often sufficient simply to provide verbal instructions and an opportunity to practice: the signs of accomplishment will then function as a reinforcer for the activities that produced them. This is usually assumed to be the situation for the physically disabled. It seems plausible that anyone who has been injured and needs to acquire new skill in order to be more effective will in fact "want" to acquire these skills and will be well reinforced by signs of achievement. From this assumption it follows that failure to progress in the acquisition of the new skill can only be interpreted as some form of personality difficulty, usually referred to as a "motivational" problem.

This problem of the individual who seems capable of acquiring more behavior but who does not acquire it is a major problem in the field of rehabilitation and is likely to be the first problem encountered by the behavior modifier who offers his services in this area. As Fishman states, "Empirical evidence substantiates the theoretical considerations that the single most important problem facing the rehabilitation worker concerns the ways and means of implementing marginal motivation" (1962, p. 28). From a behavioral point of view, however, such marginal motivation seems merely to be a case of insufficient or poorly arranged reinforcement. The basic question that should be asked is what does the patient get out of this activity? The problem of motivation is essentially a simple one. One must merely arrange the environment so that its desirable features are only available contingent upon participation and accomplishment in the rehabilitation training activity. It is in this area that the behavior modifier is making and will probably continue to make the greatest impact on the field of rehabilitation.

What reinforcers are available? First let us consider two that are natural products of the training situation. These are the attention and approval of the trainer, and the stimuli arising from the training activity itself which indicate improving ability or skill. Both of these kinds of consequences are dependent for their effectiveness on their relationship to other events—that is they are conditioned reinforcers, and therefore cannot be assumed to be effective for all individuals or for any individual at all times. However, they are probably fairly important sources for reinforcement for many of the disabled but they are not generally used as effectively as they could be. Social approval and attention by the trainer functions as a reinforcer for a number of reasons, but one important one relates to the individual's role in the authority system of the institution or social organization dealing with the client. Thus it is important that the trainer have (or appear to have) a considerable amount of autonomy and authority. Any stimuli that emphasize the trainer's subordinate position will render his approval and disapproval less effective as consequences for the client.

The most serious problem with social reinforcement, however, is the nondeliberate or spontaneous use of this reinforcer. This was mentioned above in connection with the natural tendency to attend to and show an interest in the client who is not performing as a means of inducing him to perform. Once he is engaged in whatever activity is relevant to his rehabilitation the therapist most commonly leaves him to work with another patient. The reversal of this procedure would generate considerably more participation in rehabilitation activities. In other words, if the therapist showed an interest in the patient only after he began to engage in some activity and while he was continuing to engage in it, but withdrew his interest when the patient was not engaging in the activity, the attention and interest would function as a reinforcer for the activity. As it is it functions as a reinforcer for inactivity or quitting. The situation represents another example of the same vicious circle that was described in connection with supplicative behavior. The inactivity of the client represents a stimulus situation that is aversive to the therapist. By approaching such a client and inducing him to engage in some activity the therapist is reinforced by the removal of this form of aversiveness. If the therapist's attention functions as a reinforcer for the client, the client is reinforced for his inactivity, and although he may perform as a function of the urging and instruction by the therapist his future probability of inactivity has actually been increased.

A clear example of the dramatic effects that result from reversing the normal approach to the nonperforming client is the study by Kerr and Meyerson (1964) where a group of "malingerers" in a work-hardening program were induced to become hard workers as a result of the occupational therapist's providing sympathy, interest, and suggesting rest only while they were working, and ignoring them at other times. There are many other forms of this particular vicious circle, and behavior modifiers have been concerned with the reversal of the normal pattern of interaction in a wide variety of settings. In mental hospitals patients tend to be ignored until they do something that is bizarre at which point aides, nurses, and psychologists become interested in them. The article mentioned earlier by Ayllon and Haughton describes a common example of this phenomenon and a number of other examples in the mental hospital are described in Ayllon and Michael (1959). The phenomenon is seen in ordinary educational settings with perhaps the classic case being the teacher who dismisses her pupils when they are rowdy. It is seen in institutions for the mentally retarded where a child exhibits some form of undesirable behavior and attendants terminate the behavior by restraining the child. The normal parent in dealing with his normal child often ignores the child while he is behaving well but as soon as he begins to cause trouble interacts with him in a pleasant way, and provides a form of distraction or entertainment. This pattern of interaction is indeed widespread and probably is responsible for a good deal of maladaptive, neurotic, and generally ineffective behavior on the part of people who are in some form of trouble, as well as being responsible for a good deal of wasted time on the part of the individual who "helps" them.

The other reinforcer occurring as a natural product of the training situation, the signs of increasing effectiveness for increasing skill, is also not utilized as effectively as it might be in most rehabilitation training.

For a stimulus to function as a reinforcer it should be a clear and obvious change in the environment, and the stimuli associated with improving effectiveness seldom meet this qualification. In the first place, improvement represents a relationship between a current stimulus situation and one which has occurred hours or days earlier. In addition the changes in effectiveness are quite gradual, so that today's ability compared with that of 3 weeks earlier may constitute a relationship that is quite reinforcing, but compared with yesterday's it may be hardly noticeable as a change. As a result of these difficulties it is important that the rehabilitation specialist arrange a form of record keeping for the client which will enhance the effectiveness of these stimuli. The problem is quite simple in many cases since all that is required is that the client, himself, keep a graphic record of his progress. In this way the stimulus produced by today's activity, even though only slightly different from yesterday's, can be appreciated as a further representation of a gradual increase of some sort, easily seen from observing the gradually rising curve on the graph paper. The problem is not unlike that of the person attempting to lose or gain weight but who cannot be easily reinforced by the effects of his efforts because the change is a gradual one—a situation where a graphic record of daily weight located above the bathroom scales can serve an important function. Fordyce et al. (1968) and also Goodkin (1966) made good use of this technique.

Unfortunately, a patient-kept record of progress is not always possible because of the nature of the rehabilitation activity. A client is often encouraged to attempt tasks which have a threshold skill and strength requirement. Until his skill or strength or both reach a certain level he cannot perform the task at all. However, it is usually only a matter of mechanical ingenuity to arrange some gradual approximations to the final task and once it is realized how important a record of progress is, tasks which permit such a record can be generally sought. As a general principle, tasks should be selected which permit measurable variations of smaller magnitude than the smallest amount of improvement which would be expected from daily practice. Tasks should be avoided which require a number of daily practice sessions before a measurable change can be recorded.

A special problem arises when an effort is made to strengthen muscle function below the range where the muscle moves a portion of the body, as in residual muscle training after injuries to the central nervous system. However, present electronic technology is fully capable of recording changes in muscle action over a continuum that lies considerably below the magnitude necessary to move a portion of the body, and such electronic technology would serve a useful purpose in rehabilitation training of this type. The work of Hefferline, Keenan, and Harford (1959) involved the recording of minimal muscle responses and their strengthening by reinforcement under conditions where the subject was not even aware of the muscle movement. There is no reason why this technology could not be applied to residual muscle training in such a way that the patient would have available a readily discriminable visual or auditory stimulus resulting from his muscle action even though the muscle action did not produce any movement that could be observed with the naked eye, or "felt" kinesthetically.

The effectiveness of improvement as a reinforcer should not be overestimated, however. There is no question that it probably functions as a form of reinforcement for most individuals but what is at issue is the strength of the reinforcer. In the case of many permanently disabled individuals, even the maximum improvement possible may represent only a minor accomplishment when compared with the individual's skill before he was disabled. The paraplegic who is acquiring some toe movements but who can never hope to walk or run may not be sufficiently reinforced by his accomplishment for it to maintain any very effortful behavior. In addition, for complex social reasons, increased independence may not be reinforcing at all in that the individual may lose some control of his social environment although gaining some control of his physical environment. Progress under such conditions may function as a punisher.

Another reinforcer closely related to the rehabilitation training itself is rest from the activity. Azrin (1960) has shown, although not with disabled individuals, the importance of rest pauses as reinforcers. Once again the natural training procedure does not seem to utilize rest pauses as reinforcers since a very common approach is to encourage the patient to work for a specific period of time and then take a break; or even worse, the rest is often suggested when the individual is showing signs of discontent or fatigue. The most effective procedure would be to try to arrange that a rest pause occurs after a fixed amount of work and then gradually increase the work requirement. Although it may seem paradoxical, the best time to suggest a rest break is while the client is working most effectively, as was done in the study by Kerr and Meyerson mentioned above.

The three kinds of reinforcement discussed so far are by no means adequate for all clients. For a variety of reasons social reinforcement may not be effective; signs of increasing effectiveness may represent such trivial improvement in the face of the catastrophic worsening represented by the disability that they are, at best, very weak reinforcers; and rest pauses after all can be obtained by not working at all. So what other reinforcers are available? The situation is by no means hopeless and much of behavior modification in other areas has consisted in rearranging the environment so as to make better use of available sources of reinforcement. The general approach is simply to control as many aspects of the environment as possible and to permit contact with its reinforcing features only contingent upon participation in the training activity. At first blush this seems to be a childish way to deal with an adult and it must, indeed, be handled skillfully in order not to generate emotional resistance. Some suggestions for dealing with this aspect of the problem will be made later.

The general strategy is first to survey all the activities which are engaged in frequently. If the setting is an institutional one, there are usually a number of planned recreational and social activities under the control of the staff, such as television viewing, going to a movie, a social contact with some staff member, home visits, swimming, massage, etc. In the case of the individual who is not institutionalized, one must make the survey with respect to his own particular living situation, but it is not usually difficult to find a number of things which he can do or have that can be arranged in a hierarchy of preference.

At this point it is important to introduce the concept of a token or point system. Many, perhaps most, of the activities which reinforce the normal human require a certain duration of participation for them to be effective as reinforcers. For example, swimming as a reinforcing activity requires proper dress, transportation to the pool, and at least 15 or 20 minutes of actual swimming activity in order to be a reinforcer (unless, of course, the reinforcement derives from an escape from some other activity). On the other hand, reinforcement to be maximally effective should be given often, and immediately after the unit of behavior being strengthened. Those things which can be "consumed" in small units, small edible items such as M & M candies for instance, are not of sufficient reinforcing value for most adults to maintain much activity. The solution to this problem is the solution that has been achieved within our own monetary culture. A token or point is given contingent upon the immediate activity and the individual is later charged a number of such tokens or points as the price for participating in a time-consuming and quite reinforcing activity.

An additional advantage to this procedure over the use of the reinforcing activities themselves to maintain the rehabilitative work is that one need not be so concerned to find specific events which will reinforce a particular patient at a specific time. All that is necessary is to have a wide range of reinforcing activities available, and then the patient can purchase the activity which appeals most to him. The token or point in other words, can be dispensed immediately, and in small units, but its reinforcing value does not depend very much on the momentary interest of the patient.

In addition to activities which will function as reinforcers it is, of course, possible to arrange that the points be exchanged for foods of various kind, toilet articles, clothing, etc. which are available at the institution or which are in the possession of the trainer. They can also be exchanged for green stamps or money which then could be spent outside of the institution. Financial remuneration is especially likely to be useful in the case of an individual who is so depressed that he wants nothing for himself, but is still concerned for his family. If the money can be used to defray some of the cost of his treatment, or to improve the living conditions of his family, he might be induced to engage in considerable rehabilitative activity in order to earn such money even though he would not spend it on himself. There is a danger in the use of money in that some individuals will turn over available money to others (most commonly family members) because of various social pressures, but will not find it reinforcing to earn more money. When this happens the points or tokens will lose their effectiveness as reinforcers for the patient. This is especially critical in the case of the young people who turn over their earnings to their parents. The therapist should make sure that the individual spends some of his tokens on things which the therapist is confident are reinforcing to the patient, in order that the tokens do not lose their value.

As mentioned above, it is important that the reinforcing system not be offensive to the patient and his relatives and friends, or at least no more offensive than other aspects of hospitals and similar institutions.

There are two aspects to the problem of making a point system acceptable to the patient. If an institution is operating on this basis at the time a new patient is admitted all that is required is some sort of "admission" unit where the individual is indoctrinated with respect to the goals and techniques of the institution, and gradually required to work for an increasing number of the things that he expects to receive as a matter of course. The fact that everyone works for his rewards, both in and out of the institution, plus the obvious benign purposes of the institutional staff will make the situation pretty acceptable to most new patients.

The more difficult problem is the transition from a generally free or noncontingent environment to one where all reinforcers are contingent on rehabilitative effort. However, the transition need not be made suddenly, and the constant patient turnover in most institutions will contribute to the ease of a gradual transition. The rationale for a work requirement can be made in terms of the general behavioral principles described above, although of course, expressed in commonsense terms. The overall goals of the institution and staff can be stressed: "It is to our interest and to the interest of society in general that you become as capable and effective as possible. To facilitate this we have an incentive system, not unlike the one that works so well in our democratic society, etc. etc." The high patient-staff ratio and the limited facilities can be mentioned as a basis for some form of contingency, and if, in fact, there really is no logical basis for some form of limitation, an artificial scarcity can be created. A good strategy is to start the point system with some new reinforcer which was not available before to anyone—a new swimming pool, some new personal convenience or privilege, or a new series of entertainments. With one activity used as a reinforcer for rehabilitative progress, it is not difficult to gradually add more. As new patients arrive to find a partial point system already in effect, they are especially susceptable to even further encroachments on the usual "free" environment.

Points could also be introduced as a form of pay to some patients for helping in the rehabilitation training of other patients, with the added manpower as a bonus.

Relief from pain as a form of reinforcement should also be mentioned. Although this may seem quite severe, there are circumstances where it might be quite helpful and well justified. Whaley, Kushner, and Knowles (In Press) described the use of electric shock as a pain stimulus in dealing with a case of hysterical anesthesia. Naturally the patient's voluntary participation was obtained and by "perceiving" a mild electric shock stimulus in the "anesthetic" area he could avoid receiving a more severe painful shock stimulus in a normal area. A similar form of escape and avoidance conditioning in a rehabilitation setting has been described by Ince, Sokolow, and Menon (1968). The technique was a straightforward example of escape or avoidance conditioning in which the limb capable of only minimal movement had to be moved to some degree in order to turn off or to prevent the onset of painful electric shock. Again, the subjects volunteered for the procedure and it was partially successful.

In both of these situations the experimenter produced the painful stimulus and the patient was able to terminate it by exhibiting some behavior believed relevant to the rehabilitation process. Another situation involving pain arises when the pain is produced naturally as a result of injury or illness and the experimenter provides drugs which relieve the pain. The use of such drugs as reinforcers has not been suggested but the fact that they serve as reinforcers and can, in fact, strengthen an undesirable form of behavior has been indicated by Fordyce, et al.(1968). He points out that the practice of providing pain-relieving drugs on demand, that is, when the patient asks for them as a function of the severity of the pain may well have the detrimental effect of reinforcing what Fordyce call "pain behavior"—the operant behavior by which we become aware of another person's pain. In other words, drugs on demand may function as a reinforcer for complaining about pain. He altered the procedure in such a way that the pain-relieving drugs were given on a regular time basis rather than contingent on behavior, with a considerable reduction in "pain behavior." Since this procedure was accompanied by a number of other procedural changes, the evidence can only be considered suggestive, but the wide individual differences in reaction to pain strongly suggest a significant operant component, which would be capable of strengthening by various reinforcers, especially one so powerful as a drug which relieves or reduces whatever nonoperant "pain" may exist.

In summary then, the implications of behavior modification for most rehabilitation training lie in the more explicit application of programming technology as a means of task analysis and presentation, and a more explicit use of reinforcing and punishing consequences. This latter application will probably require considerable rearrangement of most rehabilitation settings, but there is good reason to suppose that it would eliminate the "motivation problems" in much of rehabilitation work.

Although it is only a special case of skill analysis and programming, language training as in work with the adult aphasic, the congenitally deaf child, the mentally retarded, and others, is an area where the substantive component of behavior modification has far-reaching significance. In much of rehabilitation training the behavior modifier can accept the rationale for treatment and the general characteristics of the skill analysis made by the other specialists dealing with the patient. He will probably work toward a finer breakdown of the activity into its components and will be especially concerned with the effectiveness of the reinforcers and their delivery. In language training, however, the behavior modifier will usually find that much of the treatment rationale depends on a "theory of language" which he will find far too cognitive and mentalistic for his liking. Comprehensive behavioristic analyses of language are relatively new (Skinner, 1957), but it is quite apparent that they represent a drastic departure from other available interpretations and theories. In this area, then, the behavior modifier will have to develop his training rationale and can expect to receive little aid from existing approaches.

Training Regarding the Social Reactions of Others to the Disabled Person

There are many circumstances where the main inconvenience of being disabled is not the direct result of the disability but arises from the social reactions of others. It would seem to be a part of rehabilitation training to deal with this problem and, in fact, a certain amount of counseling, warning about future problems, etc. does take place in rehabilitation settings. A somewhat more deliberate approach, however, could be applied with considerable benefit.

The reactions of other individuals to the disabled fall into two categories; those whose effects are primarily emotional, and reactions which actually interfere with the disabled person's operant behavior. An example in the first category is the repugnance and embarrassment displayed by a nondisabled person as he shakes "hands" with a double amputee's lower arm prosthetic device. This reaction does not actually prevent any action on the part of the disabled individual, but may function as an emotional stimulus. A shopkeeper's refusal to allow such an amputee to handle some retail item on the grounds that he might break it is an example of the second category of reaction, and obviously interferes with the amputee's attempt to determine whether he wishes to purchase the object.

Other examples in the first category are the stares of children at a facial disfigurement, and various kinds of overheard remarks of pity or disgust. Signs that one is causing some kind of strong negative reaction or excessive curiosity on the part of another human are of considerable significance under normal conditions. Such negative reactions play a role in child training when adults use them as punishers or as warnings that punishment will follow if some change in behavior doesn't take place. They are also used among children to control behavior that is "out of line" in some respect, and continue to function in this way among adults. Discourteous stares by strangers are similarly significant in that they indicate that one is doing something wrong and that some more serious form of disapproval may take place if the wrong behavior continues. Such social stimuli are also used to develop stimulus control by pairing them with novel events, a process very clearly described by Staats (1968, pp. 10-50). When a mother expresses strong disgust at some object in the presence of her child, she increases the likelihood that in the future he, too, will have some negative emotional reaction to the object; and she also decreases the likelihood that he will touch or play with the object.

The disabled individual has been subjected to all of this training prior to his disablement, and will continue to be exposed to such functional social reactions, and to use them, himself, to control behavior and to develop stimulus control. As a result of his disability, however, he becomes the recipient of some negative social reactions which are without any significant function for him. Negative reactions to his prosthetic device cannot function as effective warning stimuli, nor as relevant punishers. Discourteous stares related to his disability do not imply that a change in his behavior is required. The fact that a parent inadvertently "conditions" her child to behave negatively toward him in some respect (and, also toward others with similar disabilities) is not something that he can react effectively to, or do anything about. The lack of practical significance will, generally, weaken the emotional effect of such social stimuli, but this is counteracted, in part, by the continued practical significance such reactions have when they are unrelated to the disability. What is involved is a set of rather diffiult discriminations; the disabled individual must continue to react to such social behavior on the part of others when it is appropriate—the hostile stares that a male amputee receives as he starts to enter the women's restroom, for example—but must stop reacting when they relate to unchangeable conditions.

This discrimination develops naturally as the individual is repeatedly exposed to "irrelevant" and "relevant" negative social reactions, but as is usually the case, the natural environment is not programmed very well. In the first place, the rate of occurrence of the irrelevant social stimuli is not great enough—particularly in the hospital and rehabilitation center where everyone is especially sensitive to this problem. In addition, relevant and irrelevant stimuli occur together frequently in the natural environment when the individual is first discharged from rehabilitation training, and this makes the discrimination an unusually difficult one. An example is the social disapproval given to the amputee when he drops something from his prosthetic hand. Furthermore, it would seem that nonreaction to irrelevant social negativity could be developed with least discomfort to the patient if he were first exposed to only mildly negative reactions and only presented with more severe ones as his reaction to the mild ones diminished. The natural environment is relatively chaotic with respect to this last factor.

It would be quite easy to design an artificial environment, a special training center, or ward, which was programmed much more effectively than the natural environment. The staff would be skillful at role playing, as in the armed forces training centers for espionage agents where capture and interrogation by enemy forces is simulated. In such centers the trainee has an opportunity to develop an appropriate emotional and operant repertoire under repeated and increasingly realistic conditions. The artificiality of the environment can be partially overcome by skillful staff participation, and by gradually fading the artificial environment into the real one.

Training the disabled to deal with the kinds of social reactions which actually interfere with his operant behavior must take a somewhat different form. Here it is important to acquire a repertoire appropriate to overcoming the interference. This, of course, varies greatly depending on the particular form of interference, and can be discovered by interviewing effective individuals with the different kinds of disabilities. In some situations reassurances as to one's willingness to assume responsibility might be sufficient. In others it may be appropriate to suggest alternative solutions to the problem at hand, for example, asking a shopkeeper to perform various operations with some object which he doesn't wish the disabled individual to handle. It is important that the disabled be familiar with his legal rights, and be fully prepared to threaten and to take legal action or to obtain help from a police officer if necessary. It is also important to be familiar with various public policies regarding the disabled; for example, it used to be the case that it was difficult to purchase an airline ticket if at the time of purchase it was made clear that the passenger would have to be carried onto the plane; but if such an individual simply showed up with his ticket, he would usually be carried on with no protest, although he often had to help the terminal personnel locate the special carrying chair used for such purposes.

Again, the acquisition of these behaviors should not be assumed to result from simply telling the disabled what he should do. An artificial environment with role-playing staff members and a set of situational problems, such as was suggested above for eliminating emotional reactions, would be the most effective way to generate a repertoire of this sort. It would be most economical, in fact, if the same artificial environment was devoted to dealing with both of these kinds of social reactions by the nondisabled.

Vocational Training

In many respects vocational training is an extension of special rehabilitation training. The individual not only learns, for example, to manipulate his artificial limb in everyday activities, but also in terms of some occupational skill. The basic strategy in such training is to utilize an effective reinforcer as a form of consequation for well-programmed activities. The same problem exists regarding effective reinforcers that was discussed above. The reinforcers that are intrinsic in the situation, social approval, signs of increasing skill, rest pauses, are not taken maximum advantage of, and furthermore, these events do not function as reinforcers for all trainees and therefore there is a good deal of "marginal motivation." The problem can be easily solved in vocational training, since consequation in the form of pay for the activity is not likely to meet any emotional or social objections. But of course the pay must be contingent on increasing effectiveness (and not simply given by the hour or by the week) in order to function as a reinforcer for skill acquisition.

The Control of Working Behavior

Equipping the disabled individual with a new vocational skill seems to be a much less difficult problem than finding his employment and keeping him employed. This is partly because the aims of most vocational training are seldom at new skills which would require a good deal of training, but rather usually attempt to make modifications on the skills the individual has already acquired or provide training in an unskilled or a semiskilled area. The problems of obtaining employment for the disabled involve in many respects broader social problems than can be dealt with in the present paper. They involve political, economic, and social strategies, including effective legislation, and it would take us too far afield to suggest a behavioral analysis of the field of public relations, advertising, lobbying, and the production of social change.

Keeping the disabled employed is a problem for which a behavioral analysis is quite relevant, however, and a probem that occupies a great deal of the effort and time of the rehabilitation counselor. Some disabled individuals, it appears, even when jobs are found for them where their job skills are fully adequate to the task, do not remain employed. This is true, of course, for the nondisabled worker as well and the statistical evidence does *not* suggest that the disabled employee is less stable than the normal employee. A behavioral analysis suggests, however, that there are some special problems involved in employing the disabled and although this analysis may not be new to most vocational counselors it may be useful to hear it put in somewhat different terms.

Let us start by considering the working behavior of the normal individual (Michael, 1968). The basic question is "What are the consequences that are responsible for an individual's coming to work, coming on time, behaving appropriately toward his fellow workers and his supervisors, performing the work task effectively, and so on?" It is useful to break this question into two parts: First, what are the consequences and contingencies that occur within the working situation itself? But since many of these are only indirectly significant to the individual, an equally important second question is what are the events outside the working situation which are responsible for the significance of those occurring within the working situation? To illustrate this double analysis, let us consider the behavior of coming to work on time. The events that occur within the working situation when one is late are usually the disapproval that one experiences from a supervisor or from fellow workers and perhaps other inconveniences related to the work itself. There may also be some form of fine involved. These are the immediate consequences and to some extent they may have reinforcing or punishing value irrespective of their relationship to other effects, but much of their significance relates to long-range variables. Disapproval by one's foreman could be tolerated if it were not for the fact that one's continued employment, or perhaps advancement, is dependent upon the foreman's favorable report. And this, too, is a value because of its intricate relationship to even more derived reinforcers and punishers relating to rent payment, food purchase, clothing, entertainment, and other events that are equally basic. There is, in other words, a long chain of derived reinforcers and punishers with those events that are most closely in contact with working behavior being of value primarily because of their relationship to other events, some of which we could call "the basic necessities of life." Of course, it is true that in our culture at the present time to lose one's job does not lead immediately to starvation, but not having money to spend certainly does generate a variety of increasingly serious inconveniences and prevents obtaining most of the rewards and satisfactions in our culture.

One of the principles of the animal laboratory and also of human behavior involving consequences is that their control, whether it be the strengthening effect of reinforcers or the weakening effect of punishers, is maximized if they are immediately contingent on the behavior that one is attempting to control. Delays in reinforcement and punishment deprive these manipulations of some of their effectiveness, and derivations in which the immediate event is of value only because of its relationship to some later occurring event also detract from the effectiveness of the consequence system.

From this point of view the ordinary working situation is not especially well designed with respect to the relationship between the immediate (unfortunately, not too immediate) consequences and the various aspects of the working behavior on the job. In general, the money that one earns is not contingent in any immediate way on the work activity except in cases of piecework. The consequences of being late, in many employment situations, are not particularly clear and the detection of tardiness is often defective. The approval that is given for a job well done may be given some considerable time after the job has been completed, and it may not be so much related to the quality of the job as to the social skills of the worker and the interpersonal relations between worker and employer.

It is only as a result of a long apprenticeship in our economic system that one can be controlled by such poorly arranged consequences, a fact which can be easily appreciated when one attempts to utilize such a system with the very young individual, the individual from some other culture, or the adult individual who has never had to work.

The relation between the consequences occurring in the work situation and the long-range consequences which are responsible for their value is fairly close in the case of money but less so for other types of consequences. The necessity of the money one earns is ordinarily well maintained within the culture. There is some delay, of course, before one is evicted or one's utilities turned off, but the relationships are generally quite effective. One can continue to borrow for a while, continue to obtain on credit for a while, but many of the consequences of being without money are immediately realized. The other variables such as approval or disapproval by one's supervisor, support of one's fellow workers, are a sloppier form of currency, and as a result their control is generally less effective.

It is probably the case that in many semiskilled or unskilled working situations a powerful form of reinforcement ultimately available is to get out of that situation into a more favorable one. There is still a good deal of upward mobility in our society, although it may not proceed as far up as it used to, and a young, ambitious worker's sensitivity to such variables as approval, effectiveness in the work situation, etc., may be closely related to potential improvement in the actual nature of his work situation. He may be attempting to become a part of management, or to work into a position which doesn't pay more but which involves a more pleasant type of work. It is also probably true that the relationship between these "ambition" variables and their ultimate payoff is considerably sloppier than the relationship between money and the things that money can buy, yet it undoubtedly plays an important role in some cases.

It should be mentioned that the general effectiveness of this whole system is sufficiently low that employers are constantly seeking ways to reduce high turnover rates, absenteeism, and general work inefficiency. It should also be stated that a good deal of the efficiency that does exist in the system is related to a complex form of social learning in which young individuals (mainly males) are gradually adapted to a way of life that requires an increasing amount of effort to maintain. They are at first encouraged and aided in the acquisition of economic responsibilities (clothes, a car, an apartment), and then further encouraged to obligate themselves socially and emotionally (girl friend, wife, children). These controls lead to more economic obligations (better car, clothes for the wife and children, better apartment, home "ownership", etc.) which can only be met by being a highly effective and stable employee. Furthermore, these controls have somewhat the characteristics of a ratchet wheel in that the aversiveness involved in reducing one's standard of living (aversiveness arising in part from the social reactions of family and friends) is much greater than the aversiveness involved in the extra effort required to fulfill some additional economic obligation and maintain the status quo. For many individuals the forward pressure of this system of controls eases only when retirement approaches and he is forced out of the system. Sometimes an individual breaks out of the system by some drastic means, such as running away and assuming a new identity, or in earlier times, becoming a "hobo"—today, perhaps, an adult "hippie."

A severe physical disability is another way in which this system of social and economic controls is disrupted. It is often the case that the individual's standard of living is considerably lowered as a result of his disability. In addition, his responsibility for maintaining it at the new lower level is considerably reduced. Either he receives some form of pension or accident insurance, or other family members, wife, older children, take over some of the head-of-household responsibilities. Once he starts working again after a period of vocational retraining and rehabilitation, the situation may be sufficiently altered that the money he earns on the job is no longer effective control of effortful and prolonged working behavior. The ambition variable may have been drastically altered by his disability. Blind workers do not customarily become foremen, since, other things being equal, the foreman who can see can generally do a better job than the one who cannot. Failure to advance is no longer a source of severe social disapproval from family and friends, and for that matter failure even to maintain a job is often acceptable in terms of the difficulties produced by the disability, the prejudices of the nondisabled employer, and other conditions. The money earned may not represent a significant portion of the family income and even when it does it may bring little personal advantage to the individual who actually earns the money. It is most likely to be simply pooled with other sources of family income, the dispensation of which the disabled individual now has less control of as a function of changed responsibility relationships within the family. Because his situation is now a form of economic crisis the disabled individual is not encouraged to take on any advancing economic responsibilities of the type which would generate new reinforcers. This is no time to purchase a new car, to indebt oneself with respect to new sources of entertainment, etc. The result of all of these factors may well be that the money earned is no longer an effective reinforcer for the individual and therefore the other forms of control that depend upon this ultimate source are greatly weakened. Appropriate behavior toward one's fellow employees and toward one's superiors in the employment situation is no longer as well maintained by approval and disapproval variables, and when this factor is combined with normal frustrations resulting from the disability itself the individual may become "emotionally unemployable" even though he has effective working skills.

There is no simple behavioral solution to this problem, but by being aware of the relevance of working behavior to the dispensation of the worker's earnings, rehabilitation workers can at least attempt to anticipate the difficulty and can offer partial solutions in some cases.

"HABILITATION": PHYSICALLY DISABLED CHILDREN, THE MENTALLY RETARDED, AND THE CULTURALLY DISADVANTAGED

Each of the three populations named in the title of this section raises some behavioral problems which have no counterpart in the rehabilitation of the physically disabled adult. For that matter, like this latter population, each of these three is composed of subpopulations which differ from one another as much as they do from the other two. However, the analysis of the rehabilitation of recently disabled adults prepares the way for a consideration of two special behavioral problems which these populations have in common: marginal motivation in education and training, and later employment instability.

The children of the poor, the mentally retarded, and disabled children (deaf, blind, crippled, cerebral palsied, and others) all, for their own special reasons, fail to benefit from ordinary child training and ordinary educational practices. However, all of these individuals *can* benefit from special training of one sort or another. The deaf child does not learn to speak under ordinary conditions, but can learn when given special training. Some mentally retarded children, if simply subjected to the usual family training practices, will never learn to dress themselves, to speak, to eat with knife, fork, and spoon, etc., but can learn these skills if given more systematic training. The culturally disadvantaged child who is not well controlled by the ordinary conditions of elementary and secondary school and, for example, does not learn to read under these conditions, can be taught to read with relatively little difficulty when subjected to special training conditions.

These special training conditions consist essentially in an effective program of tasks related in a contingent manner to effective reinforcers, and although the program and task analysis is certainly important, the lack of effective reinforcers underlies most of the training problems with these groups. The reinforcers controlling much human learning are rather complex stimulus relationships resulting from improved effectiveness and rather subtle social interactions between teacher and learner. Since the role of these events as reinforcers is not well appreciated by most instructors in the areas being considered, the fact that they are not functioning as such is most likely to be interpreted in other terms. The very young child, the brain-injured child, and the child described as mentally retarded often do not persist in adult-prescribed activities for as long as the adult would like. This failure is attributed to the child's short attention span, a trait supposedly seen quite often in children of this type. From the point of view of the concepts and methodology of the animal laboratory, the organism in question is obviously not being effectively reinforced. If a student in such an animal laboratory attempted to excuse his failure to control his subject on the grounds that the pigeon or rat has too short an attention span the student would be assigned some form of remedial training. The "attention span" of the pigeon and rat is quite remarkable, in fact, since these organisms can be induced to work for many hours each day, for most of their lives, at some rather difficult experimenter-prescribed activity.

Short attention span is another way of describing the fact that the smiles, frowns, and other verbal behavior of the adult, and the stimulus aspects of the task itself, do not remain effective reinforcers for very long with the children in question. However, there is no reason to suppose that these subjects could not maintain effortful training activity for long periods of time if they were receiving effective reinforcement for the activity. Finding effective reinforcers for children is not as difficult as for the physically disabled "unmotivated" adult, since the problems of the acceptability of the contingency system don't generally arise. There are a great many activities and objects and stimulus changes that will reinforce children whether they be physically disabled, mentally retarded, or culturally deprived. Homme (1966) describes effective reinforcement systems with normal nursery school children, children of poverty, pre-school American Indian children on a reservation, a 5-year-old nontalking retardate, and others. Lent (1968) describes a comprehensive token system for work with institutional retardates; and the work of Wolf, Giles and Hall (1968) with fifth and sixth graders illustrates an effective point system for work with the culturally disadvantaged.

Why the training conditions that work with the normal child are not functional with these special populations is an important question, but it should not be confused with the problem of developing special training conditions that will be functional with these populations. Irrespective of his "intellectual deficits" the retarded individual can be rather easily trained to do many things that he would not learn to do without special training. And irrespective of their wretched home conditions, their poor self-concept, or whatever other problems they may have, the children of the poor can be easily taught almost anything one would like them to learn if the material is well programmed and effectively reinforced. With respect to this latter group, it is especially important to avoid the erroneous notion that the social problems responsible for "cultural disadvantagement" must be dealt with before we can educate the disadvantaged child. It is also important to avoid the view that the various other effects of poverty on a particular child's behavior, those effects often described in terms of traditional personality theory, must be dealt with before he can benefit from special training programs designed to develop an effective scholastic repertoire. Other things being equal, it is probably better for unhappy children to be able to read, even though they may remain unhappy. Not being able to read will generate its own additional form of unhappiness. It may of course, be more reinforcing for many people working in the "poverty" area to work with broad cultural problems and/or children's personality problems than it is to improve the effectiveness of ordinary educational systems—especially if they have no idea how this latter goal would be achieved.

The second point of similarity between the populations dealt with in this section and the recently disabled adult consists in the inadequacy of ordinary employment variables for many members of these populations. It was stated earlier that to be a "good" employee one should really "need" the money. And a really strong "need" of this sort requires the gradual development of emotional and financial obligations. In addition, ambition variables related to improved employment conditions play a role, especially among younger employees. When an ordinary adult employee suffers a serious physical disability many of these emotional, financial, and ambition variables controlling his strong "need" for money may be disrupted, and his working behavior may deteriorate. In the case of the disabled child, the retarded, and the culturally disadvantaged, the strong "need" for money may never develop. The system of gradually increasing demands related to the maintenance of a gradually rising standard of living is apparently somewhat ineffective even for the "normal" worker, if the proportion of "good" workers among the unskilled and semiskilled levels of employment is any indication. But for the three special populations under consideration the contingencies necessary to develop increasingly effective independent working behavior are especially likely to be faulty. The disabled and retarded are subjected to an environment where the necessary reinforcers are available almost irrespective of behavior; and the poor are in an environment where there are no relevant reinforcers available.

It would not be difficult to design an environment which would develop and maintain the necessary working behaviors. It would be an institutional setting where a minimal standard of living was available free, that is without any work. This minimal condition would be one involving uninteresting but healthful meals, no forms of entertainment, a warm but hard place to sleep, little privacy, no place to store private belongings, etc. Work of various kinds (primarily educational activity to start with) would be available and the worker would receive points, tokens, and ultimately money for his job. The points or tokens could be used to improve one's living conditions—better meals, better sleeping conditions, and in this way the individual could be gradually accomodated to a higher standard of living which he would have to spend more time working to maintain. This sheltered environment would be like the "real world" in many ways, but would differ in its planned gradualness and in its prevention of drastic social disruption when the contingencies failed to control effective working behavior. In these respects the sheltered environment might seem quite similar in function to ordinary forms of partial economic support such as disability compensation, pensions, or welfare payments. There is a critical difference, however, in that this sheltered environment provides only the minimum standard of living for nothing, and requires increasingly effective behavior for all improvements.

Ultimately the demands and rewards of such a planned environment could be made as similar to the natural working situation as one desired, and if vocational training was included as a part of the institution's program the individual could be gradually phased out of the sheltered environment. In the case of the culturally disadvantaged this would be the obvious goal of such training. Some of the mentally retarded would also become independent of the institution; some would probably continue to live in the sheltered environment but work outside; and some would be "employed" in various institutional activities. The degree of dependence on the sheltered environment would depend on the extent to which the contingencies that would be in effect in the outside environment would be sufficient to maintain good working behavior once it was developed. The physically disabled child cannot be dealt with in general terms, since the contingencies ultimately available in the natural environment depend a great deal on the degree and type of disability. Some could undoubtedly become completely independent but some would re-require some form of continued support in the form of a sheltered environment.

NOTES

1. This description of individual organism methodology is, of course, greatly abbreviated. A book has been written on the subject (Sidman, 1960) as well as a number of articles, a very readable example of which is the one by Baer, Wolf, and Risley (1968).

2. The term "punishment" refers here to any stimulus change which, when contingent on behavior, weakens this behavior. "Punisher" is equivalent to "negative reinforcer" or "aversive stimulus." In this technical sense, the term does not necessarily imply physical or corporal punishment nor even the activity of another person. It is common in a behavioral context, for example, to refer to the punishments that arise from clumsy interaction with the physical environment.

3. In dealing with the "mentally ill," occupational therapy is *not* primarily concerned with the development of new motor skills, as such, but with the benefits that this activity may have in helping the patient recover from his "mental illness."

REFERENCES

Ayllon, T., & Haughton, E. Modification of symptomatic verbal behavior of mental patients. *Behavior Research and Therapy*, 1964, 2, 87-97.

Ayllon, T., & Michael, J. L. The psychiatric nurse as a behavioral engineer. *Journal of the Experimental Analysis of Behavior,* 1959, 2, 323-334.

Azrin, N. H. Use of rests as reinforcers. *Psychological Reports,* 1960, 7, 240.

Baer, D. M., Wolf, M. M., & Risley, T. R. Some current dimensions of applied behavior analysis. *Journal of Applied Behavior Analysis,* 1968, 1, 91-97.

Fishman, S. Amputation. In J. F. Garrett, and E. S. Levine, (Eds.) *Psychological practices with the physically disabled.* New York: Columbia University Press, 1962, pp. 1-50.

Fordyce, W. E., Fowler, R. S., Lehmann, J. F., & DeLateur, B. J. Some implications of learning in problems of chronic pain. *Journal of Chronic Diseases,* 1968, 21, 179-190.

Glaser, R. (Ed.) *Teaching machines and programmed learning, II.* Washington, D.C.: National Education Association, 1965.

Goodkin, R. Case studies in behavioral research in rehabilitation. *Perceptual and Motor Skills,* 1966, 23, 171-182.

Harris, F. R., Wolf, M. M., & Baer, D. M. Effects of adult social reinforcement on child behavior. *Young Children,* 1964, 20, 8-17.

Hefferline, R. F., Keenan, B., & Harford, R. A. Escape and avoidance conditioning in human subjects without their observation of the response. *Science,* 1959, 130, 1338-1339.

Homme, L. E. Contingency management. *Newsletter,* Division 12, American Psychological Association, 1966, 5, (4).

Ince, L., Sokolow, J., & Menon, M. Escape and avoidance conditioning of responses in the plegic arm of stroke patients. Paper presented at Hobart College, Geneva, New York, 1968.

Kerr, N., & Meyerson, L. Motivating working behavior in workmen's compensation clients. Paper read at American Psychological Association meeting, Los Angeles, September, 1964.

Krasner, L. Studies of the conditioning of verbal behavior. *Psychological Bulletin,* 1958, 55, 148-170.

Lent, J. R. Mimosa cottage: experiment in hope. *Psychology Today,* 1968, 2, 51-58.

Meyerson, L., Kerr, N., & Michael, J. L. Behavior Modification in rehabilitation. In S. W. Bijou, and D. M. Baer, (Eds.). *Child development: readings in experimental analysis,* New York: Appleton-Century-Crofts, 1967, Pp. 214-239.

Michael, J. L. Consequences in the control of working behavior. Paper read at Joseph P. Kennedy, Jr. Foundation Fourth International Scientific Symposium on Mental Retardation, Chicago, Illinois, 1968.

Sidman, M. *Tactics of scientific research.* New York: Basic Books, 1960.

Skinner, B. F. *Verbal behavior.* New York: Appleton-Century-Crofts, 1957.

Skinner, B. F. *The technology of teaching.* New York: Appleton-Century-Crofts, 1968.

Staats, A. W. *Learning, language, and cognition.* New York: Holt, Rinehart, and Winston, 1968.

Whaley, D. L., Kushner, M., & Knowles, P. Treatment of a case of hysterical anesthesia by escape and avoidance conditioning. *Journal of Applied Behavior Analysis*, (In Press).

Wolf, M. M., Giles, D. K., & Hall, V. Experiments with token reinforcement in a remedial classroom. *Behavior Research and Therapy*, 1968, 6, 51-64.

Wright, B. A. *Physical disability—a psychological approach*. New York: Harper and Brothers, 1960.

5: Behavior Modification, Token Economies, and Training in Clinical Psychology

LEONARD KRASNER

Role identification is a key concept in any evaluation of what implications behavior modification might have for training procedures in clinical psychology. The specifics of what kind of training, its goals and techniques, depend upon the role model framework within which the trainer or teacher works. This paper will discuss some aspects of behavior modification, its historical origin, current directions, and the role model in which training may be enhanced, especially as it may be influenced by operant conditioning procedures.

When an investigator starts to describe the application of operant conditioning procedures to real life people with problems, as we shall do when we describe the token economy program, a usual reaction from some readers is, "Here's another one of those experimentalists trying to apply rat psychology to humans; he just doesn't have the clinical experience to realize that it won't work." In effect, they raise a question which will be implied throughout this paper, namely, what is to be the scope of an individual's training which will prepare him to work professionally with disturbed people? Implicitly the investigator is being asked by his audience, "Are you now or have you ever been a clinical psychologist?" My own personal answer is that I was trained as a clinical psychologist; I still identify myself as a clinical psychologist. However, I would now equate the label of clinical psychologist with that of a behavior modifier, a professional person whose role behaviors are to be discussed implicitly and explicitly in this paper. Some of the problems involved in clinical training during my day should no longer exist in current training, although

The preparation of the material included in this paper was facilitated and supported, in part, by USPHS No. 11938 from the National Institute of Mental Health.

they have been replaced by other kinds of problems, perhaps equally complex. The role model of the clinical psychologist for which people were trained in the late 1940s when I was working on a doctorate in the graduate school at Columbia University, has altered considerably. As it was, my own training at that point was deviant for its time. At Columbia the program was primarily focused on experimental procedures. The more usual training for the clinical psychologist emphasized his clinical role; the pervading model in those days was that of the junior psychiatrist. In those prehistoric days you were trained as an experimentalist *or* as a clinician and never the twain should meet.

But I was faced with some real problems that bordered on the development of a schizophrenic reaction. On the one hand, I was interested in psychotherapy and wanted to help sick people. On the other hand, I was exposed to what was then a very exciting new development in psychology, the use of operant conditioning procedures, primarily with animals, and I could see no connection between the two. At that point, if you would ask me what kind of therapist I was, I would say, "I'm a psychoanalytically oriented psychotherapist with eclectic leanings," since this kind of label incorporated all the good words of the era.

However, I still retained my research interests and became attracted to the verbal conditioning line of investigation because it seemed at that point, in the early 1950s, that here was a way of taking into the experimental laboratory an analogue of the real life process of psychotherapy, which in itself was sacrosanct and not to be interfered with, and experimentally manipulate various variables to determine how verbal behavior could be systematically modified.

In 1958 I wrote a paper summarizing the existing verbal conditioning studies which numbered about 30 in the literature (Krasner, 1958). Proliferation and escalation quickly set in, and there are now over 500 reported studies in verbal conditioning which are exciting, mutually contradictory, give rise to interesting controversies, especially on the relation between awareness and conditionability, and which I certainly could *not* summarize at this point except with the general statement that "under certain circumstances, a preselected class of verbal behavior can be systematically manipulated by reinforcement which may be verbal, motoric, token, or vicarious" (Krasner, 1965, 1967).

My own interests, however, have moved from viewing verbal conditioning as an analogue of psychotherapy to viewing the experimental situation as "real life," to view changes in verbal behavior as real changes with measurable consequences outside the experimental laboratory (Krasner, 1966a). More generally, my interests have moved from the dyadic situation of verbal conditioning to applying the same general principles to group settings, then to larger units of behavior such as a psychiatric ward, as exemplified by the token economy program to be described, to the even broader implications of social engineering (Krasner, 1966b). This touches upon such areas as training, values, and utopias (Krasner, 1969).

At this point it would be most useful to delineate the hierarchy of terms which will define the limits of involvement; behavior influence, behavior modification, and behavior therapy.

Behavior influence, the broadest term, is defined as any situation in which there is *deliberate* control or influence being exerted on human behavior by someone in a socially sanctioned controlling role such as a research investigator or a school teacher. Formal schoolroom education would fall in this category as would psychological studies involving opinion change, or techniques of learning, or obedience, or perception, or sensory deprivation. In some instances the behavior change effected may well be socially *undesirable* such as the decrease in intellectual or perceptual acuity which may result from sensory deprivation experiments. The focus in behavior influence studies is upon the process and lawfulness of change itself, and not on an evaluation of the goodness or badness of the behavior being changed.

Behavior modification involves the application of principles derived from the psychological laboratory to the changing of *undesirable* human behaviors. Designating an individual's behavior as that which is to be changed involves a decision on someone's part evaluating the social desirability of a particular behavior in a given context. Behavior modification would include such techniques as the operant conditioning of undesirable behaviors of autistic, retarded, or normal children as exemplified by the work of Ferster, Bijou, Lovaas, or Becker; the training of parents, teachers, peers, probation officers, and nurses such as the studies of Patterson or Walder, the reduction of specific maladaptive behaviors such as the stuttering studies of Goldiamond; the structured counseling and guidance work of Krumbolz and his group; the shaping of better physical behavior in physical rehabilitation as classically demonstrated by Michael and Meyerson; the use of programmed learning procedures in the classroom; the application of institutional controls such as token economies; the application of social psychological procedures including enhancing patient expectancies such as those described in the recent Goldstein, Heller and Sechrest (1966) book; or the use of modeling and social learning procedures such as those of Bandura or the self-control procedures of Kanfer; and the sensitization, relaxation, and counterconditioning procedures developed by Wolpe and Lazarus.

The term *behavior therapy* should be reserved for the procedures most recently described by Wolpe (1958). The only reason to do so is the historical artifact of the term "behavior therapy" originally being applied by Eysenck to these procedures (Eysenck, 1959). The term "therapy" is appropriate to a disease model of abnormal behavior, *not* to a behavioral model. For the purposes of this chapter behavior therapy will be used in its recent historical context to denote the procedures derived from classical conditioning.[1]

The behavior modifier in his research and in his application to helping people does *not* view psychotherapy as a unique process, but rather a part of the broader science of human behavior. He takes seriously Astin's (1961) warning of a few years ago about the danger of being seduced by the "functional autonomy" of psychotherapy. The behavior therapist is apt to try to apply learning principles to changing human behavior but this does not mean that he is necessarily sold on any one learning theory. Rather, he is pragmatic and eclectic, but argues that all human behavior is learned and the process of learning and unlearning deviant behavior is lawful. The behavior modifier places major emphasis on the events in the environment which elecit and maintain current behavior. He is less concerned with events in the patient's childhood. He de-emphasizes or ignores the role of hypothesized internal mediating events such as the ego, the unconscious, or psychic forces. The behavior modifier views the behavior that is undesirable as that which is to be changed. He is likely to avoid using a term such as "symptom" which is indicative of an underlying disease process. Since he is to be working within a behavioral rather than a disease model of psychopathology, he is not threatened by the dangers of symptom substitution, the evidence for which he would consider inconclusive at best. The behavior modifier is likely to be optimistic, and very active in his therapist role. He is likely to view the patient-therapist interaction more in terms of teacher-student roles than doctor-patient roles. He is also very likely to attempt to affect the environmental influences on the patient by training key people in an individual's life, such as parents, peers, teachers, aides, probation officers, police, and others. By training these people with specific procedures their attitudes toward the patient and toward their own role vis-a-vis the patient are also directly affected.

To fully understand behavior modification, especially any implications for training, it is necessary to place current behavior modification studies into historical perspective.

It is a truism that in treating deviant behavior there is literally nothing new under the sun. Some of the principles involved in behavior modification such as the use of reinforcements for desired behavior go as far back as the Greeks and probably even to prehistoric man. Many of the techniques are "merely common sense" and some men, if not all, have had that for a long time. They are based on acute and accurate observation of human behavior and its consequences. Jerome Frank, in his *Persuasion and Healing* (1961), points out how many primitive healers, such as Shamans, made good use of some of the same procedures as do our current influencers of behavior.

In behavior modification, the subject is exposed to an environment that is manipulated by the therapist to provide meaningful contingencies for the subject's differential responses to stimuli. It is this last aspect, systematic, contingent environmental consequences, which is based on the theoretical and empirical work of the last 20 years, that is the distinctive mark of contemporary behavior modification (Ullmann & Krasner, 1965). However, there have been many predecessors who took the same basic attitude, that of retraining behavior, and who utilized, albeit not always systematically, many, if not all, of the techniques now used by behavior modifiers.

If a single specific starting point had to be designated, it would probably be the Greeks, whose temple psychiatry involved an elaborate scheme of *social influence* including the suggestion of previous cures, rituals, drugs, etc., to foster a new course of behavior. The suppliant was considered basically normal and personally responsible; that is, failure to obtain relief was considered an indication of impiety rather than of sickness over which he had no control.

Pinel's concept of the maladaptive person as one to be treated as normal and responsive to the treatment as other people led to the concepts of moral treatment, which can be considered as a prime example of behavior modification. In moral treatment the person was expected to play a normal role rather than a sick one. A rewarding environment, but not necessarily a permissive one, was developed.

Of course, Mesmer and Freud, each in his own way, developed further the general approach involving the procedures of using environmental change to alter behavior. However, the direct precursors of the present behavior therapies are in the works of Pavlov, Sechenov, Bechterev, and Bykhow, on the one hand, and Thorndike, Hull, Mowrer, and Skinner on the other. More clearly than anyone else, John Watson deserves credit in psychology for pointing out the wide social implications of Pavlov's work, for generating interest in it, and for providing early examples of its use with humans.

In 1924, a major contribution was made by William Burnham, whose book, *The Normal Mind*, anticipated many of the current procedures used by behavior modifiers, particularly those involved with associating new responses to environmental stimuli such as the Wolpeans. The year 1924 also saw the appearance of Mary Cover Jones' paper involving laboratory studies of the conditioning and deconditioning of children's fears, using methods similar to Wolpean reciprocal inhibition. From that time to the present there has been a small, but steady stream of behavior modifiers, such as Dunlap, Hollingsworth, Guthrie, Herzberg, Jersild, Holmes, and Mowrer.

After World War II, there was a series of books and papers which translated psychoanalytic concepts into the language of learning therapy, such as the work of Dollard, Miller, Mowrer, Shaw, and Shoben, but these writings led to a new way of *talking* about therapy, not a new way of doing or investigating therapy. In the 1950s and 1960s, two distinct types of behavior modification procedures emerged, one based on Skinnerian operant conditioning, and the other based on Hull and Pavlov. The latter procedures were developed by Wolpe as presented in his 1958 book, *Psychotherapy by Reciprocal Inhibition.* The term "behavior therapy" was first used by Eysenck in an article in 1959 to refer specifically to Wolpe's work, and since then has merged into the broader concept of behavior modification. In 1963, a journal, *Behavior Research and Therapy* edited by Eysenck and Rachman, began to be published. Since then many journal articles, research studies, and anthologies have appeared summarizing current work (Franks, 1964; Krasner & Ullmann, 1965; Ullmann & Krasner, 1969).

The more specific background of the token economy program is in the early operant work of Skinner (1938). The basic ingredient of the operant conditioning paradigm is the use of environmental cues to reinforce behavior with a view to strengthening desirable behavior. The basis is the development in the experimental laboratory of laws of behavior which apply to organisms from lowest to highest. Its first application to disturbed or deviant behavior was probably Fuller's (1949) operant conditioning of a "vegetative idiot," and subsequent applications ranged from Fuller's conditioning of the very simple behavior of arm raising to the application to larger and larger units of behavior including the social and economic behavior of psychiatric patients in a society (Skinner, 1948; Mertens, 1967).

Currently there are three types of research investigators in the area of behavior modification; the Skinnerians, the Wolpeans, and the eclectic modifiers who may use various combinations of operant and classical procedures together with other laboratory derived procedures involving behavior influence and social learning such as modeling, role-taking, placebo, attitude change, sensory deprivation, hypnosis, and milieu control.

A behavior modifier then can be identified as a professional individual who uses a behavioral model and techniques and, equally as important, who is willing to label himself as such. In several graduate clinical psychology training programs, the focus is on the kinds of procedures avowedly necessary to train behavior modifiers.

It may be predicted, at this point, that behavior modification will eventually change rather drastically the basic conceptions of the field of psychotherapy. Their impact is now first being felt, and within 10 or 15 years many of the present techniques of psychotherapy will be generally acknowledged to be archaic, ineffective, and inadequate. If this is so, then training in behavior modification must focus on preparing people to be able to be flexible enough to change as necessary and to be able to bring their talents and background to the new problems they will face.

Eventually there will evolve at least three general types of psychotherapeutic procedures: first, those in which people will pay for friendship, companionship, love, affection, and general attention to their affairs. The second type will be behavior modification in which individuals will seek specific ways of changing their behavior which is disturbing to themselves or others. In this category the individual will be taken seriously in his verbalizations as to the nature of his problem. If he reports a variety of disturbing behaviors, such as stuttering, fears, anxiety, excessive drinking, aggressive or withdrawn behavior, these will be the behaviors with which the behavior modifier will work. As therapist, he will not be concerned with a reconstruction of the individual's personality, but will expect that as behavior changes, other people will respond differently to the individual, elicit different behaviors, resulting in a "different" person. The third type of procedure will explicitly involve social engineering, the changing of social institutions to affect groups of individuals. The social institutions involved may range from mental hospitals to "pockets of poverty" and the procedures may range from "token economies" to poverty programs. It is this kind of procedure which will fulfill the ultimate role of behavior modification as a social movement (Krasner, 1969; Ullmann, 1969). All three of these forms of "help" are quite legitimate functions, but each should be clearly labeled by the practitioner so that an individual knows what type of program he is about to enter and what he may expect from it.

In order to investigate the impact of training a human behavior modifier we must point out at least four types of reaction to "behavior modification" elicited from practicing psychotherapists. First, there are those therapists who are avowed modifiers of behavior and see their own role in terms of training the individual to learn new behaviors and to learn to control his own environment. Second, there are those therapists who have used modification techniques, albeit, perhaps, not systematically or deliberately; yet they have evolved into such procedures after frustration with other approaches. Their reaction, after hearing descriptions of behavior techniques, is that they have been doing something like that for a long time, and they may express surprise to find themselves labeled behavior modifiers. The reaction of a third group of psychotherapists is that the operant approach represents nothing new and that traditional therapeutic processes can be translated into learning terms and vice versa and that "we're all in the same boat; there are no differences that can't be arbitrated and let's go off together into the eclectic-we're-all-doing-the-same-thing-anyway-wonderland." Here I would differ sharply. There are real differences between these approaches which are matters of *alternatives,* not of finding a common meeting ground.

The fourth group of psychotherapists includes both those who deny the relevance of a learning approach to psychotherapy and those who decry what they call manipulation of behavior. Here is a large block of therapists who, be they psychoanalysts, existentialists, nondirective, or eclectic, will have nothing to do with an approach that for them seems destructive of the values for which they are doing psychotherapy. To change undesirable, "symptomatic" behavior or to influence contingently seems vastly different than to "effect basic personality changes," or to strengthen the ego. The attitudes in this group range from live and let live to continual decrying of the behaviorists as the arch enemy of man.

In discussing the procedures involving changing of human behavior it makes more sense to refer to them as behavior modification rather than as psychotherapy. In literal terms, psychotherapy means treatment of the mind or soul. There is the often reiterated, albeit battered, contention that psychotherapy involves a doctor-patient relationship within a medical model of psychopathology (Szasz, 1961). On the other hand, a term such as behavior modification expresses directly what is involved in this situation, the changing of human behavior without having to carry the burden of years of controversy and confusion as to goals and procedures.

The training of the therapist in behavioral techniques involves interpreting the helping situation in a far different way. The role conceptualization of the behavior modifier is different from that of the traditional psychotherapist. The behavior modifier views himself as a scientist and as a technician; he acknowledges his responsibility for the modification of another human being's behavior. He is an educator, a teacher, not a physician who heals disease.

The influence of the behavioral approach has supplied experimental evidence that argues strongly against the notion of deviant behavior being conceptualized as a mental illness or disease (Ullmann & Krasner, 1969). Psychosis and neurosis are not unique behaviors discrete from normal, but rather they are extensions and aspects of normal behavior, understandable in terms of conditioning, social learning, and modeling. This is not to say that some deviant behavior may not result from a legitimate disease process. For example, the physiological changes brought about by a narcotic such as heroin places such physiological demands upon the organism that certain types of behavior logically follow; whereas, for example, in most neuroses, the individual is *reacting* to environmental stimuli. The locus of the elicitation of change in one instance is internal and in the other, external. The former then is primarily a medical problem; the latter is primarily an educational problem. This distinction is important in determining how the therapist will approach his task. The behavior modifier, influenced by learning theory, sees the locus of behavior control as external; the traditional therapist, influenced by disease models, views the locus of control as internal.

One of the major implications of behavior modification procedures is in the training of the key people such as parents, attendants, or peers in the children's (or adults') environment. In the token economies of Ayllon and Azrin (1965) or Atthowe and Krasner (1968), for example, the careful spelling out of the contingencies determines the behavior not only of the patients but of the staff. The staff get immediate feedback that they are doing something worthwhile. This results in increased confidence and satisfaction in their jobs.

Most behavior modifiers stress the importance of training parents in general behavior principles so that they are in a position to obtain some control over their environment; namely, the behavior of their children. This is exemplified in the title of a paper written by a group at the University of Washington, "Mothers as Behavior Therapists for their Own Children" (Wahler, Winkel, Peterson, & Morrison, 1965). They summarized their findings as follows:

> An attempt was made to modify the deviant behavior of three children by producing specific changes in the behavior of their mothers. It was demonstrated that a mother's reactions to her child's behavior may be systematically modified, at least within confines of an experimental setting, and these modifications may produce marked changes in her child's deviant behavior (p. 113).

Walder (1966) reported the successful teaching of techniques of extinction, positive reinforcement, and shaping to parents of autistic children.

Problems and procedures of assessment in behavior modification have received increased emphasis recently. An illustration is a paper by Ferster (1965) in which the assessment procedure utilized systematic observation in the home of an autistic child. Ferster observed that none of the parents' behavior in respect to any behavior of the child resulted in contingencies or consequences that could possibly maintain behavior; literally, the child did not have to work for anything; it was a "nonreactive" environment. The observational techniques he used offers many possibilities of systematic observation. Kanfer and Saslow (1956) have recently presented a schemata which may be of use in the eventual development of behavioral assessment procedures, the need for which is now of major importance. Weiss (1968) has also recently extended the development of operant assessment procedures.

The token economy program which was originated by Ayllon presents many important training and application opportunities. We have recently reported on such a program (Atthowe & Krasner, 1968), and in this paper will only cover certain pertinant aspects of these programs which are illustrative of the application of behavior modification procedures.

A token economy has at least three aspects which define its composition:

1. The designation by institutional authorities of certain behaviors as good or desirable, hence reinforcable. This involves clear value determination on the part of the behavior modifier as to what are desirable behaviors.
2. An object with a degree of value to it, a medium of exchange, an object that "stands for" something else, an object with backup reinforcers behind it. These may be small cards shaped like credit cards (which we have used), small metallic coins, poker chips, marks on a piece of paper, or even green stamps.
3. Ways and means for utilizing the tokens, the backup reinforcers themselves. These are the good things in life, the desirable things for a given individual, which may range from food to being able to sit peacefully in a chair.

The goals of our program were as follows:

1. To shape and guide certain behaviors which are deemed to be desirable in hospitalized patients.
2. On a broader level, to help these patients in spending the rest of their lives in a productive, satisfying environment in which they will be able to function as fully responsible individuals. That is, to be able to achieve the optimal utilization of their abilities and talents.
3. To maximize the satisfaction of the staff who interact with these patients and to minimize the kinds of annoyances and inconveniences so typical of this kind of human interaction.
4. To determine how far the behavior of institutionalized patients can be changed in the direction of a more productive life. Could we set up a utopian society?
5. To teach patients a new social role, that of a good citizen in his present community.
6. To teach patients to make the kinds of determinations they have found so difficult to make in the past; what kinds of behavior pay off in their society.
7. To teach patients that they can control others in such a way that this control is socially acceptable to others.
8. To serve as a source of training in behavior modification for staff and students.

This program was initiated several years ago at the Veterans Administration Hospital, Palo Alto. In terms of the basic behavior principles involved, that of the use of systematic contingent reinforcement, our procedures and orientation were very similar to those described by Ayllon and Michael (1959) and Ayllon and Azrin (1965). However there were some major differences between the two programs which are based on viewing behavior modification in the context of social engineering. Ayllon and Azrin's ward in the state hospital was a completely controlled one; they had complete control of all environmental stimuli. We, in contrast, were interested in determining if a token program could be set up in a less controlled environment. Could we compete with the outside world? One of the first things we did in inaugurating the program was to open the ward so that an individual could come or go freely, *if, of course,* he had the correct number of tokens.

The ward on which the program started was one comprising 80 patients averaging 58 years of age and 24 years of hospitalization. Most have been labeled schizophrenic or organic brain involvement at some point in their career. But whatever deviant behavior had brought them into the hospital in the distant past was no longer relevant. The full impact of institutionalization had made itself felt.

Although we have been getting significant changes in various target behaviors, in the ratings of behavior, and in general ward appearance, I wish to stress the points which are most relevant to this paper. First our aim was *not* to get the patients out of the hospital but to help them attain a better life in the hospital, literally to make maximum use of whatever talent or ability they had. We wanted to create a better society. As to what constitutes a better life represents a value decision on the part of the designers of the society. For example, we think that it is better that an individual do a productive day's work such as cleaning or repairing old furniture or typing than it is for him to merely sit peacefully in a chair. However, the choice is his as a responsible person. If he wishes to sit in a chair, he may do so provided he has earned the tokens permitting this. In fact, we are saying he has no inalienable right to be sick. Even his right to a bed in the evening must be earned.

We found that as you begin to control an economy even on a limited basis, you begin to encounter many of the same problems you encounter in the *unreal* world of the outside. People hoard tokens; people steal tokens. A banking system must be devised so that people may save tokens. There should be a purpose for saving such as passes to visit that unreal world outside. We even developed a special prestige group, which enabled individuals to leave the token system and have all of its privileges with the equivalent of a Carte Blanche or Diners Club card.

We wanted to determine if our kind of economy, the token way, could survive in a world in which the same kinds of good things in life were available, but without contingencies. Some of these good things such as candy or cigarettes could be purchased with something called money, a green token-like piece of paper. Thus, on an economic basis, our tokens had to be cheaper to compete with the other system.

How do you demonstrate the efficacy of a social system? By its products; in this case, its people. This is why there was a large token payoff for appearance, neatness, being shaved, dressed in business suit and tie (if you can't tell the patient from the staff without a score card, you will most likely react to him as if he were normal just like you). If the patients are productive by eliciting good ratings from their work supervisors, then, to utilize a word high in the academic vocabulary, the patient is highly "visible," and this augers well for the perceived success of an institutional program.

Whereas aides and nurses may be initially reluctant to participate in a program which looks like it might entail a lot of work and is *different*, a considerable amount of prestige is soon accrued to individuals working in such programs and a tremendous amount of satisfaction occasioned by feedback on observing that there is a relationship between what they are doing as aides or nurses and patient behavior. They begin to discover that although it is the tokens which are controlling behavior, there is also a gradual restoration of the social reinforcing qualities of their behavior to which the patient is now responding. Throughout, wherever possible, we have paired the tokengiving situation with social reinforcement. When the individual is given a token, it is accompanied by a verbal statement explaining the contingencies and a social reinforcer such as "I'm pleased," and "that's good." This serves a dual purpose of helping the patient learn or relearn to respond to social reinforcement as most people do, and it also serves to train the aide in appropriate behavior and to alert him to appropriate patient behavior to respond to and how to do it effectively.

In terms of the success of our program in its social movement context, we have been reinforced by obvious kinds of reactions, the most gratifying of which was the adoption of token economy as a way of life by two other wards in the hospital.

But where do we go from here? We are in the process of planning a token program which will have as its goal the return of the patient to the community to live a productive life and to improve the community itself. The problems here are different from the ones we started with since it is almost axiomtaic that the behaviors that pay off in a hospital setting are not always those that pay off on the outside. Nor of course is there the systematic control of reinforcement outside as in the hospital. However this brings us to questions of design of social events so as to elicit maximal reinforcement for a maximal number of people, and this involves the training of the individuals on the outside, in society, as to how to interact with these people. The behavior modifier must be trained so that he has the vision and the techniques to undertake tasks such as these.

Similar token programs have been initiated in a number of institutions throughout the country, particularly those working with retarded children, psychotics, delinquent adolescents, job corps volunteers, and alcoholics. (Burchard, 1966; Girardeau & Spradlin, 1964; Lent, 1965). A study by O'Leary and Becker (1967) extending the token economy into the classroom further illustrates how a behavior modification program can begin to affect values of key societal figures such as teachers and have consequent effect on a major social institution, the schoolroom.

If there is to be an eventual social impact of the behavior modification "movement" there must be major effort made to train younger people with the likelihood that improved techniques, more carefully controlled research, and newer fields of application will emerge from their fresher and less blinded efforts. Just as 10 years ago it would have been impossible to predict the specifics of the kind of research being reported under the aegis of behavior modification today, it is unlikely that one could predict today the studies and applications 10 years hence, other than that they will represent drastic change from today, in principles, assessment and modification procedures and even in implicit values, goals and purposes.

To be prepared for the eventual future research which will make the major breakthroughs to come, the behavior modifier must be trained to observe behavior and its consequences. In our token economy we spent considerable time in first observing the ward and determining what behaviors were of high value to the patient by the frequency with which they occurred. These were then incorporated into the token program as something which had to be earned. That is, if the behavior of sitting on the ward was valued by the patient as indicated by the frequent occurrence of the behavior in our assessment period, then the patient could continue this behavior if he had earned enough tokens to pay for it, or, in fact, for any of the other good things in life. The observed frequency of undesirable behaviors in the assessment period can serve as the baseline to determine the effectiveness of the experimental procedures.

The behavior modifier must also be prepared for research programs which will merge the laboratory and real life. Here again the token economy studies are illustrative. Our token economy study was designed to be a merger of research, training, and service, and many of the recent studies such as those of Ferster, Lovaas, Bijou, and Ayllon represent a unique combination of research and service, as well as training.

Further, the implications of a token economy are not limited to work with institutionalized patients. If you work with basic principles of behavior they should apply to all behaviors and all people; but we are not dealing with a mere mechanical application of techniques from one situation to another. For example, a technique, such as translating reinforcement via tokens, successful with elderly long-term patients, labeled schizophrenic, might *not* work with an outpatient neurotic, who lives in a money token economy all the time anyway. But the principles behind the token involve an analysis of the reinforcing events in an individual's life that maintain behaviors. This kind of analysis of behavior, based on careful observation or reports of the real life setting, would be the basis for therapeutic endeavors with the nonhospitalized individual. He could learn to change his own behavior in such a way as to elicit different and more rewarding behaviors from others in his daily life. Goldiamond (1965) has recently demonstrated this with college students and "neurotic" problems.

The behavior modifier uses "techniques" to change behavior. This does not mean that he is in any way mechanical or robot-like although he may well use mechanical aids in his therapeutic program. The words "mechanical" and "robot" continually are brought up in critiques of behavior modification procedures. They are accused of dehumanizing man. Such criticisms do not adequately consider the goals and techniques of behavior modification. For example, using an illustration from token economy programs, the goal of the program is to enable hospitalized individuals to obtain greater control over their own environment. By pointing out the discriminative cues to which they should react, and reinforcing them for such reaction, we are helping them to be freer individuals. We would argue that freedom for an individual means having a greater range of behaviors available in his repertoire. If you are faced with a disturbing situation and there is only *one* way in which you can behave, then you are less free than an individual faced with the same situation and having *two* or more behaviors available. Nor should we be disturbed by the use of mechanical devices in the conditioning procedure. These allow for the precision often necessary in conditioning of which human reaction time is incapable.

An illustration is the ingenious device of Watson (1965) in his work in toilet training mentally retarded children. An aide could, as he had in the past, continue to sit and observe the child's toilet behavior and reinforce for the proper behavior, but this is time-consuming, inefficient, and from the point of view of the aide, unpleasant. Why not mechanize it as Watson did, using a photoelectric cell in the toilet bowl which activated a machine dispensing tokens. On the other hand, there are many types of functions that cannot be readily mechanized in which human judgmental decisions are necessary and, in fact, desirable. Does the patient appear neat, clean, and shaven today, warranting a token? Further, what is neat for one patient may represent a major advance for him, whereas a comparable neatness in another may be regression. Only the decision of another person, using his ability to give tokens, can be made to help shape the patient's behavior in a desirable direction. Lang's (1965) MOM machine illustrates that in some instances a machine properly programmed can desensitize an individual to certain problems as effectively, perhaps even more so, than an individual human therapist. Colby's (1965) "Doctor Machine" although primarily a psychoanalytic "doctor machine" should soon be able to "think" and perform as effectively as any good psychoanalyst, the machine having received much the same training.

A recent paper by Truax (1966) illustrates attitudes about the issue of mechanization. Truax, himself dedicated to the nondirective school, did a series of analyses of a successful psychotherapeutic case seen by Carl Rogers. Truax felt that his data analysis could be decisive in determining whether Skinner or Rogers was right about the directiveness of psychotherapy. Truax's experimental evidence enabled him to conclude that insofar as he could determine Skinner seemed to be right about psychotherapy.

> The present findings point to the presence of significant differential reinforcement effects imbedded in the translations of client-centered psychotherapy. Since differential reinforcement is one of the procedures used in operant research to alter (or control) behavior, the findings suggest that the therapist, in this case Rogers, implicitly alters (or controls) the patient's behavior in the therapeutic setting. To this extent, then, the evidence weighs in favor of the view proposed by Skinner rather than that of Rogers. The present findings are not consistent with Rogers' view that relatively uniform conditions which are globally "facilitative of personal growth and integration," are offered to patients in a manner not contingent upon the patient's behavior. (Truax, 1966, p. 7)

However, Truax could not refrain from concluding his article with an attack on the view that the therapist is a "social reinforcement machine," since if he were he could not communicate, even contingently, warmth and empathy.

> As the communication of any "reinforcing machine" qualities would by definition mean a low level of empathy and warmth, the present viewpoint is in full agreement with Schonbar's (1964) statement that "as a therapist I am no more a 'reinforcing machine' than my patient is a 'talking pigeon.'" (Truax, 1966, p. 8)

A "social reinforcement machine" (Krasner, 1962) is a descriptive phrase which I find useful in describing the role of the therapist in that it carries with it the implication of a finely trained human being who is making use of social reinforcement principles in such a way as to systematically affect human behavior. "Machine," of course, has many different definitions; included among these is that machine is used to signify "a device, often complex, for doing work beyond human physical or mental limitations or faster than human hand or mind." In other words, the psychotherapist, by virtue of his training, reacts quickly, and in many instances reacts automatically, in terms of the kinds of stimuli to which he has been trained to react. In this respect, all therapists are social reinforcement machines, but this view is usually denied or deliberately avoided.

In terms of their implications for the training of the behavior modifier, neither the operant conditioning techniques and procedures developed from the laboratory nor the classical desensitization procedure can stand alone, without being supplemented by a broader behavior influence process. From a practical point of view the modifier of human behavior who views himself as obtaining his sustenance from the psychological laboratory must merge in his practice the experimental work deriving from the social psychology of behavior influence. In other words, the operant and classical learning techniques are completely consistent with theory and research in such areas as modeling, expectancy, experimenter bias, hypnosis, sensory deprivation, all of which also involve the systematic modification of human behavior. As an illustration, in a recent exciting text by Goldstein, Heller and Sechrest (1966) the authors formulate the results of social psychological research into general hypotheses useful for the behavior modifier. These involve specific recommendations about tactics and approaches to be used by the psychotherapist at various stages of psychotherapeutic interaction.

Finally, in contrast to a generally optimistic chapter, we end on a note of strong caution. The behavior modification procedures must be validated by experimental evidence as must any other approach. There are many questions to be answered in terms of therapist variables, patient variables, and task variables. For what patients and behaviors are what techniques and therapists most effective? Problems of generalization have been barely touched upon. Many of the actual procedures used may bear little resemblance to the basic learning or behavior experiments of the laboratory; many theoretical issues remain to be explained. The behavior modifier must still demonstrate that when change is effected, it is a function of the specific procedures used, over and above what changes could be effected by the usual placebo variables. Yet therapists are impatient and understandably so, and hearing of new techniques, with optimistic claims, are apt to adopt the techniques, which sometimes look deceptively simple, without the training in approach and attitude, and without awareness of the difficulties, subtleties, and multivariables involved.

Finally, I would hope that behavior modification will not go the way of cultism. It should not and will not if two of its basic tenets are adhered to: it must maintain its contacts with, receive its nourishment from, suggest problems for, and merge with the research laboratory; it must accept the eventual verdict of research investigation. If specific procedures are ineffective in specific circumstances with specific patients, they should be abandoned and not enshrined in the therapists' hall of fame. It should be this mutual interaction and merger between laboratory and real life that will in the long run represent the real strength of behavior modification. The task of the designers of graduate training programs in clinical psychology now must focus on incorporating these general principles of behavior modification in their programs. The clinical psychologist of tomorrow is the neophyte behavior modifier of today.

NOTE

1. Recent historical surveys indicate that the origins of the term "behavior therapy" go back to it's use in the early 1950s to apply to Lindsley's and Skinner's application of operant technology to psychotic patients.

REFERENCES

Astin, A. W. The functional autonomy of psychotherapy. *American Psychologist,* 1961, 16, 75-78.

Atthowe, J. W., & Krasner, L. A preliminary report of the application of contingent reinforcement procedures (token economy) on a "chronic psychiatric ward." *Journal of Abnormal Psychology,* 1968, 73, 37-43.

Ayllon, T., & Azrin, N. H. The measurement and reinforcement of behavior of psychotics. *Journal of the Experimental Analysis of Behavior,* 1965, 8, 357-383.

Ayllon, T., & Michael, J. The psychiatric nurse as a behavioral engineer. *Journal of the Experimental Analysis of Behavior,* 1959, 2, 323-334.

Burchard, J. D. A residential program of behavior modification. Paper presented at meeting of the American Psychological Association, New York City, September, 1966.

Burnham, W. H. *The normal mind,* New York: Appleton, 1924.

Colby, K. M. Things to come: designing neurotic computers. In L. Krasner and L. P. Ullmann (Eds.). *Research in behavior modification.* New York: Holt, Rinehart and Winston, 1965.

Eysenck, H. J. Learning theory and behaviour therapy. *Journal of Mental Science,* 1959, 105, 61-75.

Ferster, C. B. Interim progress report: Linwood Project. Institute for Behavioral Research, Silver Springs, Md., 1965.

Frank, J. D. *Persuasion and healing.* Baltimore: Johns Hopkins Press, 1961.

Franks, C. M. (Ed.). *Conditioning techniques in clinical practice and research.* New York: Springer, 1964.

Fuller, P. R. Operant conditioning of a vegetative human organism. *American Journal of Psychology,* 1949, 62, 587-590.

Girardeau, F. L., & Spradlin, J. E. Token rewards in a cottage program. *Mental Retardation*, 1964, 2, 345-351.

Goldiamond, I. Self-control procedures in personal behavior problems. *Psychological Reports*, 1965, 17, 851-868.

Goldstein, A. P., Heller, K., & Sechrest, L. B. *Psychotherapy and the psychology of behavior change.* New York: Wiley, 1966.

Jones, M. C. The elimination of children's fears. *Journal of Experimental Psychology*, 1924, 7, 382-390.

Kanfer, F. H., & Saslow, G. Behavioral analysis: an alternative to diagnostic classification. *Archives of General Psychiatry*, 1965, 12, 529-538.

Krasner, L. Studies of the conditioning of verbal behavior. *Psychological Bulletin*, 1958, 55, 148-170.

Krasner, L. The therapist as a social reinforcement machine. In H. H. Strupp and L. Luborsky (Eds.). *Research in Psychotherapy, Vol. II.* Washington, D.C.: American Psychological Assoc., 1962.

Krasner, L. Verbal conditioning and psychotherapy. In L. Krasner and L. P. Ullmann (Eds.), *Research in behavior modification.* New York: Holt, Rinehart and Winston, 1965.

Krasner, L. The translation of operant conditioning procedures from the experimental laboratory to the psychotherapeutic interaction. Paper presented at the meeting of the American Psychological Association, New York, September, 1966. (a)

Krasner, L. The behavioral scientist and social responsibility: No place to hide. *Journal of Social Issues*, 1966, 21, 9-30. (b)

Krasner, L. Verbal operant conditioning and awareness. In K. Salzinger (Ed.), *Research in verbal behavior and some neurophysiological implications.* New York: Academic Press, 1967.

Krasner, L. Behavior modification—Values and training. In C. R. Franks (Ed.), *Behavior therapy.* New York: McGraw-Hill, 1969.

Krasner, L., & Ullmann, L. P. (Eds.), *Research in behavior modification.* New York: Holt, Rinehart and Winston, 1965.

Lang, P. J. Some mechanisms of fear reduction: a laboratory analysis of desensitization therapy. Paper presented at the meeting of the American Psychological Association, Chicago, September, 1965.

Lent, J. The application of operant procedures in the modification of behaviors of retarded children in a free social situation. Paper presented at the meeting of the American Association for the Advancement of Science, Berkeley, California, 1965.

Mertens, G. C. Behavioral planning. Unpublished manuscript. St. Cloud State College, St. Cloud, Minnesota, 1967.

O'Leary, K. D. & Becker, W. C. Behavior modification of an adjustment class: a token reinforcement program. *Exceptional Children*, 1967, 33, 637-642.

Schonbar, R. A. A practitioner's critique of psychotherapy research. Paper presented at the meeting of the American Psychological Association, Los Angeles, September, 1964.

Skinner, B. F. *The behavior of organisms.* New York: Appleton-Century-Crofts, 1938.

Skinner, B. F. *Walden two*. New York: Macmillan, 1948.

Szasz, T. S. *The myth of mental illness*. New York: Harper, 1961.

Truax, C. B. Reinforcement and nonreinforcement in Rogerian psychotherapy. *Journal of Abnormal Psychology*, 1966, 71, 1-9.

Ullmann, L. P. Behavior modification as social movement. In C. R. Franks (Ed.), *Behavior therapy*. New York: McGraw-Hill, 1969.

Ullmann, L. P., & Krasner, L. (Eds.), *Case studies in behavior modification*. New York: Holt, Rinehart and Winston, 1965.

Ullmann, L. P., & Krasner, L. *A psychological approach to abnormal behavior*. New York: Prentice Hall, 1969.

Wahler, R. G., Winkel, G. H., Peterson, R. F., & Morrison, D. C. Mothers as behavior therapists for their own children. *Behavior Research and Therapy*, 1965, 3, 113-124.

Walder, L. O. Teaching parents to modify the behaviors of their autistic children. Paper presented at the meeting of the American Psychological Association, New York, September, 1966.

Watson, L. S. Application of operant conditioning techniques to institutionalized severely and profoundly retarded children. Paper presented at the meeting of the American Psychological Association, Chicago, September, 1965.

Weiss, R. L. Operant conditioning techniques in psychological assessment. In P. W. McReynolds (Ed.), *Advances in psychological assessment*. Palo Alto: Science and Behavior Book, 1968.

Wolpe, J. *Psychotherapy by reciprocal inhibition*. Stanford: Stanford University Press, 1958.

6: Human Aggression

ROGER E. ULRICH

JUDITH ELBERT FAVELL

Human aggression is one of man's most persistent and difficult problems. From the beginning of history, he has from time to time hurt or killed his fellows. Prehistoric cracked skulls and crude weapons testify to the ancient roots of his aggression. Together with religious-philosophical writings, accounts of war constitute a major part of the literary evidence concerning the development of "civilization." Today, aggression is more serious and dangerous than ever, and in spite of centuries of concern, little has actually been done to develop effective controls.

Our ignorance of the causes of aggression is a major factor for this failure. Because aggression is so complex, controlling it has always been especially difficult. In addition, we have consistently taken obtuse approaches to the nature of aggression. Like many behavioral problems, aggression has most often been regarded as behavior springing spontaneously from the individual. A man may be considered aggressive because he is of a particular race or simply because aggressiveness is part of his "personality." Or the existence of a biologically determined aggressive "drive" may be assumed. This drive is then expected to inevitably express itself in one way or another. Thus, in spite of the seriousness of the problem, the tendency has often been to regard aggression as an unfortunate, but unavoidable, attribute of "human nature."

The data reported in this paper result from the efforts of many investigators. The contribution of certain persons, however, cannot be adequately catalogued by simply citing their names and a date at the end of a sentence. This especially holds true for N. H. Azrin, Director of the Behavior Research Laboratory at Anna State Hospital. However, there are others who must also receive special recognition for the contributions their research has made to our understanding of the causes of aggression. Ronald Hutchinson, Donald Hake, John Mabry and Thomas Stachnik are all persons with whom the senior author at one time or another worked closely on

We will describe, however, a view of aggression which does not make these assumptions. Rather, it seeks the causes of aggression in the organism's environment. This is not to say that heredity has no effect on aggression; however, this approach is concerned primarily with environmental stimuli. The potential usefulness of this approach lies in the fact that environmental causes of aggression can be objectively identified, studied, and eventually controlled. As we gain knowledge and control of the causes, we gain control of the behavior itself.

Although the research reported here employed human subjects, it is an outgrowth of work in animal aggression. We will briefly review some of this animal research to provide background for this study and to suggest directions for future research with human subjects.

AGGRESSION IN ANIMALS

There are a variety of scientific approaches to the study of animal aggression. Naturalists (e.g., Calhoun, 1948, 1950; Carpenter, 1934, 1940, 1942; Crew & Mirsksia, 1932; Eibl-Eibesfeldt, 1961; Guhl, 1953) have described the aggressive behavior of a wide range of species in natural conditions or in laboratory settings designed to simulate natural conditions. Their descriptions cover the topography of both overt aggressive behavior and associated "threat" or "tournament" displays. In addition, naturalists have described the influence which factors such as sex, season, food deprivation, and amount of available space have on the frequency and form of aggression. Various social patterns established by aggressive incidents, such as dominance hierarchies and territorial systems, have also been described.

Physiologists have been concerned with the role played by various internal mechanisms in relation to aggression (e.g., Delgado, 1963; Hess, 1954; Hess & Akert, 1955; Hutchinson & Renfrew, 1966; Masserman, 1950, 1964; Ranson, 1934; von Holst & von Saint Paul, 1963; Wasman & Flynn, 1962). A major finding in their investigations has been that stimulation

the aggression research and to whom we are extremely indebted. Douglas Anger and Kay Mueller deserve special credit for their help in relation to the preparation of this manuscript. To George Hunt, Jim Bernard, Sharon Lane Surratt, Don Patterson, Marshall Wolfe, and Marilla Scott Svinicki, our thanks for assisting with the experiments and graphs. To Marilyn Arnett, Carole Ulrich, Tom DeLoach, and Judy Buelke for their careful editing, proofing and typing, we extend our sincerest thanks.

Support for a large portion of the research reported in this paper came from the National Institute of Mental Health (Grant No. MH 08841-01; 2Rol-MH 11976-02A1; MH 12882-01), the Illinois Psychiatric Training and Research Authority (Grant No. 17-177: 1964-1965), the Office of Naval Research (Contract No. N00014-67-A-0421-0001, NR 171-807) and the Western Michigan University Research Fund.

of the hypothalamus will produce aggressive behavior of various types.

Another approach has been taken by behavioral scientists. Working in the laboratory they have analyzed the effects of various environmental events on aggressive behavior.

Essentially, this paper will reflect the work of laboratory scientists whose major concern was the analysis of two types of environmental stimuli which are responsible for aggression in animals: aversive stimuli and reinforcing stimuli.

Aggression and Aversive Stimuli

Aversive stimuli are those events which an animal will work to escape or avoid or which will suppress the responses upon which they are contingent. From time to time, we may also use the word *pain* interchangeably with *aversive stimuli*. Use of the word *pain* is not intended to imply a phenomenological definition rather than the behavioral definition already given; it is merely a more convenient term.

One of the first observations of the fact that aversive stimuli would cause fighting was by O'Kelly and Steckle (1939). They found that rats, when shocked, would pair off and fight. This fighting would continue beyond shock termination unless the rats were returned to their home cage, where they would resume their normal behavior. Although some replication of the "O'Kelly-Steckle reaction" followed (Daniel, 1943), this interesting line of investigation received little further attention at the time.

The next study of note was done in 1948 by Neil Miller. Miller's experiment was designed to shape and maintain fighting by reinforcing successive approximations with termination of electric shock. An attempt to explore aggression using a method similar to that employed by Miller led to some of the more recent research on pain and aggression. Two rats were placed in a chamber in which the grid floor could be electrified. Fighting was to be shaped by reinforcing successive approximations with termination of shock. However, soon after the shock was turned on, the rats reared on their hind feet and began fighting even before the shock was terminated. This phenomenon occurred repeatedly during subsequent shock presentations. The rats needed no training to fight when shocked; fighting appeared to be an unlearned response to pain.

The implications of these observations led to a long series of experimental investigations of aggression.[1] Before presenting an overview of this research, a general behavioral definition of aggression is necessary. In choosing behaviors we term aggressive, we must confine ourselves to observable movements associated with the presentation of aversive or conditioned aversive stimulation to another organism. When these responses are directed toward inanimate objects, they also are categorized as aggressive. In addition, we include in our definition behaviors which are functionally related to more overt aggressive behavior. For example, striking or biting movements made by fighting animals might not connect with their opponents, but these movements are typically a prelude to that contact and are produced by the same stimuli. Similarly, certain stereotyped behavior frequently occurs in animals as a precursor to, or substitute for overt aggression (e.g., tournament fighting, Eibl-Eibesfeldt, 1961). Since these behaviors occur in sequences and seem to be controlled by the same stimuli as overt aggression, they are included as part of the general aggression phenomenon.

We are aware that this definition will allow for a wide variety of responses to be labeled aggressive and thus more specific operational definitions are necessary for an experimental analysis. Indeed, such definitions are critical if we are to understand the relationships between the behaviors termed aggressive and the environmental conditions which produce them. Most experiments cited in this paper provide such definitions. It must be remembered, however, that the word "aggression" used in the general sense is not a precise term. Thus, the question frequently asked of whether or not something is really aggression is not appropriate since it implies the existence of "true" aggression. Aggression in this paper is defined by specific behaviors and the conditions which produce them.

Much of the initial research on aggression was concerned with the effect of intensity, frequency and duration of shock (Azrin, Hutchinson, & Hake, 1963; Azrin, Ulrich, Hutchinson, & Norman, 1964; Ulrich & Azrin, 1962; Ulrich, Wolff, & Azrin, 1964). In general, intermediate values of these parameters were most effective in producing aggression.

However, a number of other variables were found to effect aggression. For example, reduction in floor space and increase in the number of rats in the chamber were found to increase aggression (Ulrich & Azrin, 1962). The presence of male sex hormone appeared to augment aggression (Hutchinson, Ulrich, & Azrin, 1965), while sensory impairment decreased it (Flory, Ulrich, & Wolff, 1965). It was also found that animals will attack members of other species as well as their own (Azrin, Hutchinson, & Hake, 1963; Azrin, Hutchinson, & Sallery, 1964; Ulrich & Azrin, 1962; Ulrich, Wolff, & Azrin, 1964), and some animals would attack inanimate objects (Azrin, Hntchinson, & Sallery, 1964; Hutchinson, Azrin, & Hake, 1966; Ulrich & Azrin, 1962). The reaction was also found to be extremely resistant to fatigue (Ulrich & Azrin, 1962). The fact that it has been produced experimentally in numerous species attests to its generality.

Stimuli other than electric shock seem sufficient to produce similar aggressive reactions. Azrin, Hake and Hutchinson (1965) found that a blow or pinch to the tail of a squirrel monkey will produce attack upon a cloth-covered ball. Paired rats will fight when placed on a preheated metal floor (Ulrich & Azrin, 1962). Withdrawing or withholding positive reinforcers can also cause aggression. Azrin, Hutchinson and Hake (1966) found that discontinuation of food reinforcement (extinction) produced aggression in pigeons. A similar finding is reported by Boshka, Weisman and Thor (1966), who noted an increase in aggression in addicted rats who were denied morphine.

These stimuli appear to produce aggression without prior conditioning or learning. However, it is also possible that neutral stimuli can be conditioned according to the classical or Pavlovian paradigm (Pavlov, 1927). For example, Ulrich, Hutchinson and Azrin (1965) noted that fighting occurred, in the absence of shock, between animals that had previously been paired and shocked but were housed separately. It appeared that the "other animal" had become the CS for fighting. Other experimental efforts produced fighting in response to a buzzer that had been paired with shock (Creer, Hitzing, & Schaeffer, 1966; Vernon & Ulrich, 1966).

Aggression and Reinforcing Stimuli

Although some aggression appears as a function of preceding aversive stimuli, much aggression seems to be emitted independent of identifiable preceding stimuli. In these cases the probable "cause" of aggression is the stimulus consequences which have followed similar occurrences of that behavior in the past. Stimuli such as these, which increase the future probability of the behavior upon which they are contingent, are known as positive reinforcers. Withdrawal of aversive stimuli also reinforces behavior. These stimuli are known as negative reinforcers. The general procedure is called operant conditioning (Skinner, 1938).

Positive reinforcement has been used on several occasions to produce and maintain aggression. In one case (Ulrich, Johnston, Richardson, & Wolff, 1963), fighting was reinforced with water. Rats were first individually trained to go to a water magazine at the onset of a buzzer and light. Fighting behavior was subsequently conditioned by making the buzzer, light and water contingent upon movements by the experimental animal toward the head of the control animal. Through this process of shaping, vigorous fighting movements were eventually made by one rat toward another.

In a similar study by Reynolds, Catania and Skinner (1963), a stable pattern of aggression was established by reinforcing a food-deprived pigeon with grain. More recent studies have shown that intracranial stimulation can be used to reinforce the attack of one rat against another. Indeed, rats can be conditioned not only to fight other rats, but cats and squirrel monkeys as well (Stachnik, Ulrich, & Mabry, 1966a, 1966b).

These studies clearly show that fighting behavior can be conditioned through positive reinforcement. In addition, it was found that such behavior apparently became more than simply an operant response strengthened by reinforcement. Once aggression was increased by operant conditioning, fighting eventually occurred which had many of the qualities typical of aggression produced by aversive stimuli.

Negative reinforcement probably has a similar effect on aggression. However, the study of this phenomenon is complicated by the fact that the same stimuli whose withdrawal is reinforcing can produce aggression. In such cases, it becomes difficult to separate the effects of negative reinforcement from those of the aversive stimulus. However, recent findings by Azrin, Hutchinson and Hake (1967) suggest that termination of the aversive stimulus after the onset of aggression can intensify the aggressive response. Thus, negative reinforcement does appear to increase aggression.

Other Areas of Research in Animal Aggression

Two other areas in the recent study of animal aggression deserve mention. One is the effect of aggression itself as a reinforcer. After the presentation of an aversive stimulus, if there is no appropriate object for attack in the animal's vicinity, the animal will emit an operant response in order to obtain one. The effect was studied in monkeys by Azrin, Hutchinson and McLaughlin (1965) who showed that, when shocked, a monkey would pull a chain which resulted in presentation of an inanimate object for attack.

The relationship between the aggressive response to pain and another typical response, that of escape or avoidance, has also been studied in our laboratory. This work was designed to see if an animal would press a bar to escape or avoid shock, or if he would attack instead. A number of these studies have been conducted (Azrin, Hutchinson, & Hake, 1967; Ulrich, 1967b; Ulrich & Craine, 1964; Ulrich, Stachnik, Brierton, & Mabry, 1966). Although the animals would often fight rather than perform the escape or avoidance response, the extent to which they would fight depended on a variety of factors.

These studies showed that it was not meaningful to speak of either aversively controlled operants such as escape or aversively controlled fighting as having a prepotency over the other without specifying the attending conditions. Whether an animal will fight or escape probably depends on a complex interaction of heredity, past history and the present stimulus conditions.

In summary, we have seen that experimental work on aggression in animals has established both aversive stimuli and reinforcing stimuli as important factors. In the next section we will report some research on human aggression. This research is presented both because it is an outgrowth of the animal research reviewed above and because it is representative of a potentially fruitful direction for future human research.

HUMAN AGGRESSION

Much of the aggression research on animals (Lorenz, 1966) as well as with humans (Buss, 1961) rests on the assumption, mentioned earlier, that aggression is most closely related to an internal state in the organism. The approach is represented in humans by various tests devised to measure these states. Two such tests are the Siegel Manifest Hostility Scale and the Buss Hostility Scale. Such measures of aggression are used in various descriptive and correlational studies which attempt to relate aggression to such factors as academic achievement, sex, hostility, etc. One problem that arises is that the definition of variables such as hostility is often unclear. In addition, the relationship of these variables to actual aggressive behavior is difficult to determine. Even if we could establish the nature of hostility and its relationship to aggression, we would still be faced with discovering and controlling the variables responsible for hostility. This takes us back to environment.

Indeed, some studies of human aggression have concentrated less on internal states and more on environmental variables. For instance, Sears, Hovland and Miller (1940) studied the effects of various degrees of sleep deprivation on aggressive responding. There have also been attempts to study reinforcement of aggression in children (Cowan & Walters, 1963; Hops & Walters, 1963; Walters & Brown, 1963). Another popular line of investigation which should be mentioned follows the hypothesis that frustration produces aggression (Dollard, et al., 1939). The problem so far has been in specifying both the frustrating event and the aggressive response.

The experiments reported below might be considered studies of frustration as a cause of aggression. However, they are methodologically closer to the animal research already described and grew out of attempts to find aggressive reactions in humans similar to those in animals. Our first efforts along these lines were casual. A game of musical chairs involving prizes for getting a chair seemed to produce more aggression than one in which no extraneous reinforcement was given. Children reinforced for stacking blocks would often physically attack a stooge who had followed our instructions to knock the blocks down.

In these free-play experiments, it was very difficult to control the actual precipitating event and also difficult to specify or measure the resulting aggressive responses. However, in the experiments described here, the environment was arranged in such a way that both the independent variables, i.e. the frustrating events, and the dependent variables, i.e. the aggressive responses, could be specified, controlled and counted. Briefly stated, the frustrating event was disruption of a task for which the subject had been previously reinforced. The aggressive response was the press of a button which the subject was told would have a similar disruptive effect on another child, involved with an identical task in another room.

Subjects used in the first of two studies were one female and three male 10-year-olds, selected randomly from a list submitted by a local elementary school. Parents and subjects were told initially that the study involved a comparison of performances on a simple motor task for which the subjects would receive a daily maximum of $2.00.

The experimental chamber was a booth (8 ft. by 4 ft.) placed in a large room (17 ft. by 10 ft.). One side of the booth was open and allowed unrestricted observation of the subjects from behind a one way mirror located at the opposite end of the room. A multiconductor cable, which extended from the chamber to the control room, allowed for remote control of both the manual and automatic stimulus conditions as well as for the recording of the subject's behavior. The experimenters manually operated a Davis reinforcement dispenser and the device for blocking positive reinforcement.

The subjects' apparatus (Figure 6.1) consisted of a sheet of plywood (2 ft. by 3 ft.) mounted on four low-tension springs atop a table 30 inches high. Centered at the rear of the plywood was a synchronous motor. A piece of bent brass tubing enveloping an "off-balance" weight was attached to the armature shaft of the motor, causing it to vibrate when running.

The task, involving the erection of a stack of small rubber cylinders (bottle stoppers) on circles drawn on the spring-mounted table, was performed within an area 1 foot square near the front of the table. Additional stoppers were available in a small box attached to the left side of the table. A 100-watt signal light on the wall facing the subject indicated the beginning of each trial. Available to the right of the subject was a 3-watt feedback light attached to a momentary-contact response button which he was told would shake the table of another individual who was performing a similar task in a nearby room. Positioned in front of the table was a metal stool to which a left hand glove was attached.

The subjects were initially given the following instructions:

> This is a test to see how fast and how well you can use your hand. I'm going to explain the instructions, then demonstrate the experiment and finally let you try it.
>
> The first part of the experiment is to put your left hand in this glove. Now you look at this light. When it flashes you must place these stoppers on the little white circles, this way. When you have completed that, making sure that you remove your hand from the last stopper, like

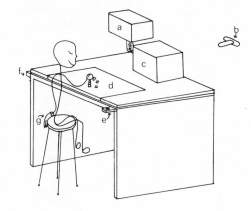

A. DAVIS UNIVERSAL FEEDER

B. SIGNAL LIGHT

C. MOTOR

D. STACKING AREA

E. FEEDBACK LIGHT & BUTTON

F. BOX OF EXTRA CYLINDERS

G. GLOVE

FIGURE 6.1   *Diagram of the table upon which the stacking task was performed and the encased motor which vibrated the table top. The feeder was mounted to the left to allow visual accessibility of the glass receptacle while prohibiting convenient touching. The response button and feedback light are fixed to the right of the subject.*

this, you are ready to begin stacking. Begin stacking the first five stoppers with the smaller end down on this white circle. When you have completed the first stack, you may begin on the second stack. When all ten stoppers are stacked, you must remove your hand from the table for 3 seconds. You will then receive a reward in this glass jar. Leave the money in the jar until I come in at the end of the period and give it to you. Now let us go through it again. (Here the instructions were repeated until it was clear that the child understood what he was to do.)

Finally, the children were told:

There is another person in another booth who is also stacking stoppers. When you press this button, his table will shake. He also has a button that will shake your table like this. However, to keep his table shaking you must press the button many times, like this. If you don't, this little light will not flash and his table will not shake. Now you try it.

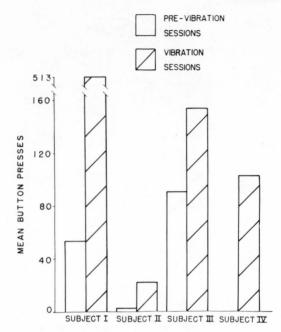

FIGURE 6.2 *Means of total button presses for each subject during previbration and vibration sessions.*

The subjects were first given 14 sessions, each composed of 20 trials. Sessions 1-4 were nonvibration sessions during which baseline data on button presses were collected. Ten experimental or vibrational sessions followed. Five sequences of intermittent, 4-second-duration, table vibrations were programmed during the 20 trials of each of these sessions. A sequence was defined by the frequency of vibrations for each session, as well as by the point at which vibrations occurred within a trial. Thus, within any one sequence, vibrations were randomly produced over the 20 trials and at various stages of progress in the individual's stacking. Each subject received different arrangements of these sequences. When the blocks fell either accidently or by design, no reinforcement was given. With no accidental failures the maximum earned per session was $1.60 (Sequence I); the minimum, $.80 (Sequence V).

The length of each session depended upon the rapidity with which the subject completed the 20 trials of stacking. Each child participated 5 days per week for 3 weeks. Upon conclusion of the standard procedure, four variations of the procedure were effected:

1. A return to the previbration procedure.
2. Presentation of vibrations during each of a number of trials.
3. Nonreinforcement of stacking completion.
4. Combinations of the preceding three.

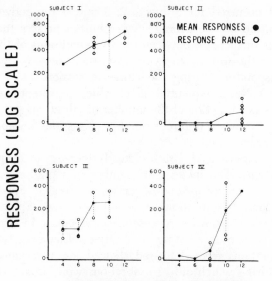

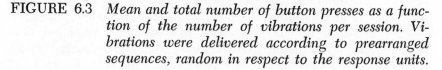

VIBRATIONS PER SESSION

FIGURE 6.3 *Mean and total number of button presses as a function of the number of vibrations per session. Vibrations were delivered according to prearranged sequences, random in respect to the response units.*

Each subject received unique combinations of the variations mentioned above, and no identical sessions were repeated on the same individual. During these sessions the length of each experimental period varied.

To conclude the study, one of the experimenters, whom the subjects had never met, conducted an interview with each subject.

Results indicate that the dependent variable, button presses, increases in frequency as a function of disruptive vibrations. Figure 6.2 shows mean number of button presses for each subject under the previbration and vibration conditions. Subject 1 emitted a mean rate of approximately 50 button presses for the previbration sessions and a mean rate of 513 responses during the vibration sessions. Subject 2 showed an average of only 3 responses during the previbration sessions and 20 during the experimental phase. Subject 3's responses in the previbration condition averaged 90 and increased to a mean of 142 in the vibration periods. Subject 4 showed a response increase from 0 in the previbration phase to an average of 105 during the vibration sessions.

Differences in increases of response rate between previbration and vibration sessions for each subject differed greatly. For example, Subject 1 showed not only the greatest total responses, but also the highest percentage of increase between the previbration and vibration conditions (851.8 percent). Likewise, increases of 633.3 percent, 70.3 percent and

103.4 percent occurred for Subjects 2, 3 and 4 respectively. Although Subject 4 emitted on the average fewer button presses than Subject 3, the percentage of increase between the two conditions of the experiment was higher for the former. In every case, there occurred an increase in aggressive responding during the vibration session.

Figure 6.3 shows sequential effect which represent mean and total button presses as a function of the number of vibrations per session. Each subject's graph shows a different number of sessions because of the five vibration sequences used.

Subject 1 experienced a rather steady increase in frequency of disruptive vibrations. The increase in number of vibrations, however, did not produce an increase in total responses per session. For instance, in a session in which 10 vibrations were administered, Subject 1 emitted approximately 230 responses, representing a decrease in comparison with each of four sessions presenting 8 vibrations. Likewise, two sessions in which 12 vibrations were delivered showed lower response totals than one session during which only 10 vibrations were programmed.

With Subject 2, no differences are seen in button pressing in response to 4, 6 and 8 vibrations per session. However, mean responses increased under the 10 and 12 vibration conditions. The five randomly assigned sessions in which 12 table vibrations were delivered produced total responses to this vibration frequency ranging from 0 to approximately 80.

Subject 3 shows equal response averages as a function of both 4 and 6 vibrations. A sharp increase in responding is seen with 8 vibrations, and this average is maintained under the 10 vibration conditions. As with the other subjects, the total responses per session do not follow the identical pattern of increase seen in plotting mean responses. However, the sessions displaying the lowest totals of button presses as a function of 10 and 12 vibrations still represent an increase over the sessions in which the highest totals of responses were produced as a function of 4 and 6 vibrations.

Subject 4's average number of responses increased steadily as a function of the frequency of vibrations, with the exception of the slight decrease under the 6 vibration condition. Although the range of total responses per session as a function of 8, and particularly of 10 vibrations, showed variance, the lowest total number of button presses occurring within a 10 vibration session is still higher than the session with the highest number of responses under the 8 vibration condition.

A more refined analysis is represented in Figure 6.4. In this graph, totals for previbration and vibration sessions have been divided into button presses occurring as a function of each of the three stimulus events: vibration, reinforcement and accidental failure.

Subject 1 exhibited a higher total number of responses to vibrations than to reinforcement in 6 of the 10 experimental sessions. Of these 4 other points, 3 occurred during the last three sessions. The ninth session also showed a lower number of responses to vibrations than to accidental

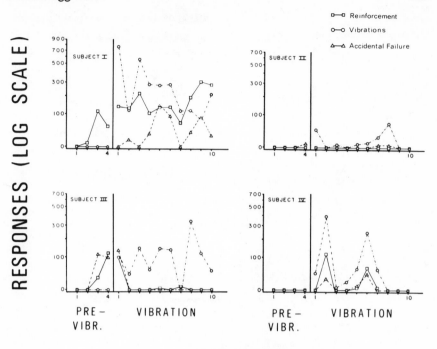

FIGURE 6.4 *Button presses as a function of three stimulus events: vibration, reinforcement and accidental failure. Button presses were considered functionally related to one of the three when emitted following the onset of that event, but before the onset of the next event. Previbration and vibration sessions are shown.*

failure, which had produced the lowest frequency of button pressing, except in session 5.

Button presses following reinforcement and accidental failure remained at near 0 throughout the experimental procedure for Subject 2. The number of responses following programmed vibrations was more variable and slightly greater. Subject 2 did not respond at all during sessions 2, 4, 9 and 10.

Subject 3's graph displays an overall greater frequency of button pressing in response to vibration than to the other stimulus events, the exception being sessions 1 and 7. Variability in responding to table vibrations increased markedly during sessions 7 and 8, then returned to a level and pattern similar to that seen in the first six sessions, although decreasing slightly.

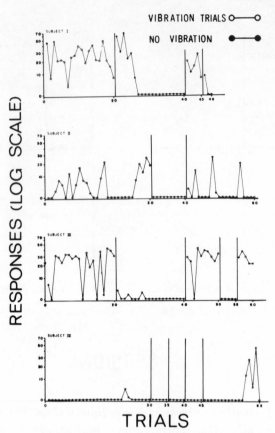

VIBRATION TRIALS O——O

NO VIBRATION ●——●

RESPONSES (LOG SCALE)

TRIALS

FIGURE 6.5   *Representative sessions for each of the subjects dur-*
ing random vibration of three experimental condi-
tions. The condition of nonreinforcement was added
during certain trials. This varied procedure was in
effect during four sessions for each subject and fol-
lowed the ten vibration sessions depicted in the
preceding figure. Vertical lines indicate a change
of experimental conditions.

The record for Subject 4 indicates an oscillating but higher number
of responses following vibrations than accidental failure or reinforcement in the first 7 sessions. Responding thereafter decreased to 0 for all
three conditions. The pattern of button pressing across sessions is virtually
identical for all events, regardless of number of responses.

Following the 10 experimental sessions, the experimenters randomly
varied the conditions for each subject within each of four daily sessions.
Sample performances under various conditions are shown in Figure 6.5.

The figure presents evidence of the high degree of control disruptive vibrations had over the behavior of button pressing for Subject 1. Although the number of presses following each vibration varied considerably, button pressing continued to trials beyond termination of vibrations (trial 20), thereafter keeping a stable level of 0. Reinstatement of vibrations produced a concomitant increase in pressing, again reversed by the withdrawal of this condition.

Subject 2 showed a high degree of variability in number of responses during the first 20 vibration trials. The nonvibration procedure was initiated following 4 trials of relatively high and stable button pressing in response to vibrations and resulted in no responses during this phase. When the vibration condition was reinstated, sporadic responding, interspersed with trials of 0 button pressing, was produced.

When Subject 3 was subjected to continuous vibrations, responding rapidly assumed high and stable values varying from 20 to 45 responses per trial, with the exception of trials 11, 15 and 17. After vibrations were discontinued, button pressing decreased substantially, stabilizing at a level of 0. Reintroduction of vibrations resulted in responding similar in frequency and pattern to the first 20 vibration trials, except for the deviant point at trial 43. Elimination of vibrations immediately returned responding to 0, and a final re-presentation of table vibration produced a corresponding increase in button pressing.

The data for Subject 4 show that the few presses that did occur appeared subsequent to table vibrations.

Concluding the experiment, each subject was interviewed by one of the experimenters, whom the subjects had never seen. The following are responses to the question, "Why did you press the button on your table?"

Subject 1 answered that he, "pressed the button even though the other person was a nice guy," because he "just wanted to be mean," but he wasn't angry.

Subject 2 commented that she "liked the money very much" and that her "partner didn't want her to have it for some reason." She said that button pressing made her "feel better" but she was never "mad."

Subject 3 stated that button pressing helped him "work off annoyance" when the other subject "got mad at me" and shook the table. He said that he was "mad only when the machine broke and didn't give dimes," but in general "just felt annoyed."

Subject 4 said that he shook the other child's table on days when he lost a baseball game, but refrained when he won or was going swimming after the session. He indicated that he "felt sad" when he pressed the button, but that the other subject always "started it."

The preceding experiment was later replicated to investigate the effect of session length, amount of reinforcement and distribution of vibration.

By increasing the number of trials and the length of time required for completion of each task, the total session was lengthened to approximately 50 minutes. This revision was instituted to examine frequency of button pressing as a function of an increase in the amount of time the subjects were exposed to the series of disruptive vibrations. By decreasing the size of each reinforcement from a dime to a nickel, an attempt was made to minimize an accumulation of money, thus maintaining its effectiveness as a reinforcer and insuring that disruption of its attainment remained sufficiently aversive.

In order to avoid an artificial experimental environment, vibrations were delivered intermittently on a variable interval schedule of 1½ minutes, regardless of whether stacking was in progress. Table vibrations which occurred during periods when the subject was relining stoppers or waiting for the signal light following reinforcement were not considered to disrupt the task and, therefore, were not considered as discrete trials. This alteration was arranged in an attempt to eliminate cues that might indicate the nonexistence of a second subject. In addition, it provided an opportunity to evaluate any differences between frequency of button pressing as a function of disruptive vibrations as opposed to vibrations that did not disrupt completion of stacking.

Two 10-year-old subjects, one male and one female, were again randomly selected from a list submitted by a local elementary school. Both parents and subjects were told that the experiment involved performance of a motor task for which the children could earn a daily maximum of $1.50 per session, attending three times per week.

The apparatus used in this second experiment was identical to that in the first study, with the exception of the following additions. A VI timer and microswitch were wired to the vibration mechanism, and a VI 1½ minute tape was used to deliver vibrations. A cumulative recorder measured trial time, rate of button presses, and whether the button pressing followed reinforcement, accidental failure or vibrations. Ten silver cylinders were placed on the subject's table on the left and ten white cylinders were positioned to the right of the stacking area for use in the task. One nickel was delivered following each successful completion of the cylinder-stacking task.

Instructions were identical with respect to the purpose of the button and the operation of the apparatus. In this replication, however, the subject was required to stack two stacks of the five white cylinders, reline those and complete two identical stacks of the silver cylinders. Baseline data on the rate of button pressing, number of reinforcements received and session length were initially recorded. Following this, experimental sessions, each composed of 30 trials, were begun. As in the first study, a trial was terminated by either delivery of reinforcement, occurrence of accidental failure or disruption by a vibration. Reinforcement followed successful completion of all four stacks.

In Figure 6.6, the mean number of total button presses following reinforcement, accidental failure and vibrations for previbration and vibration sessions is shown for each subject. Responses to vibrations in experimental periods are broken down into those which occurred sub-sequent to vibrations which disrupted reinforcement and those which did not.

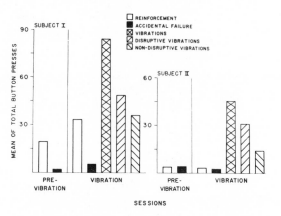

FIGURE 6.6   *Mean number of button presses following reinforce-ment, accidental failure, and vibration. Responses to vibration are broken down into those to disruptive and those to nondisruptive vibration.*

In the case of Subject 1, button pressing in response to accidental failure occurred minimally with a mean of less than 3 in previbration and 6 in vibration sessions. Responding which followed reinforcement had a higher frequency, the mean increasing from approximately 19 in pre-vibration to 33 in experimental sessions. A markedly higher rate was emitted as a function of table vibrations with a mean of nearly 84. In addition, it can be noted that vibrations which disrupted the task, thus precluding the delivery of a reinforcer, had a somewhat higher mean incidence, 50, than those which did not interfere with stacking, 40.

Subject 2 showed a similarly low average number of aggressive re-sponses to both accidental failure and reinforcement. Specifically, rein-forcement evoked a mean of 5 button presses in the previbration phase and an average of 3 responses during all vibration sessions. Accidental failure produced a mean of 5 for previbration and less than 3 button presses for vibration sessions. Not only does average responding to vibra-tions, 45 presses per session, evidence an increase over that to reinforce-ment or accidental failure, but also average button presses in response to both disruptive and nondisruptive vibrations show higher frequencies

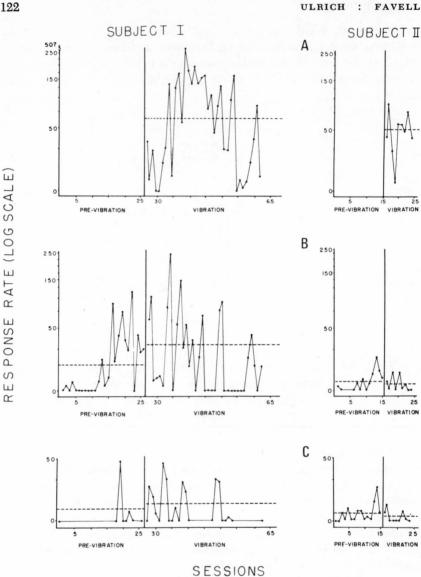

FIGURE 6.7   *Button presses divided into three function cate-*
            gories: those emitted as a function of reinforcement,
            accidental failure and vibration. Previbration ses-
            sions are indicated for each subject.

than to the other conditions. Responding to disruptive vibrations reached
an average of 31 per session, whereas mean presses to nondisruptive vibrations were approximately 12.

Figure 6.7 differentiates the response of button pressing into three functional categories: those emitted immediately following (A) vibration, (B) reinforcement and (C) accidental failure.

In the case of Subject 1, responding to accidental failure (Figure 6.7c) is minimal throughout the experiment, only twice exceeding pressing on an equivalent day as a function of reinforcement and vibration. Button pressing following reinforcement (Figure 6.7b) occurred more frequently and with marked variability during the previbration period. During the initial 8 sessions under the experimental condition, the frequency of button pressing in response to reinforcement was higher than that in response to vibration (Figure 6.7a) in all but 2 of the sessions. Subsequent responding to reinforcement fell lower than that of vibrations throughout the remainder of the experiment with the exception of 3 of the last 5 sessions. The frequency of pressing following vibration began to follow a decreasing trend after the high point at session 38.

Subject 2 represents a clearer difference in responding as a function of vibrations (Figure 6.7a) as opposed to reinforcement (Figure 6.7b) or accidental failure (Figure 6.7c). The latter conditions occasioned intermittent minimal responding in comparison with the uniformly higher rates following table vibrations.

It was seen from the data that button presses were produced and maintained despite the fact that no reinforcing consequences (other than operation of the feedback light) were programmed by the experimenters. Retaliatory button presses were in no way instrumental in decreasing or terminating disruptive vibrations. Two possible explanations of this behavior can be found in the research with animals reviewed earlier.

First, it is possible to regard this aggression as a response to aversive events, similar to the aggression produced by rats in response to electric shock or by monkeys and pigeons when placed on extinction schedules. Another way of looking at the behavior is to regard it as its own reinforcer. Since aversive events have been shown to make aggression itself reinforcing in animals, it is possible that the frustrating table vibrations produced a similar motivational condition for the children, making the supposedly aggressive button presses somehow reinforcing.

Another possible explanation of the button pressing is that it received fortuitous reinforcement from the fact that many of them occurred while the 4-second table vibration was still in progress. In this case, button presses would be followed by termination of the aversive vibrations and hence be negatively reinforced. Although this explanation does not tell us much about the initial occurrence of these button presses, it is lent strength by data which suggest the formation of a discrimination. While initially some subjects responded after reinforcement at a rate greater than or equal to responding after vibrations, responding to vibrations subsequently increased and were more consistently maintained than were responses following reinforcement. It should be noted, however, that button pressing also could, and often did, precede reinforcement. If the reinforcement explanation was used to account for the button pressing, one would have expected more responding to have occurred prior to reinforcement while the table was not being vibrated. This was not the case.

Another cautious explanation concerning the aggressiveness manifested in button pressing is that button pressing, instead of representing an aggressive response, became an alternative activity when vibrations made continuation of the task impossible. It should be remembered, however, that the same 10-second delay prior to the onset of the light signaling that the subjects could resume stacking followed reinforcement and accidental failure as well as vibrations. Thus, this explanation would not account for differences in level of responding following these different stimulus events which showed the highest responding following vibrations.

We should, of course, be careful to conclude that responding was maintained solely to disrupt the hypothetical other subject. The instructions may not have been credible, or in some other way may have been nonfunctional in controlling the differential frequencies of responding to vibrations. On the other hand, the instructions may have been construed as a mandate concerning retaliation. The reasons that postreinforcement responding occurred are not completely clear, although it may be related to the overall aversiveness of the situation. Such responding might also be related to earlier vibrations.

One can see then that there could be a number of possible explanations for the behavior produced by vibrations. Nevertheless, the data, especially that shown in Figure 6.5, indicate a definite functional relationship between vibrations and button presses. Aggression did occur more frequently and reliably to the vibration circumstances throughout both experiments. Although it is unreasonable to expect that an area as complex as human aggression can be clarified by one set of experiments, we feel that the data do indicate that a specific behavior (button pressing) can legitimately be referred to as aggression and that it was functionally related to vibrations.

The main importance of this work lies more in its experimental approach to aggression. It shows that it is possible to avoid a purely topographical description of the phenomenon by employing an arbitrarily defined aggressive response, such as button pressing, and that this response can be functionally related in time to classes of events, such as making reinforcement impossible.

The aggression research utilizing infrahuman subjects has steadily isolated and related classes of environmental and behavioral events. Using similar laboratory procedures and controls, an examination of the degree of generality between infrahuman and human organisms should be increasingly possible. We can hope eventually to gain the understanding and control of the environmental causes of human aggression needed to reduce its occurrence.

CONCLUSIONS AND IMPLICATIONS

In this paper we have presented evidence which indicates that certain environmental events are important causes of aggression in both animals and humans. To date, research has concentrated on procedures effective in producing aggression; little attention has been given, even in animal research, to ways of stopping it. This line of work was once described by a philosopher-friend as a collection of data on "how to start wars." However, the initial step in any effort to prevent or eliminate a problem involves discovering conditions which produce or maintain it. As we have seen, a substantial amount of work has been done with animals and similar experimental progress with human subjects is beginning.

The dichotomy between animals and man is often overemphasized. In actuality, the differences we find behaviorally between man and monkey probably relate more to our reluctance or inability to create similar experimental conditions for the two, rather than to any organismic variables. Or it may be the history of human subjects that makes their aggression data more variable than animal data, rather than some inherent complexity within the organism. With this in mind, let us speculate as to how research on both animal and human aggression might apply to the control of the serious and immediate problems that confront us.

Generally speaking, there are three ways to prevent or suppress the occurrence of undesirable behavior. The first is to withhold or discontinue the stimuli that control its occurrence. The second is to punish the behavior, i.e., present an aversive stimulus contingent upon the response. The third is to reinforce behavior incompatible with the response to be eliminated. For instance, if we wish to eliminate sitting, we reinforce standing.

Two types of environmental events known to cause aggression in animals are aversive stimuli and positively reinforcing stimuli. It seems reasonable to assume that stimuli causing physical pain, as well as the withdrawal or blocking of positive reinforcement, will produce aggression in men as well as animals. Indeed, the research reported here indicates that the blocking of positive reinforcement can produce aggression in humans.

One possible method for reducing human aggression, then, lies in the reduction of the aversive stimuli that cause it. Although we know that it is impossible and probably undesirable to eliminate all aversive stimuli from our environment, there are still many such stimuli which are needlessly maintained by our society. A proliferation of examples can be found in our slums. Slum dwellers are more often hungry, cold and hurt than other members of society and, in addition, much of their socially acceptable behavior is met by aversive consequences. In attempts to find a job or a better home, they are often met with social rejection from which they escape by discontinuing the search for an advanced position. Indeed, the lack of opportunity experienced by some of our citizens to obtain the positive reinforcers common to others is perhaps aversive enough to cause aggression. It is no wonder, then, that the rate of violent or overtly aggressive criminal acts is higher in slums than elsewhere in our society. This picture of slum living is certainly not a revelation to anyone. Yet it is in areas like these that we might experiment, at least on a gross scale, in reducing human aggression. The fact that crime is also on the increase in suburbia indicates that simply eliminating all obvious social ills will not be a cure-all for aggression. It should also be stressed that the increase in crime in other than slum areas does not make the previous analysis invalid. In any event, it seems a worthy undertaking to try to eliminate some aversive stimuli from our physical environment and social institutions.

Other stimuli which probably cause aggression in men as well as in animals are positive reinforcers. Reinforcement has been shown to affect many human behaviors. Cultural differences in aggressiveness of men and women support this contention. In the Tchambuli culture, for example, where males are passive and females aggressive, male children probably receive little or no reinforcement for aggressive behavior, while female aggression is often reinforced (Mead, 1935). In our own society, boys are more often reinforced for aggressive behavior, such as playing with guns, winning in sports or "sticking up" for their sisters. Some children are taught that it is wrong to display temper or to get into a fight, while some are reinforced when they physically defeat other children. Thus, operant conditioning seems to increase or decrease human aggressive behavior.

As we noted above, this has been shown experimentally. Children rewarded for hitting responses in a play situation subsequently showed more interpersonal physical aggression than did children who had not been so rewarded (Cowan & Walters, 1963; Walters & Brown, 1963).

Another way of decreasing aggression is pointed up by these observations. If we were to cease our reinforcement of aggressive behavior, we could expect to eliminate aggression which is maintained by these consequences. We should note in this regard that extinction of behavior sometimes produces a temporary increase in that behavior. In addition, extinction itself has been shown to cause aggression in animals (Azrin, Hutchinson, & Hake, 1966). In any event, it would seem best to avoid shaping aggression. When dealing with ongoing aggression, extinction is probably a feasible method of control.

We can see reinforcement of aggression at work, not only in the family that reinforces the children for "defending themselves," but in our society's glorification of the soldier and in the many successfully aggressive heroes that appear on television and in the movies. Some of this operant aggression is maintained for good reason. Our government, for example, undoubtedly considers the awarding of combat medals necessary to our nation's defense. Indeed, few of us would dare to rear a completely nonaggressive child and send him into our society. However, even "adaptive" aggression can have unpleasant side effects. For example, a businessman emitting aggressive responses while fighting for a better place in the company may produce counteraggression in his co-workers. The fact still stands that one way of reducing aggression is to withhold consequences that might support it.

It may also be possible to decrease aggression by punishing it. This sort of control leads to extremely complex stimulus situations, and it is not clear what kinds of stimuli will accomplish it. As noted above, the fact that aversive stimuli can produce aggression makes their use a questionable technique for decreasing aggression. We have frequently noted, however, that pain-produced aggression can be suppressed in monkeys when the retaliation of the more powerful monkey is sufficiently punishing. We also anecdotally note that the threat of punishment sometimes suppresses our aggression or prompts us to find more suitable objects for attack.

Risley found that actual physical punishment used on a little girl did not produce aggression (Risley, 1968). Based on this finding, he appears to suggest that warning statements which point out that punishment procedures may, in fact, increase rather than eliminate aggressive behaviors can now be taken less seriously. He states, "These findings (with his punished subject) serve to limit the generality of extrapolations from past research which contraindicates the use of punishment" (p. 34).

At this point it should once again be made very clear that we are not suggesting that punishment is not an effective method of behavior control nor that it will *always* cause obvious aggression. We are instead following the results of a vast body of research which shows that the probability of aggression is higher under aversive conditions.

These facts should be considered when using punishment. Although humans do not always attack other humans when hurt, the classic story of the disgruntled employee kicking his desk instead of his boss may hold some truth. We may feel like striking the baby when we stick a pin in our finger in an attempt to fasten a diaper, but we have had experiences which lower the probability that aggression will actually break through. The little girl in the Risley study may have had just such experiences.

It is still not completely predictable as to exactly when pain will produce aggression and when it will not. Many variables can effect the pain-aggression phenomenon. The fact that pain has produced fighting in numerous species is at least one good reason for looking, whenever possible, to positive reinforcement as a control technique. At this point in the history of aggression research, it might be more dangerous to use the fact that one punished person did not fight as a reason for becoming less cautious about possible aggressive side effects from punishment than it would be to lean toward over-concern.

The third method for reducing the occurrence of behavior is to strengthen an incompatible response. From the effectiveness of this method in reducing other operant behavior, we would expect it to be effective in controlling aggression. In fact, Brown and Elliott (1965) had some success along these lines. They instructed nursery school teachers to ignore aggression and reinforce cooperation as much as possible. There was a reduction in aggression during the periods when this procedure was in effect, apparently as a direct result. One would hope that attempts to control aggression would include not only nonreinforcement of aggression but also meaures designed to establish effective, incompatible, nonaggressive behavior.

It is our contention that the aggression in the world today is a lawful, natural result of the conditions this world imposes upon man, who has various hereditarily-determined possibilities. There are reasons for race riots and there are reasons for man's tendency to resort to bombs and bullets. If we would have such behavior cease, we must alter the conditions of which it is a function. Although human aggression remains an extremely complex problem, it is felt that data from the experimental analysis of animal aggression do allow a greater understanding of the phenomenon and also provide the seeds for some of the first real breakthroughs contributing to effective control.

This does not mean that the answer to global warfare will emanate solely from the animal laboratory or from homes where mothers never use punishment or never reinforce aggressive behavior. In fact, it is difficult to see how we can ever expect to completely remove all reinforcement for competition. But again, there are times when reinforcement for cooperation would do nicely instead. Scientists should and will continue to collect data on this and other interesting questions and we can all hope that the information gathered will one day filter out to those who have assumed responsibility for social control.

At this point, the issue of application becomes most critical. Behavioral scientists know how to control behavior. Political leaders and the powers behind them also have much practical knowledge on this same topic but, in addition, often have the power to change conditions in ways that the scientist only talks about. If we, as scientists, desire to produce different behaviors in our society, then it is time to explore ways of gaining more effective control of relevant environmental variables.

None of us could tolerate working in a laboratory that prohibited altering the experimental conditions. Yet we talk about applying our findings within various social institutions, which represent little more than larger laboratories, but without the higher degree of control required to conduct large experiments. We might work long hours on a child's aggression and have it all wasted unless we can alter the conditions which produce and maintain it. The same thing is true in state mental hospitals, public schools, etc. The fruits of science are realized not only when behaviorial principles are discovered, but also when scientists, such as those whose works are contained in this book, gain effective control over larger portions of the environment and thus allow an effective application of these principles.

Our laboratories were once sufficient if they could hold several animal chambers, a housing unit and a few relay racks. Then the chambers grew in size to accommodate subjects as large as humans. Later they expanded again to accommodate more than one human and finally whole groups.

We suggest that scientists must continue doing research on aggression, not only in the chambers already in operation, but also with an eye toward exploring how to expand and experiment with populations chambered by entire hospitals, universities, school systems, industries, and possibly, someday, even cities and countries.

NOTE

1. More detailed reviews of this general research area can be found in Ulrich (1966, 1967a) and Azrin (1967).

REFERENCES

Azrin, N. H. Pain and aggression. *Psychology Today,* 1967, 1, 26-33.

Azrin, N. H., Hake, D. F., & Hutchinson, R. R. Elicitation of aggression by a physical blow. *Journal of the Experimental Analysis of Behavior,* 1965, 8, 55-57.

Azrin, N. H., Hutchinson, R. R., & Hake, D. F. Pain-induced fighting in the squirrel monkey. *Journal of the Experimental Analysis of Behavior,* 1963, 6, 620-621.

Azrin, N. H., Hutchinson, R. R., & Hake, D. F. Extinction-induced aggression. *Journal of the Experimental Analysis of Behavior,* 1966, 9, 191-204.

Azrin, N. H., Hutchinson, R. R., & Hake, D. F. Attack, avoidance and escape reactions to aversive shock. *Journal of the Experimental Analysis of Behavior*, 1967, 10, 131-148.

Azrin, N. H., Hutchinson, R. R., & McLaughlin, R. The opportunity for aggression as an operant reinforcer during aversive stimulation. *Journal of the Experimental Analysis of Behavior*, 1965, 8, 171-180.

Azrin, N. H., Hutchinson, R. R., & Sallery, R. D. Pain-aggression toward inanimate objects. *Journal of the Experimental Analysis of Behavior*, 1964, 7, 223-227.

Azrin, N. H., Ulrich, R. E., Hutchinson, R. R., & Norman, D. G. Effect of shock duration on shock-induced fighting. *Journal of the Experimental Analysis of Behavior*, 1964, 7, 9-11.

Boshka, S., Weisman, M., & Thor, D. H. A technique for inducing aggression in rats utilizing morphine withdrawal. *Psychological Record*, 1966, 16, 541-543.

Brown, P. & Elliot, R. Control of aggression in a nursery school class. *Journal of Experimental Child Psychology*, 1965, 2, 103-107.

Buss, A. H. *The psychology of aggression*. New York: John Wiley, 1961.

Calhoun, J. B. The development and role of social status among wild Norway rats. *Anatomical Record*, 1948, 101, 694.

Calhoun, J. B. The study of wild animals under controlled conditions. *Annals of the New York Academy of Sciences*, 1950, 51, 1113-1122.

Carpenter, C. R. A field study of the behavior and social relations of howling monkeys. *Comparative Psychology Monograph*, 1934, 48, 1-168.

Carpenter, C. R. A field study in Siam of the behavior and social relations of the gibbon (*Hylobates lar.*). *Comparative Psychology monograph*, 1940, 84, 1-212.

Carpenter, C. R. Sexual behavior of free-ranging rhesus monkeys (*Macaca mulata*). *Journal of Comparative Psychology*, 1942, 33, 113-162.

Cowan, P. A. & Walter, R. H. Studies of reinforcement of aggression: I. Effects of scheduling. *Child Development*, 1963, 34, 543-551.

Creer, T. L., Hitzing, E. W., & Schaeffer, R. W. Classical conditioning of reflexive fighting. *Psychonomic Science*, 1966, 4, 89-90.

Crew, F. A. E. & Mirsksia, L. The effects of density on an adult mouse population. *Biol. Generalis*, 1932, 7, 239-250.

Daniel, W. J. An experimental note on the O'Kelly-Steckle reaction. *Journal of Comparative Psychology*, 1943, 35, 267-268.

Delgado, J. Cerebral heterostimulation in a monkey colony. *Science*, 1963, 141, 161-163.

Dollard, J., Doob, L., Miller, N., Mowrer, O., & Sears, R. *Frustration and aggression*. New Haven: Yale University Press, 1939.

Eibl-Eibesfeldt, I. The fighting behavior of animals. *Scientific American*, 1961, 203, 112-122.

Flory, R. K., Ulrich, R. E., & Wolff, P. C. The effects of visual impairment on aggressive behavior. *Psychological Record*, 1965, 15, 185-190.

Guhl, A. M. Social behavior of the domestic fowl. *Kansas Agricultural Experimental Station*, 1953.

Hess, W. R. *Diencephalon. Automic and extrapyramidal functions.* New York: Grune and Stratton, 1954.

Hess, W. R. & Akert, K. Experimental data on the role of hypothalamus in mechanisms of emotional behavior. *Archives of Neurological Psychiatry,* 1955, 73, 127-129.

Hops, H. & Walters, R. H. Studies of reinforcement of aggression: II. Effects of emotionally-arousing antecedent conditions. *Child Development,* 1963, 34, 553-562.

Hutchinson, R. R., Azrin, N. H., & Hake, D. F. An automatic method for the study of aggression in squirrel monkeys. *Journal of the Experimental Analysis of Behavior,* 1966, 9, 233-237.

Hutchinson, R. R. & Renfrew, J. Stalking attack and eating behaviors elicited from the same sites in the hypothalamus, *Journal of Comparative and Physiological Psychology,* 1966, 61, 360-367.

Hutchinson, R. R., Ulrich, R. E., & Azrin, N. H. Effects of age and related factors on the pain-aggression reaction. *Journal of Comparative and Physiological Psychology,* 1965, 59, 365-369.

Lorenz, K. *On aggression,* New York: Harcourt, Brace & World, Inc., 1966.

Masserman, J. H. A biodynamic psychoanalytic approach to the problems of feeling and emotion. In M. L. Reymert (Ed.), *Feeling and emotions.* New York: McGraw Hill, 1950.

Masserman, J. H. *Behavior and neurosis.* New York: Hafner Publishing, 1964.

Mead, M. *Sex and temperament in three primitive societies.* New York: Morrow, 1935.

Miller, N. E. Theory and experiment relating psychoanalytic displacement to stimulus-response generalization. *Journal of Abnormal and Social Psychology,* 1948, 43, 155-178.

O'Kelly, L. E., & Steckle, L. C. A note on long-enduring emotional responses in the rat. *Journal of Psychology,* 1939, 8, 125-131.

Pavlov, I. P. *Conditioned reflexes.* New York: Oxford University Press, 1927.

Ranson, S. W. The hypothalamus: its significance for visceral innervation and emotional expression. *Transactions College of Physicians of Philadelphia,* 1934, 222-224.

Reynolds, G. S., Catania, A. C., & Skinner, B. F. Conditioned and unconditioned aggression in pigeons. *Journal of the Experimental Analysis of Behavior,* 1963, 1, 73-74.

Risley, T. R. The effects and side effects of punishing the autistic behavior of a deviant child. *Journal of Applied Behavior Analysis,* 1968, 1, 21-34.

Sears, R. R., Hovland, C. I., & Miller, N. E. Minor studies of aggression: I. Measurement of aggressive behavior. *Journal of Psychology.* 1940, 9, 275-294.

Skinner, B. F. *The behavior of organisms.* New York: Appleton-Century-Crofts, 1938.

Stachnik, T. J., Ulrich, R. E., & Mabry, J. H. Reinforcement of aggression through intracranial stimulation. *Psychonomic Science,* 1966, 5, 101-102. (a)

Stachnik, T. J., Ulrich, R. E., & Mabry, J. H. Reinforcement of intra- and inter-species aggression with intracranial stimulation. *American Zoologist,* 1966, 6, 663-668. (b)

Ulrich, R. E. Pain-aggression. In G. E. Kimble (Ed.), *Foundations of conditioning and learning.* New York: Appleton-Century-Crofts, 1967. (a)

Ulrich, R. E. Interaction between reflexive fighting and cooperative escape. *Journal of the Experimental Analysis of Behavior,* 1967, 10, 311-317. (b)

Ulrich, R. E. Pain as a cause of aggression. *American Zoologist,* 1966, 6, 643-662.

Ulrich, R. E. & Azrin, N. H. Reflexive fighting in response to aversive stimulation. *Journal of the Experimental Analysis of Behavior,* 1962, 5, 511-520.

Ulrich, R. E. & Craine, W. H. Behavior: Persistence of shock-induced aggression. *Science,* 1964, 143, 970-973.

Ulrich, R. E., Hutchinson, R. R., & Azrin, N. H. Pain-elicited aggression. *Psychological Record,* 1965, 15, 111-126.

Ulrich, R. E., Johnston, M., Richardson, J., & Wolff, P. C. The operant conditioning of fighting behavior in rats. *Psychological Record,* 1963, 13, 465-470.

Ulrich, R. E., Stachnik, T. J., Brierton, G. R., & Mabry, J. H. Fighting and avoidance in response to aversive stimulation. *Behaviour,* 1966, 26, 124-129.

Ulrich, R. E., Wolff, P. C., & Azrin, N. H. Shock as an elicitor of intra- and inter-species fighting behaviour. *Animal Behaviour,* 1964, 12, 14-15.

Vernon, W. & Ulrich, R. E. Classical conditioning of pain-elicited aggression. *Science,* 1966, 152, 668-669.

von Holst, E. & von Saint Paul, U. On the functional organization of drives. *Animal Behavior,* 1963, 11, 1-20.

Walters, R. H. & Brown, M. Studies of reinforcement of aggression: III. Transfer of responses to an interpersonal situation. *Child Development,* 1963, 34, 563-571.

Wasman, M. & Flynn, J. Directed attack elicited from hypothalamus. *Archives of Neurology,* 1962, 6, 220-227.

7 : Reciprocity and Coercion: Two Facets of Social Systems

GERALD R. PATTERSON
JOHN B. REID

The present report outlines a conceptual framework, based on social reinforcement theory, for the analysis of some aspects of dyadic interactions. Within this framework, two mechanisms are posited as important characteristics of social interchange; these are "reciprocity" and "coercion." The major function of this paper is to demonstrate the heuristic value of utilizing these two constructs, not only for the investigation of dyadic interaction, but for the description and observation of more complex social systems as well.

"Reciprocity" describes dyadic interaction in which the persons A and B reinforce each other, at an equitable rate. In this interaction, positive reinforcers maintain the behavior of both persons. "Coercion," on the other hand, refers to interaction in which aversive stimuli control the behavior of one person and positive reinforcers maintain the behavior of the other. Both "reciprocity" and "coercion" are held to be stable patterns of dyadic interaction which characterize much of the interaction in families.

The present paper defines some of the conditions which produce variations in reciprocity and coercion. An attempt is also made to outline the relation between variations in these processes and associated changes in rate of deviant child behaviors. In addition, this report might

The project was supported by PHS 08009. The senior author also wishes to acknowledge the cumulative effect of the persistent "gadfly behaviours" of R. Littman. More recently, a similar function has been served for both authors, by R. Weiss, R. Ziller, F. Kanfer, and W. Sheppard. The writers particularly want to thank R. Weiss, W. Sheppard, D. Peabody, and C. Dicken, for their critical responses to the manuscript. Their effort to save us from ourselves not only resulted in alterations in our previous effort, but led to the development of some additional hypotheses as well.

be viewed as a position paper which asserts that the social environment must be the primary focus of the behavior modifier who is interested in the development of intervention programs for the noninstitutionalized child. It is necessary to develop not only a conceptual framework for investigating the parameters which govern the dispensing of reinforcers in target social environments, but it is also crucial to develop a technology which will effectively alter the behavior of the dispenser himself. This report outlines a preliminary effort to develop both a conceptual framework and a set of correlated engineering procedures.

The attempt to conceptualize, investigate, and manipulate the family in which the deviant child lives has constituted the core of the traditional approaches to family intervention (Ackerman, 1958; Bell, 1961). A similar stance is also reflected in the more recent efforts of the behavior modifiers. Some of these investigators have trained the parents to alter the behavior of their own child. Parental retraining has been the focus of attention in several investigations which have produced significant changes in the behavior of schizophrenic and autistic children (Ray, 1965; Wahler, Winkel, Peterson, & Morrison, 1965; Wolf, Mees, & Risley, 1964), retarded children (Lindsley, 1966), delinquent adolescents (Thorne, Tharp, & Wetzel, in press) and for the types of children commonly referred to outpatient child guidance clinics (Hawkins, Peterson, Schweid, & Bijou, 1966; O'Leary, O'Leary, & Becker, 1967; Patterson & Brodsky, 1966; Patterson, Hawkins, McNeal, & Phelps, 1967; Shah, 1967; Straughan, 1964).

Probably the most extensive efforts to re-program the reinforcing behavior of social agents in the child's milieu have focused upon the classroom teacher. The earlier efforts of Zimmerman and Zimmerman (1962) were followed by others (Allen, Hart, Buell, Harris, & Wolf, 1964; Harris, Johnson, Kelly, & Wolf, 1964; Hart, Allen, Buell, Harris, & Wolf, 1964) in demonstrating that teacher-dispensed reinforcers could be dramatically successful in altering the behavior in the classroom setting. More recently, an impressive technology has been developed in which the teacher "controls" the deviant behavior of whole classrooms of children by dispensing tokens (Becker, Madsen, Arnold, & Thomas, 1967; Birnbauer, Bijou, Wolf, & Kidder, 1965; Haring & Hayden, 1966; Hotchkiss, 1966; Krumboltz & Goodwin, 1966; Quay, Sprague, Werry, & McQueen, 1967). The studies applying the operant paradigm to retraining parents and teachers constitute an exciting beginning in the development of sophisticated social engineering. The procedures outlined in these studies are described in language which maximizes the possibility of replication; the observation data, which constitute the criteria for evaluating the outcome of intervention, provide clear support for their efficiency.

It is hoped that the application of the operant paradigm to the problem of dyadic interaction will provide the basis for the development of a social engineering technology capable of handling even more complex problems with the same degree of efficiency.[1] In the discussion which follows, the coercion and reciprocity constructs will be more precisely defined, and observation data, collected in family settings, will be presented which provide tests for some of the relevant hypotheses. In the last section, some engineering procedures for family intervention will be outlined, together with observation data demonstrating the effect of these interventions.

The Coercion Construct

It is assumed that members of the family or the peer group can, and frequently do, reinforce deviant behaviors. Direct support for this assumption has been provided by observation data which showed that both teachers and peers provided social reinforcers for hyperactive behaviors occurring in the classroom (Anderson, 1964; Ebner, 1967; Grindee, 1964; Hall, Lund, & Jackson, 1968; Hotchkiss, 1966). The peers and teacher are very likely to attend to the behavior of the disruptive child when he walks around the classroom or when he makes noise. Their attention serves as a powerful reinforcer for these behaviors. Observations have also shown that the peer group reinforces delinquent behaviors in institutional settings (Buehler, Patterson, & Furness, 1966), and that mothers reinforce hyperactive and negativistic behaviors in the home (Hawkins et al., 1966; O'Leary et al., 1967). The recent monograph by Patterson, Littman, and Bricker (1967) showed that members of the peer group provide the reinforcing contingencies necessary for both maintenance and acquisition of one class of deviant child behaviors. The reinforcers for aggressive behaviors included such consequences as crying, withdrawing from the disputed territory, or giving up the prized object.

These statements would imply that, for example, a mother strengthens the very temper tantrum behaviors in her child which she claims make her "miserable." It is perhaps disconcerting to think of the victim of an aggressive act as providing a positive reinforcer for the very response which produces pain for him. However, the observation data just cited suggest that these contingencies are in fact provided by the "victim" of many forms of deviant child behavior. The coercion hypotheses attempt to explain why it is that a person who is the target of some forms of deviant behavior finds himself in the position of reinforcing these behaviors. The hypotheses also describe the contingencies which maintain the reinforcing behavior of the target.

To illustrate the coercion hypotheses, let us assume that person A interacts with B and A emits a mand. Typically, the reinforcer for a mand, or command, is compliance (Skinner, 1957). The behavior of the

person who complies is maintained by positive reinforcers supplied by
the person who emitted the mand. However, in a coercive interaction the
contingencies provided for the maintenance of the manding behaviors
are radically altered. For example, A shouts to his mother in the supermarket, "I want an ice cream cone." In coercive interaction, noncompliance is punished; if, for example, the mother does not comply, this will
produce an increase in the rate or amplitude of the manding behavior.
In the example the child is likely not only to continue his demands for a
cone, but in addition, he is likely to *raise the volume*. After a series of
such interactions the initial mand can serve as a discriminative stimulus,
setting the occasion for avoidance (compliant) behaviors. Once the
child has trained the mother, it is necessary only to present the first mand
in the chain in order to produce compliant behavior. Periodic presentation of the aversive stimuli will serve to maintain the compliant behaviors at high strength.

In this form of coercive interaction, noncompliance is punished. By
the same token, *compliance is reinforced*. The second hypothesis refers
to the effect of terminating the mand behaviors. Presumably the termination of these behaviors corresponds to the withdrawal of an aversive
stimulus. The event which produces the withdrawal of the aversive stimulus is the compliant response of the target. When the mother buys the
ice cream cone, the deviant mand terminates. The reinforcer for the
child was the ice cream cone. The reinforcing contingency for the
mother was the termination of the "scene" in the supermarket. Taken
together, the two hypotheses account for the reinforcing contingencies
which maintain the behavior both of the Person-who-mands and the
behavior of the Person-who-complies. These two sets of contingencies
constitute the main outlines of the Coercion Construct.

There is a quality associated with mand behaviors in general which
is of some interest. When contrasted to non-mand behaviors it seems
that the effect of a mand is to make the world respond more predictably.
For one thing, a mand seems more likely to produce an *immediate* and
specified consequence. In contrast, most non-mand social behaviors may
or may not produce an immediate positive consequence, nor is it always
possible to predict the particular class of consequences. The mand, in
forcing a particular consequence, greatly constrains the variety of behaviors which can be presented by the other member of an interaction.
It was this constrained quality of the mand-compliance interaction that
led the writers to choose the label "Coercion" for the construct. The
greater degree of control effected is undoubtedly a function of the
aversive contingencies provided. For most mands, the aversive consequences resulting from noncompliance are ordinarily rather mild or non-
existent. It also seems true that most societies are carefully programmed
for the provision of positive social consequences for compliance with

normal mands. For example, the rules for saying "Thank you" are well specified. Compliance with a deviant mand is probably less likely to be provided with a positive reinforcer. The consequence of noncompliance for coercive mands are more painful. It is this latter quality which provides the deviant mander with greater control over the behavior of the individual with whom he interacts.

It seems likely that coercion would be more characteristic of the individual who has not yet developed the skilled social repertoires which serve to produce predictable consequences from the social environment. In that context, younger children should be more likely to use coercive mands than would older children. Although no data are available which provide a direct test, an observation study reported by Charlesworth and Hartup (1967) is relevant. Their data showed that 34 percent of the consequences supplied in the interactions among 4-year-old children were characterized as submissive. Observation data from a report by Patterson, *et al.* (1967) showed that assertive mand behaviors were reinforced an average of 80 percent of the time by preschool children. These studies clearly demonstrate that young children use coercive mands and are reinforced for doing so.

The research literature also provides some support for the hypothesis that noncompliance produces increases in the rate of occurrence of coercive mands. In a classroom situation (Hammerlynck, Donely, & Heller, 1967), the teacher and the peer groups were trained to ignore the hyperactive behaviors of a 13-year-old boy. Baseline observation of inappropriate verbal behaviors alone showed an average output of 1.2 deviant responses per minute. During the "extinction" period, the responses showed a 30 percent increase in rate maintained over a period of 2 weeks! Similar findings were reported by Becker et al. (1967) when a teacher was trained to ignore a child's deviant behaviors. There is no reason, theoretically speaking, why a deviant mand cannot be extinguished. The practical difficulty lies more in the fact that the mands are probably acquired under conditions of variable ratio reinforcement such that these behaviors are highly resistant to extinction. Also, and more to the point, it is extremely difficult to train someone to tolerate the aversive chains of behavior that would be run off under prolonged extinction conditions. It is probable that only well trained, nondirective play therapists and other kinds of Christian martyrs possess the requisite skills for this type of endeavor. Parenthetically, it should be noted that these increases in mands would be shortlived if the extinction programs were accompanied by parallel programs in which the child were being positively reinforced for behaviors which compete with the occurrence of the coercive mands (Becker et al., 1967; Quay et al., 1967).

It is of some interest to relate the coercion hypotheses to the problem of defining "deviant" child behavior. Within the present framework, that one kind of child who is likely to be labelled as deviant is one who *frequently* uses coercive mands. An extreme example might be the self-destructive behaviors displayed by some hospitalized children. The data provided by Lovaas, Freitag, Gold, & Kassorla (1965) showed such behaviors as head banging literally *force* the well socialized nurse to respond with sympathy and concern. The *deviant* person is one who coerces too often and in too many situations. It is interesting in this regard that the research carried out by Jennings (1950) showed that "attention-getting" behavior was ascribed 13 times as often to the less popular child as compared to the popular child. Most "deviant children" are a melange of coercive mands; they are referred for at least four or five different problem behaviors (Macfarlane, Allen, & Honzik, 1962). This suggests that there is probably a saturation point, which varies somewhat from family to family, beyond which the members of the social system refuse to be coerced further. When that point is reached, the child is labelled as "deviant" and is either institutionalized or referred for professional help. One might say, then, that many kinds of "pathology" represent forms of coercion which are no longer tolerated.[2]

It seems to the writers that the coercive mechanism is likely to characterize the interactions of children who fall into the very broad category of "Conduct Disorders." The behaviors which are so labelled generally represent very active modes of intercourse with the social environment. Factor analyses of a wide range of data are consistent in identifying a conduct disorder dimension. These data range from referral problems (Jenkins & Glickman, 1944), parents' and teachers' ratings of their children's behavior (Becker, 1960; Peterson, 1961; Quay, 1964; Quay & Quay, 1965), to actual observation of the child's behavior (Patterson, 1964). Presumably the behaviors described in these factor studies function as coercive mands and are maintained by similar sets of consequences.

It is quite clear that the general outlines of a coercion hypothesis have long been a part of the clinical literature, particularly in some of the socially-oriented theories of personality. Probably Alfred Adler in his book, *Social interest: A challenge to mankind* (published in 1927) provided the best known examples. In that publication he presented an excellent description of the coercive child

> . . . whenever the mother abounds all too evidently with excessive affection and behavior, thought, and action, and even speech, superfluous for the child, then he will be more readily inclined to develop as a parasite (exploiter) and look to the other persons for everything he wants. He will continually press forward to be the creator of every scene and seek to have everyone at his beck and call. He will display egoistic tendencies and regard it as his right to suppress other people . . . *to take and not to give* . . . (p. 149-150).

Much of what Adler would label as attention seeking behaviors would be akin to coercive mands.

Contemporary personality theorists such as Leary (1957) and Szasz (1961) also postulate a dominance-submission relationship which is similar in some respects to the coercion hypothesis. In his discussions, Leary referred to the fact that dominance *elicits* submission. This relationship is formally similar to the functional analysis of mands and compliance outlined in the coercion hypotheses.

The implications of the coercion hypotheses will be discussed in the context which includes the reciprocity hypothesis. The next section outlines the reciprocity hypothesis.

The Reciprocity Hypothesis

"janeloves   all who loveher   at all, including rickey Hall . . ."

Typewriter doodling by
Jane Patterson (7 years of age, 2/67)

The idea that social interaction is in part governed by some reciprocal exchange of "goods" has been implicit in most discussions about social institutions and societies. Indeed the realization that men could better manipulate their physical environment by "cooperating" and "exchanging" probably provides a basis for the formation of every social unit. Although a part of the conventional wisdom for some time, the idea of reciprocity has been systematized into a formal construct only recently by social psychologists such as Homans (1961) and Thibaut and Kelley (1959). The view of reciprocity held by these theorists could be described as a "social economics." Two members of a dyadic interaction exchange "goods" which provide mutual support for the activities of each of the members involved. The goods exchanged are broadly defined and refer to a variety of reinforcers ranging from social approval, money and interest, to "services" and "favors." The reinforcing effectiveness, or value, of these reinforcing events vary as a function of a number of parameters including the availability of the reinforcer and a "cost" variable. Cost, for example, varies as a function of the effort required to elicit the reinforcer and the number of alternatives given up in accepting this reward. The present report differs from these earlier formulations in that it represents a more limited set of variables (positive and aversive consequences); and the definitions are cast primarily within the framework of operant conditioning.

As used here, the term reciprocity also refers to that "balance of trade" which exists in most social interactions. Specifically, the term refers to an equity in the giving and receiving of positive and aversive consequences which occur in most social interactions. The first hypothesis refers to the assumption that reciprocity in fact exists, in most dyadic interactions. This would require that, over a series of interactions, two persons reinforce or punish each other for approximately the same proportion of behaviors. For example, if person A reinforces B for 50 percent of the interactions which B has with A, then A, in turn, will *receive* about the same proportion of positive reinforcers from B. The actual proportion which person A gives varies depending upon which member of the family is involved. The proportions of giving and receiving should vary systematically for all combinations of dyads. The person who gives (proportionately) the least to A, should receive proportionately the least from A; and the person who gives A the most should receive the most. Data will be provided which test this hypothesis.

In view of the earlier discussion of the Coercion Construct, it would seem reasonable to assume that most children characterized as "conduct disorders" would tend to be nonreciprocal in their interactions within the family. Specifically, it is hypothesized that the rate of output of the deviant child behaviors will covary with the children's deviations from reciprocity. Observation data collected within families will be provided as a test of this hypothesis.

Existing surveys of the empirical literature demonstrate that social reinforcers, of various kinds, can be used to maintain an impressive variety of human behaviors ranging from eating to defecating, from button pressing to using plural nouns, and from cooperating to hitting. Many of these studies were recently reviewed in the volumes edited by Honig (1966) and Verhave (1966). In these studies, social reinforcers were dispensed unilaterally by one person to maintain the behavior of a second person. However, such studies provide only a limited basis from which to analyze the most complex problems involved in two-person *interactions* in which *both* persons reinforce each other.

Aside from earlier pioneering efforts by Sidowski (1957), and Azrin and Lindsley (1956), the most extensive investigation of two-person interaction within a social learning paradigm has been that reported by Lindsley (1963) and Cohen and Lindsley (1964). In Lindsley's procedure, two persons, responding in adjoining rooms, pressed levers to obtain pennies as reinforcers. If A responded within 0.5 seconds of B's response, one or both of the subjects might be reinforced depending upon what kind of social interaction was being studied (cooperation, competition, or leadership). The discrimination learning was significantly accelerated when the subjects were told that the occurrence of one signal connotated the response of a person in the adjoining room and that the occurrence of a second signal indicated that the other person was being reinforced.

However, to understand social interaction, it will be necessary to understand not only that A reinforces B, and B reinforces A, and that these contingencies maintain interaction, but in addition we must know the *conditions* under *which* these two individuals *will provide* the necessary reinforcement. *When* do people reinforce or punish each other? Who reinforces or punishes A? Under what conditions will he reinforce, not reinforce, or punish B? Why does he stop providing these consequences? When does B begin to provide consequences for A? As Weiss (1965) so succinctly put it, we must understand the "grammar of social interaction." In the section which follows, these general questions will be considered within the context of positive social reinforcers.

Speculations about the variables which determine these positive reinforcement contingencies suggest a sequence of problems to be discussed, first of which is the specification of the conditions under which persons A and B will *begin* to reinforce each other. To discuss this question, it is necessary to first assume that both A and B have well established repertoires of *social behaviors.* The repertoire of social behaviors is thought of as being rank ordered from the most to the least frequently occurring behaviors. Presumably, these frequencies could be established by the simple expedient of observing the individual over a period of days as he responds and interacts in his own social environment. As used in the present discussion, the term "hierarchy" will refer to the rank ordered list of social behaviors characterizing an individual. The ranks which characterize the various response classes are established partially as a function of a history of repeated reinforcement for these behaviors. It is further assumed that events or behaviors which have in the past been contiguous with reinforcement, will, when they occur in the future, be more likely to elicit *attending behaviors* (Walters & Parke, 1964). For example, if the child is a habitue of the baseball diamond, it is likely that he has received a good deal of reinforcement for these behaviors. Even when not playing, seeing other children engaged in the game would elicit his close attention. Similarly, a man is very likely to attend to a discussion about matters which pertain to his work or his hobbies.

To some extent, of course, the fact that two persons were trained in the same culture would lead to the prediction that there would be *some* overlap in their repertoires of social behaviors. For short periods of time almost any combination of two persons is likely to provide mutual reinforcement for each other's behavior. This may relate to the fact, repeatedly pointed out by social psychologists, that "proximity" is one of the primary determinants for friendship selections (Hare, 1962; Lott & Lott, 1965). However, extended interactions, or friendship pairings, are most likely to occur as a function of overlapping hierarchies for behaviors which are major sources of reinforcement for both persons involved. This would suggest, of course, that friendship pairings are partially made on the basis of similarities of interests, work, and hobbies. Interacting with another person with similar interests would not only increase the probability that you will attend to his behavior and thereby reinforce him, but it also increases the probability that he will reinforce you.[3] This general hypothesis has also been suggested by Byrne, Griffet and Stefaveak (1967) who also provide some data for its support.

The *overlapping of repertoires* of social behaviors may explain part of the process involved in initiating reinforcing contingencies in social interactions.[4] Using only the variables outlined thus far, A emits behaviors similar to those which exist in the repertoire of B which would presumably elicit the attention of B. However, as the explanation stands, B would attend to (reinforce) the behavior of A in perpetuity until A either dropped from exhaustion or until B could no longer hold his head up to attend. Social interaction consists ordinarily of an exchange in which A reinforces while B listens, alternating with B reinforcing while A listens. To generate a paradigm for this latter pattern of behaviors, it is necessary to introduce an additional variable; the variable is satiation.

Repeated presentation of a stimulus reduces the likelihood that the organism will orient or attend to that stimulus. Under conditions of repeated presentation of social reinforcers (Gewirtz & Baer, 1958; Jessor, 1951) the stimuli also become less effective in controlling behavior. It is assumed that habituation and satiation effects are regular concomitants of social interaction. As A continues to respond and present behaviors which sample B's repertoire, B eventually habituates; he begins to shift restlessly in his chair, or stare about the room. As he removes his attention, the behavior of A "weakens" and if B's extinction procedure continues, A eventually terminates his discourse. To some extent, one aspect of social skill involves the ability to discriminate and respond appropriately to these precursors of "extinction."

When A stops, it is B's turn to talk. If B now presents behaviors which are high on A's hierarchy of social behaviors, then A will "automatically" attend to what he is saying. B will continue to be reinforced by A's attending until A, in turn, habituates, stops attending, and eventually extinguishes B. This formulation would apply only to the presentation of a rather limited class of social consequences. While "attending behaviors" are probably the most frequently occurring class of positive social reinforcers, it may well be that other classes of reinforcers are of equal importance. For example, consequences such as "smile," "touch or caress," "praise and approval" might occupy a unique status in the determination of some classes of social behavior. Be that as it may, it seems true that the formulation just given would not describe the reciprocal give and take of these behaviors and that some effort should be made to rectify this omission.

This kind of give and take creates a situation in which both alternation and reciprocity of reinforcers become a "natural" characteristic of

social interaction. Although some social interactions would be characterized by coercive behaviors and their concomitant negative reinforcement schedules, most social interactions should be characterized by a
set of contingencies which result in each individual "giving" and "receiving" about the same relative ratio of positive social reinforcers. For
example, within a family the member who most often reinforcers the
behaviors of other persons would himself most often receive positive
social reinforcers from others. The data in the results section to follow
will provide a test of these, and related hypotheses.

The notion that similarities in behaviors determine duration of social
interaction and friendships has a long history of consistent support by
research in social psychology (Newcomb, 1961; Precker, 1952). There
are an impressive series of observation studies (Charlesworth & Hartup,
1967; Hartup, Glazer, & Charlesworth, 1967) which provide a direct
test for some of the hypotheses outlined here.[5] It would also be expected
that the differences in social repertoires of boys and girls would be
reflected in the amount of cross-sex reinforcement which would characterize the interactions. The data showed that boys reinforced boys more
often than they did girls, and conversely girls gave more positive reinforcements to girls than they did to boys (Charlesworth & Hartup, 1967).
The observation of preschool interaction by Fagot (1967) also supported these findings. Her data also showed that the female teachers
in one nursery school positively reinforced the play behaviors of preschool children 80 percent when they were engaged in female activities
and 20 percent when engaged in male activities. The comparable data
from a second school was 98 percent and 2 percent, respectively. These
preliminary studies offer tentative but consistent support for the
hypothesis that the degree of similarity between repertoires of social
behaviors covaries with the frequency of occurrence of reinforcers forthcoming in an interchange between person A and person B.

In speculating about the outcome of an extended series of reciprocal
interchanges between A and B, it seems likely that both persons would
"shape" each other to be *increasingly similar*. The behaviors of A which
are most likely to elicit reinforcement from B are those behaviors which
are already present in the repertoire of B. Extended interactions should
produce a situation in which the two persons become increasingly
similar. For example, one might expect that the selection of a spouse
would be partially based upon similarities in interests, attitudes, and
values. The empirical literature provides support for the hypothesis
(Fisher & Fisher, 1967; Tharp, 1963). However, confirmation of the
present hypothesis would also require that the couples become increasingly similar as time progresses. As pointed out in the review by Tharp
(1963), the data attesting to the possibility of the two spouses "shaping"
each other may be confounded by the possibility that the more dis-

similar spouses are least likely to remain married. A more adequate test
of the hypothesis is provided by the data from the research report by
Newcomb (1961). In that study, students who had no previous contacts
with each other were provided with dormitory facilities. As the study
lasted over a period of months, it was possible to examine the "friendship" pairing, while at the same time evaluating changes in attitudes and
values. The data provided a clear demonstration that over time, members
of a friendship pair were most likely to show converging changes in
measures of attitude and values.

Recently a series of experimental studies carried out by Rosenfeld
(1966, 1967) provide powerful support for some of the general features
of the exchange theory. His data showed that, for example, when the
experimenter increased the frequency of his verbal and nonverbal social
reinforcers, the subjects being interviewed displayed reciprocal increases
in the frequencies of these behavior. Kendon (1965) also demonstrated
that members of a dyad maintain an equity in the length of time they
spend looking at each other. In a study by Rosenfeld (1966) subjects
in one group were instructed to behave in such a way as to seek approval
and in another to avoid approval from the other member of the dyad.
These instructions produced massive alterations in the behaviors of both
members of the dyad with regards to the frequencies of gestures, smiles,
and the overall interaction rates. One interesting sidelight to this study
also provides some confirmation of the assumed relation between an
individual's reinforcing capacities and his perceived attractiveness by
those with whom he interacts. In the Rosenfeld study the correlation between the subjects' ratings on attractiveness and their rate of positive
head nods was .70.

In the section which follows, procedures and data are presented
which provide a partial test for some of the hypotheses resulting from
these speculations about reciprocity. The data and procedures represent
only a preliminary effort to establish the meaning of the two constructs,
reciprocity and coercion. While laboratory studies are currently under
way, the bulk of the available data were drawn from observations made
in the homes of families who had produced deviant children.

Procedures and Data Relevant to the Reciprocity
and Coercion Hypotheses

Procedures. The observation data used to test the hypotheses were
obtained in the home. The families had applied to the University of
Oregon Psychology Clinic for professional assistance. Upon request, they
gave permission to members of the research team to come into their
homes and collect data during a 2 to 3 week baseline observation period.[6]
The observations were made in the home at approximately the same

hours each day, generally between 4 and 7 P.M., when all members of the family were present. During the observation period the members of the family were required to interact in the kitchen and an adjoining room. The data were collected 4 days a week, approximately 1 hour each day by one or two observers.

Each observer was equipped with a clip board on which an interval timing device was mounted. Both a visual (light) and an auditory stimulus (earphone) were dispensed to the observer at 30-second intervals. On those occasions when the reliability data were being collected by two or more observers, the timing devices could be synchronized.

Each of the observers in the home was provided with a list of randomly ordered members of the family. In the earlier studies each member was observed for a 5-minute interval on each cycle. Following an analysis of the amount of data necessary to establish reliable estimates for behavioral events, it was deemed necessary to increase the daily sampling of behavior to a minimum of 10 minutes of data for each member of the family.

When observing any member of the family, both his behavior and the consequences elicited from other family members were coded. To facilitate the coding of such events, a list of 21 behaviors were operationally defined, providing a rough classification of most of the social behaviors which had occurred in families previously observed. These response classes included such behaviors as: yell, talk, physically aggressive, self-stimulation, silly, play, social activity, dependence, and command. The list of 12 coded consequences included such behaviors as attend, ignore, approval, physical contact (positive and aversive), noncompliance, disapproval. The 12-page manual describing this coding system will be provided upon request.

The data-collecting procedures provided for a recording of the rate of occurrence of various behaviors and consequences. They also described the *continuous sequence* of these behaviors, the reactions elicited from other members, initiations to the individual and the consequences which he provided for their behavior. The continuous sequence of interaction was coded on lined paper. Every 30 seconds the observer was signalled and moved down to the next line. Pacing the observers in this fashion made it possible to measure the rate of occurrence of the variables.

After reading the coding manual, each new observer accompanied one of the staff while he observed several families to familiarize himself with the code system. After 2 or 3 hours, his agreement with one of the experienced staff members was assessed.[7] The percent agreement was tabulated on an event-by-event basis. These percentages ranged from 51.6 to 96.7 across five families and various combinations of five observers (Reid, 1967). The median percentage agreement was 84.5 which was very high indeed, considering the complexity of the data being coded.

The next problem concerns the adequacy of the sampling of the interaction events. The general form of the question would be, "How *much* data must be sampled in the family setting in order to establish reliable estimates of variables, such as the average output of deviant behavior, the average number of positive and negative reinforcers, interactions, and initiations?" The 24 members of the five families were observed during baseline periods of 2 weeks. Due to illness or absence from the home, the actual amount of time each person was observed ranged from 60 to 75 minutes. The odd and even numbered 5-minute blocks of time were used to calculate a stability coefficient for each of these variables. The Spearman Brown (odd-even reliability) estimates for the full scale coefficients were: number of initiations .73; number of interactions .65; number of positive social reinforcers .70; number of negative social consequences .70; and the rate of occurrence of deviant behavior .78.

In the more current studies, each member is being observed for 10 minutes in each session rather than for the 5-minute samples used in these first families. The effect of this increase should be to provide more stable estimates of the variables.

There is one additional methodological problem associated with the use of observational procedures. It seems reasonable to suppose that the presence of observers within the home would significantly affect the interaction among members of the family. To test this, a pilot study was initiated in which a mother was trained to use the data-collecting procedure described earlier.[8] She observed her husband and three daughters in their home; they were unaware of the fact that they were being observed. Each member of the family was observed by the mother for 15 minutes on 5 consecutive days. Then a member of our research staff observed the father and the three daughters for 5 consecutive days. The data showed that the interactions among family members occurring under conditions of "observer present" produced an increase in the frequency of positive social reinforcers and a decrease in negative reinforcers. In the second pilot study, four families were involved, three serving as experimental families. Except for the mother remaining in the room where the outside observer was present, the design was similar to the first pilot study. A fourth family served as a control in that the mother collected the data for all ten sessions. The data showed a complex interaction between baseline levels for rate of interaction and the effects produced by the presence of the observer. Individuals who displayed high base rates of interaction when the mother was observing significantly decreased their interaction rate when the outside observer was present. Low base rate interactors increased their rates when the outside observer was present. The Mann Whitney U test showed this interaction to be significant at P less than .008.

The results obtained in a study using fifteen families replicated the results obtained in the second pilot study (Patterson & Harris, 1968). The data from the latter study also showed a nonsignificant increase in rate of deviant behavior during the ten sessions.

R. B. Bechtel (1967) also noted that the presence of an observer influenced the behavior of adults even in such a comparatively neutral setting as a museum.

The Results. The data presented in this section should perhaps be thought of as more illustrative than confirmatory. In view of the fact that the investigation from which the data were obtained had only been under way for 5 months, the data serve mainly the function of illustrating the procedures which will eventually provide more appropriate tests of the hypotheses outlined earlier.

The à priori classification of consequences into categories of positive, negative, and neutral was based upon relevant laboratory findings which identified the effects of similar contingencies upon behavior. However, it will be necessary to determine empirically for each family what behavioral events in fact produce the effects one would expect of positive, negative or neutral consequences. By way of illustration, these effects were tested for three of the children in one family. On each occasion that a child was talking, both the consequence and the response occurring in the next episode were tabulated. The prediction was that if the response "talking" was positively reinforced, it should increase the likelihood that the same response would occur in the next episode. Several hundred such events were tabulated for each individual child. For child A, the probability that the response talking would persist into the next episode was .42 if the previous consequence had been either aversive or non-reinforcing. For the same child the probability was .64 that the response would persist following positive reinforcement. The comparative probabilities for the remaining children were as follows: .53 nonreinforcing and .69 positive reinforcement; .33 nonreinforcement and .53 positive reinforcement. The measure of response strength did reflect the slight increase, which is what would be predicted. In passing, it is interesting to note that the magnitude of the reinforcement effect varied from one child to another.[9] Eventually such an analysis will be carried out for each member of the families being investigated as a check upon the à priori classification of consequences into positive, aversive, and neutral categories.

It was hypothesized earlier that there would be an equity holding for the giving and receiving of positive social reinforcers within families. If interaction is maintained on a continuing basis, an analysis of the interaction should demonstrate that reciprocity holds among all of the dyads within the family. Presumably, one would expect to obtain such findings for both normal and deviant families.

Reid (1967) used a correlational analysis to test the hypothesis that within families, the individual should give the largest proportion of social reinforcers to the member of the family from whom he receives the largest proportion of social reinforcers and give the least to the member from whom he receives the least. If the reciprocity hypothesis is correct, one would predict that a positive correlation would be obtained for the "giving" and "getting" of social reinforcers for each member of the family. The magnitude of the "reciprocity correlations" computed for each of the 24 members from the five families varied a great deal from individual to individual; but as shown in Reid's analysis, the data supported the hypothesis.

While such an analysis is of interest, it tends to obfuscate some features of the data which are highly relevant to the reciprocity hypothesis. These additional components may be obtained from an analysis of the interaction among dyads within the context of the family as a social system. It might be, for example, that when interacting with the father, each member of the family reinforces at ten times his ordinary rate. While maintaining their ordinal ranks *vis à vis* the amount of social reinforcement, they give and receive in their interactions with the father. A "reciprocity correlation" would show that, in these interactions, the child who gave the most received the most from the father. However, the positive correlations would not give any indication of the enormous increase in dispensing social reinforcers which characterized all of the children in interacting with the father.

G. G. Bechtel (1968) has devised a statistical model which provides a more meaningful test and also tests for differences among family members in their giving and receiving capacities. The statistical model is based upon a paired-compositions layout; the outcome of the hypotheses tested is expressed in analysis of variance terms. The Bechtel model was applied to the family interaction data from 36 individuals in seven families. All of the families were referred because of "out of control" problems characterizing one or more of the children. The data for the analysis were based upon the ten baseline observation sessions in the homes of the families. The results of the analysis are presented in Table 1 below and are expressed as F values. The F tests relevant to the reciprocity hypothesis are presented under the column heading "symmetry" and the subheading "positive." A significant F value would indicate that there were significant inequities holding among some dyads within the family. A nonsignificant F value, on the other hand, indicates that the system was balanced or symmetric. The specific prediction would be that all, or most, of the F values would be nonsignificant.

The data in Table 1 indicated that within three of the families (Ru, Jo, and Ro) there were significant differences in the amounts of social reinforcement given to family members. An analysis of the variance of the subjects tested for differences among four major groups: mothers, fathers, deviant children, and all other siblings. The Kruskall-Wallis one-way analysis of variance produced an H of 6.4 which was minimally significant at P less than .095. The mothers "gave" the most social reinforcers (2.59 per minute) and the fathers gave the least (1.05 per minute). A similar analysis of the differences among family members in the "receiving" of social reinforcers showed that the deviant children received a disproportionate share; however, the analysis of variance showed the differences among groups to be nonsignificant.

As outlined earlier, some moment-by-moment aspects of the interaction patterns characterizing the deviant child should be "nonreciprocal." During a temper tantrum the child is dispensing high rates of aversive stimuli and receiving positive reinforcement in return. However, it is hypothesized that in the long run the other member of the dyad reciprocates by punishing the deviant child in some way. Thus, as far as the deviant child is concerned, the data should show that a kind of talon law is maintained in which the victimizer is also, in the last analysis, himself victimized. Nonreciprocal interactions should be found only for social agents who can dispense high amplitude aversive stimuli for any attempt on the part of the other to make punishment contingent upon their behavior. While in some families this may be true of the deviant child, it is most likely to be the parent who is able to sustain such nonreciprocal interactions.

The data in Table 1 showed that three families were significantly

TABLE 1 *Analysis of variance for seven families.*

Family	N	Positive Consequences		Aversive Consequences		Symmetry		Rate Deviant Behavior per Person per minute
		Give	Receive	Give	Receive	Positive	Aversive	
Sj	8	.76	.96	1.03	1.61	1.23	.64	.18
Ru	4	11.20*	3.40	27.15*	23.89*	2.53	9.56*	.19
Jo	4	34.99**	38.88**	12.21*	.42	.13	10.49*	.33
Le	4	2.66	.49	1.51	5.53	2.20	2.51	.16
Kn	6	.58	.47	4.10*	19.11**	.70	8.04**	.22
Rh	4	5.53	4.98	1.75	3.21	1.63	2.18	.33
Ro	6	3.70*	1.58	5.41*	4.33*	.96	1.28	.67

* P less than .05
** P less than .01

asymmetric in the exchange of aversive consequences. In analyzing the data from the dyads, it is clear that the social agent contributing most to the asymmetry varies from one family to another. For example, in the Kn family it was the father who contributed most to the imbalance, while in the Jo and Ru families, it was the mother and the deviant child, respectively.

While the data showed that the deviant child did in fact dispense the highest rate of aversive stimuli (.40 per minute), the Kruskal-Wallis analysis indicated that the differences among the four groups of agents were not significant. The analysis of differences in receiving aversive consequences produced a similar conclusion; while the deviant child received more aversive stimuli from other family members (.45 per minute), the differences were not significant. The lack of significant findings in the analysis for aversive consequences constitutes a partial disconfirmation of the coercion hypothesis in that it was predicted that the deviant child would dispense significantly more aversive stimuli than other members of the family.

The data from all four analyses were consistent in showing the father to be the *uninvolved* member of the family. Not only did the father dispense the least positive social reinforcement (1.05 per minute), but he also dispensed the lowest rate of aversive consequences (.26 per minute). In addition, the consequences which he received also reflect his status as "visiting stranger," in that the fathers tended to receive the lowest rates of social reinforcers (1.59 per minute) and the lowest rate of aversive consequences (.10 per minute). These findings are of particular interest in that they complement some of the findings expressed in the clinical literature to the effect that fathers tend to play a secondary role in family interaction.

THE ACQUISITION OF DEVIANT BEHAVIOR

Responsiveness to social stimuli is a pivotal variable in the formulation which follows. Effective training programs for either deviant or adaptive social behaviors assume that the behavior is under the control of social stimuli. A review of the empirical literature shows that there are marked individual differences in responsiveness to social stimuli (Patterson, 1969). It seems likely that these differences reflect variations in physiological responsiveness (Freedman, 1965), as well as differences in conditioning histories. The extensive, and exciting, recent work on attachment suggests that a number of aspects of caretaking activities relate to differences in responsiveness. For example, differences in the *amount* of caretaking was shown to be a significant variable in the research by Rheingold (1956), while the amount of interaction and the responsiveness of the parents were found to be significant variables in the study by Schaeffer and Emerson (1964). The studies carried out by and reviewed by Cairns (1966) showed "mere" contiguity produced attachment. Harlow's (1958) well-known studies have demonstrated that both contact comfort and, to a lesser degree, food-dispensing, contribute to attachment. As yet, there have not been systematic attempts to integrate the findings from such diverse procedures, subject populations, and criterion measures. However, the theorizing presented by Gewirtz (1965) represents a promising beginning to providing a theory of attachment.

The fact that the child has been trained to respond to social reinforcers not only provides a basis for socialization, but also creates the first step in a chain of circumstances which can lead to deviant behaviors. In this situation, behaviors which in the past had produced social reinforcers are temporarily ineffective, which is to say that the child is placed on an extinction schedule. There is ample evidence to suggest that even brief periods of 5 minutes or less on extinction produces marked emotional reactions in infants (Sheppard, 1969). Presumably, for older children, more prolonged extinction intervals would produce disruptions in behavior and other concomitants of an emotional state. The point to be developed within the discussion which follows is that such extinction periods occur *frequently* in the life of the normal child and that these occurrences provide one basis for the acquisition of several varieties of deviant behavior.

Although such deprivation intervals occur in the life of adults as well as children, it is assumed that they most frequently characterize the interaction of the preschool child. The assumption rests primarily upon speculations about the differences between the older and the younger child in availability of "dispensers." During the first 3 or 4 years of his life, the child has not yet been trained to obtain much of his reinforcement from the peer group or from adults other than his parents. If there are no older siblings available, then the two dispensers, the mother and the father, may constitute the primary source of supply for these younger children. There are a number of events which occur in the development of most families that serve to temporarily disrupt the parents' giving of social reinforcers to the child. For example, the birth of a sibling is a situation in which both the mother and father are probably less able to dispense social reinforcers. Although the "crisis" may only persist for a week or two, it may represent a period of marked reduction in the availability of social reinforcers for the child. Doubtless, during such a crisis many child behaviors are placed on partial extinction schedules. Other types of stress involving the parents would also serve to produce similar effects, for example, moving to a new city, economic difficulties, or marital strife. A more dramatic example, albeit one which occurs less frequently, would be the hospitalization of the child for some short term period. The younger child has ordinarily not been trained to obtain his social reinforcers from adults other than his parents; for this reason, hospitalization may represent, initially at least, a massive deprivation and/or extinction period. The data from investigations such as those carried out by Prugh, Staub, Sands, Kirshbaum, and Lenchan (1953) provide dramatic descriptions of the emotional behaviors which accompany the initial phases in short term hospitalization. Interestingly enough, their data also showed that the children who were skilled in eliciting social reinforcers from the nursing staff showed fewer of these emotional behaviors.

The hypothesis is that these states occur more frequently in the life of the very young child than for the older child. If these states also provide an as yet unspecified basis for the acquisition of deviant behavior, then it would follow that younger children are likely to display higher rates of deviant behaviors than older children. The data provided in the study by Macfarlane et al. (1962) showed that this was, in fact, the case; mothers reported higher rates of deviant behaviors for younger children than for older children.

Some extinction schedules may result from temporary disruption in the availability of the one or two dispensers which provide for the younger child. However, partial extinction can occur for older children and adults as well, even though there are a greater number of dispensers available to them. The re-occurring deprivations for these older individuals involve primarily a lack of skill on their part. These are individuals whose behavioral repertoires are extremely limited. In the light of the earlier discussion, such a limitation would mean that there would be little about their behavior that would overlap with the repretoires of social behaviors possessed by the "dispensers in the social environment." This would lead to the prediction that the behaviors of such individuals would elicit less reinforcement. The retarded child would be an example which comes readily to mind. Such a child should possess some degree of overlap in his repertoire; but, to a large extent, the complex training in social skills has probably been absent and many of the "eliciting" behaviors are absent from his repretoire. The observation study by Harris (1966) showed that retarded children did, in fact, interact with each other less than did nonretarded children of comparable age. By the same token, it would be predicted that for normal children, increasing age should provide increasingly complex social repertoires which, in turn, provide the basis for more frequent reinforcement and interactions. The data from the study by Harris (1966) showed that for the normal child, social interaction did increase significantly from nursery school through the third grade. The observation study by Charlesworth and Hartup (1967) also showed that older children provide more frequent social reinforcement for each other's behavior than do younger children.

A recent publication by Patterson and Fagot (1967) suggests one other set of antecedents which may also increase the likelihood of extinction and deprivation states. The data showed that some children are selectively responsive in that they responded to social reinforcers from some agents and not others. Boys who were responsive only to the social reinforcers of their mothers and not their fathers or peers, were more likely to be described as deviant by their teachers. In the present context, it would seem that the person who is selectively responsive to the social reinforcers of only a limited set of social agents would be more likely to find himself on extinction schedules.

Finally, there is a third set of alternatives which theoretically is available to the child confronted with an extinction schedule. This alternative requires the previous acquisition of highly complex social skills such as achievement behaviors, performing, or entertaining. Presumably, this set of alternatives is not available for most children because the contingencies for their acquisition are not always available nor clearly structured. The data by Hartup et al. (1967) showed that the social skills which accompany high sociometric status in the peer group did, in fact, accompany high rates of social reinforcement dispensed by peers to that individual. Under conditions of deprivation then, highly adaptive social behaviors *could* be strengthened. However, this seems a reasonable alternative only for those children who *already* have these skilled behaviors in their repertoire, or for children who live in an environment which is programmed to provide this type of training.

It is of some interest to speculate about the kind of family that would most likely provide the combination of short-term extinction conditions and reinforcing contingencies which would produce deviant child behaviors. It seems likely, for example, that while some families may be characterized by frequent extinction periods for the child, that some of these same families might develop well-structured reinforcement contingencies which produce achievement-oriented responses or some other form of socially adaptive behavior. In such a home, when the child is placed upon short term deprivation, the most likely outcome is not an increase in deviant mands but in "working harder." For example, for any given family, it would be necessary to have a general description of the reinforcement "programs" *and* some knowledge of the extinction schedules in order to make a prediction about the output of deviant behavior.

The senior author actually learned about the extinction-coercion-deviant behavior hypotheses from his golden retriever dog, Eric. From long acquaintance, in many settings Eric and the writer had developed overlapping hierarchies of behaviors; and in this sense were good friends. He greeted the writer each night, waiting at the gate for him to stop and talk to him. Then, together they would walk to the door. During a period of some stress in the writer's professional life he would come through the gate, and in his preoccupied state, ignore his erstwhile friend. Eric would run along beside him and bump his head into his hand until he patted him. As things progressed and the writer became steadily more preoccupied, it was necessary for Eric to increase the amplitude of his manding behaviors. After a week of this kind of shaping, Eric began to greet him by bounding through the air like a gazelle. He would retreat before the writer, bounding up in the air as if on a pogo stick. Literally they met, eye to eye, at which time the writer would reach out and absentmindedly pat him on the head. In this manner Eric forced a response. As soon as he was patted on the head, he would terminate the behaviors. What finally brought the phenomenon to the writer's attention were the complaints of his young daughter and her friends. They had suddenly become badly frightened by this gazelle-like hunting dog who was coercing reinforcers from them at a fantastic rate. Even the milkman, long since habituated to normal dog behaviors, was coerced into reinforcing him. The writer terminated Eric's illicit interactions by standing immobile until he ceased to bound. When he sat down, he was immediately reinforced. After repeated training trials he still possesses a slight "loping" gait; Eric has been extinguished for his cross-species behavior.

As it was the case for the writer, parents who are under stress would more likely provide such extinction schedules than would nonstressed parents. While the relation between parental stress and child deprivation would be far from perfect, the general assumption is given indirect support by the data from a number of investigations. Probably the best data are the studies which demonstrate that the parents of children referred to child guidance clinics have significantly more deviant MMPI profiles than are found in "normal" populations (Liverant, 1959; Wolking, Quast, & Lawton, 1964). The present writers are suggesting that deviant parents are more likely to react to the child in such a manner as to place him on periodic extinction schedules. Our own brief experience with these parents also suggests that deviant parents are perhaps unlikely to provide the structure which is necessary to train the child in adaptive social behavior.

It is hypothesized that the home in which the father is absent, or in which both parents are rather diffuse and disorganized individuals, the initial occurrence of coercive manding behaviors will tend to be overlooked. A well structured household would provide an aversive consequence for such behavior early in the acquisition process. However, in the unstructured household the parents neglect to provide such consequences. By this omission, they permit a sibling who is being victimized to provide the necessary positive consequences. It is very likely that such households *also* neglect the provision of positive social reinforcers for socially adaptive behaviors.

Rather early in the development of the out-of-control child the parents begin unsystematic use of punishment, but it is used so poorly that it does not reduce the rate of deviant behaviors. As the parents and other family members find the behaviors increasingly aversive, they may come to label the child as "bad." Both the family and members of the peer group may avoid interacting with him as much as possible. As a result, he in turn may increase the rate or amplitude of the coercive behaviors and begin to describe himself as "bad."

Assuming even the partial validity of such a speculative case history, it would be a vast oversimplification to identify the primary antecedent as the "emotionally disturbed parent." As indicated in the review of the research literature by Fontana (1966) and Frank (1965) the fact that the parent was disturbed was neither a necessary nor sufficient condition for the acquisition of these behaviors in the child. It seems reasonable to suspect that a lack of structure may characterize many homes other than those of parents who describe themselves as disturbed.

Whatever the circumstances surrounding the first few stages in the acquisition of the deviant behavior, it is assumed that once the behaviors have been acquired, the culture will likely provide reinforcers for their maintenance. Data from a growing series of observation studies show that "normal" people within the child's social environment provide positive reinforcers for an astonishing array of deviant behaviors. These contingencies have been observed for hyperactive behaviors by a number of investigators in the classroom (Ebner, 1967; Anderson, 1964; Grindee, 1964) and the home (Hawkins et al., 1966); for aggressive behaviors in the nursery school (Patterson et al., 1967) and for delinquent behaviors in institutional settings (Buehler et al., 1966). Although the environment seems to respond with alacrity to coercive mands, and thus support them, it also seems to be the case that there are statutes of limitation holding for some forms of these behaviors. For example, there are very few adolescents who *whine* and *cry* when their mother leaves for the evening. While it may be that the adolescent still applies coercive mands, the *topology* of the responses has changed since the earlier years when he, in fact, did whine and cry on such occasions. It is interesting to note that several of the longitudinal studies have provided data which demonstrate that specific deviant behaviors or personality traits are not highly stable over the extended interval between years of 5 and 15 (Bayley & Schaefer, 1963; Macfarlane et al., 1962). The data from the Macfarlane study also showed that the specific classes of deviant behaviors changed over time. However, the *number* of *problems* reported at age 6 correlated .73 with the number of problems shown by the boys during early adolescence. These findings suggest that the "persistently deviant" child may acquire his status as deviant as a function of his general tendency to use coercive mands as a means of maintaining dyadic interactions. He may always have a large number of problems even though the specific topology of mand behaviors themselves might shift over the years. "Coercive manding" may, for children, be a stable personality trait.

In the section which follows, some preliminary procedures are described which are designed to alter contingencies supplied by a family and a peer group. These alterations change the occurrence of deviant behaviors displayed by a 10-year-old boy. Observation data are provided which demonstrate the changes in output of deviant behavior within the family and in the classroom. The data were analyzed to test the effect of the intervention program upon interaction patterns within the family.

SOME APPLICATIONS TO SOCIAL ENGINEERING

Estimation of Reciprocity for a Social System

In applying the reciprocity paradigm to the conceptualization of the family as a social system, it was decided to view a family as a collection of dyads; each dyad contributed two pieces of information for each set of consequences. Combining the data for either set of consequences for all dayads would constitute a description of a social system. The information used to describe each dyad was the number of positive and aversive consequences "given" by A in his interactions with B and the number of reinforcers received by A in his interactions with B for all dyads in the family.[10]

The family was observed over a 2-month baseline period using the coding system described earlier. During this period, each of the eight family members were observed for a total of 80 minutes. Each family member was also observed for a total of 20 minutes during the last 2 weeks of intervention. The Bechtel model was used to describe the family system prior to, and at termination of, the intervention program. The section which follows describes the family, the intervention program, and the analysis of the data.

Reprogramming the Famliy

The following material is an example of a set of social engineering procedures which are designed to produce not only immediate changes in the output of deviant behaviors in the home and school, but also produce long term changes in the schedules of positive reinforcement provided by the family and by the peer group as well. An attempt was made to change reinforcing contingencies among family members.

Family.   The family consisted of a middleaged husband and wife living on a marginal income with their six children. Both parents, and all of the children, were thought to be retarded in varying degrees. The family lived in the "industrial area" at the edge of town along a busy thoroughfare. The rented house was in very poor condition; the appointments within the home were in keeping with the setting. The father supported his family by working as an unskilled laborer in one of the local plywood mills.

The family has been known to the community for some time through a variety of social agencies. The school had complained bitterly for years that the children were being "starved," in that the mother did not provide adequate luncheons for them. There were also a series of angry interchanges with the juvenile court; both parents felt that the courts, police department, and schools were unfair in their dealings with the Sj children.

The identified deviant child was Sean, 10 years of age. Placed in a special class, the teachers described him as being a loner who was rejected by peers. He was also accused of lying and stealing.

The parents complained that he would seldom tell anyone where he was going, but would simply disappear. On occasion, these disappearances were followed by the appearance of firetrucks and a barrage of questions by members of the police department. It was claimed that Sean had set fire to cars parked in the neighborhood. The parents disbelieved the claims of the police department and angrily defended Sean. He had also been accused of setting fire to the neighbors' houses, and on one occasion, was in the immediate vicinity when a pulpit in the local church was consumed by flames.

Two weeks of baseline observation data constituted the assessment procedure and served as a basis for planning an intervention program. The observations showed, for example, that when Sean returned from school, he often initiated a series of contacts with the various members of the family, but that almost invariably he was ignored or mildly punished for these behaviors. Following such a series of "extinction" trials, he would usually leave the house for a period of time. His leaving was seldom noticed, for most of the people in the family seemed deeply committed to staring fixedly at the television screen. Often, as Sean walked by, his father would reach out and place his arm about Sean's shoulders without looking at him, or speaking to him. There was no particular behavior on Sean's part that produced this noncontingent reinforcement. Sean, for his part, seldom reinforced the behavior of other persons in the family. He received fairly high rates of reinforcement, but these were contingent upon mildly coercive behaviors such as teasing or threats.

Most of the social reinforcers which were observed were "low key" such as "listening" or "attending." In several hours of observation, high incentive reinforcers such as praise, approval, smile or laugh occurred at a rate of only .035 per minute! In some important sense, these people simply did not interact with each other. Their rate of aversive consequences was an average of .15 such consequences per person per minute. This is somewhat lower than even the best behaved families that we have observed; it was as if no one were involved enough to punish or to reinforce. Presumably, destroying cars would produce exciting and reinforcing consequences in an otherwise rather nonreinforcing environment.

The data for the giving and receiving of both positive and aversive consequences among all dyads was summarized for the baseline period. The data in either matrix comprise a composition layout since, for example, the rate of reinforcement dispensed by family member A to family member B may be a function of the *sum* of A's dispensing capacity and B's attractiveness. G. Bechtel's model, in addition to testing for differences among family members in giving and receiving capacities also tests the hypothesis of additivity (or scalability) for the composition layout. This hypothesis would be that the true pairwise rate E (s_{ab}) was completely dependent upon the sum of A's dispensing capacity and B's receiving capacity. The fourth hypothesis tested concerned the symmetry, or balance, holding for the giving and receiving of social consequences among each pair of family members. Table 7.2 summarizes the least squares estimates and the tests for each of the four hypotheses from the data on positive consequences. An interaction which produced "normal social activity" was tabulated as positively consequated. For example, sitting and watching television with another member of the family would be counted as a reinforced response. However, in the case of the Sj family, this type of interaction accounted for such a disproportionate share of the total social interaction that it was decided to drop this class of consequences from the present analysis. For this reason, the analysis outlined in Table 2 will differ somewhat from the results previously presented in Table 1 for the Sj family.

The data showed that there were significant differences among family members in the giving of social reinforcers. The father and the youngest

TABLE 2   *Analysis of variance of baseline data for the Sj family: Positive reinforcement.*

Source	SS	df	MS	F
Scaling of giving capacity	975.56	7	139.37	3.61*
Scaling of receiving capacity	9287.86	8	1160.98	30.05***
Interaction	5164.33	20	258.22	6.68***
Asymmetry	68.36	8	8.55	.22
Error	811.36	21	38.64	

* P less than .05
** P less than .01
*** P less than .001

boy dispensed the highest frequency and Sean, the identified deviant child, dispensed the least. There were also significant differences among family members in the receiving of social reinforcers; inspection of the data suggested that Sean and the youngest boy in the family received disproportionate shares. These data are illustrative of the interchanges which presumably characterize the coercive-manding child. In the household, Sean was moderately aggressive and out-of-control but sufficient to coerce an impressive corner on the market for the available supply of social reinforcers. In keeping with the coercion hypothesis, he tended to give, in return, less than "his share."

The highly significant interaction effect indicated that although significant differences did occur among family members in the giving and receiving of social reinforcers, these differences did not, in fact, account for all of the transactional data. In some cases, the transactions assumed some unique output as a function of a particular dyad. For example, the father gave a very low rate of reinforcement to an adolescent daughter who otherwise received a good deal from other family members.

The symmetry analysis indicates that the family was "in balance," *vis á vis* the exchange of positive social reinforcers among dyads. The only member of the family who might have been characterized as "non reciprocal" would have been Sean, but this imbalance held primarily for his interactions with his parents. The imbalance for these two dyads was not enough to produce a significant imbalance for the system.

The summary of the analysis for the aversive consequences are presented in Table 7.3. The data show that although there were differences among family members in the receiving of aversive consequences, these trends were not significant. Inspection of the data suggests that Sean, the father, and one of the adolescent daughters were all receiving disproportionate amounts of aversive consequences. Interestingly enough it was the mother who received less than her due share.

The Intervention Programs. As a general format, the intervention programs for families consist of four phases, each of which is arranged

TABLE 3 *Analysis of variance of baseline data for the Sj family: Aversive consequences.*

Source	SS	df	MS	F
Scaling of giving capacity	130.08	7	18.58	1.01
Scaling of receiving capacity	720.16	8	90.02	4.90*
Interaction	350.10	20	17.51	.96
Asymmetry	8.97	8	1.12	.06
Error	385.77	21	18.37	

* P less than .01

in a contingent fashion. The family must complete the one phase before the next is presented. In the first phase, the parents are asked to respond to an earlier version of the programmed textbook for parents which outlines social learning principles and general intervention procedures (Patterson & Gullion, 1968). When both parents have completed the textbook, they are then trained to observe either each other's or the behavior of their children. In phase three, intervention programs are demonstrated in the home and members of the family are trained to use them. When the data show, and the family agree, that "things are going better," the formal procedures are gradually withdrawn. During this latter phase, telephone follow-ups are made each day covering specific points in the intervention program. Over a period of weeks, the calls become increasingly less frequent. At the termination of these calls, a 6-month follow-up procedure is initiated; during this time the family is observed 2 hours each month. The sequence of procedures for the classroom setting are somewhat different from those employed in the home and will be described in a later section.

When given the programmed text to read, Mr. and Mrs. Sj were instructed to call as soon as they completed the task. No calls were forthcoming, so the writer called and was given a long list of reasons why they had not been able to complete the assignment. After several such interchanges, it finally dawned upon us that for these two parents, reading would be an onerous assignment; for the father, it might very well be impossible. For this reason, D. Shaw, the other member of the clinical team working with this family, constructed a tape recording of the programmed text. In the tape each frame was presented, and following a moment's silence, the "correct response" was given. We triumphantly called the parents and announced the availability of the tape, and requested that they come in and avail themselves of the fruits of our labors. They broke three appointments in as many days. At this point, fate, and Sean, intervened; he burned another car and was promptly incarcerated in the local Detention facilities. When notified of this, we urged the juvenile court to release him contingent only upon the parents' cooperation in the program. As soon as they were notified of these contingencies, the parents promptly fulfilled their responsibilities by responding to the text in one evening. (Mr. Sj dictated his answers.)

In the next phase, the experimenters went to the home and trained both parents to record the occurrence of three events: the frequency with which the children (including Sean) complied or resisted request; the frequency with which the other spouse positively reinforced adaptive child behavior; and the frequency with which the spouse received positive reinforcers from the family. The parents were given a wrist counter and encouraged to make their observations at a regular time interval each day. They were to observe each of these events during the time interval and write down the appropriate number. Each afternoon, a member of the clinical team called to obtain the data. In this training, it was necessary to actually hand shape the father to discriminate the presence or absence of a social reinforcer. Three training sessions in the home of an hour each were required before anything approximating adequate data were obtained from the parents. Even then, neither of the experimenters were convinced that the parents were carefully attending to the behaviors.

There were three general intervention programs undertaken in the home. Two of them were designed to train the family to increase the reinforcement schedules for Sean's socially adaptive behavior and the third was designed to produce alterations in reciprocity patterns for the family as a whole.

The first two programs demonstrated to the family, and particularly to the parents, that Sean's behavior was under their control, and at the same time, decreased the frequency of his withdrawal from the family. As he found the family to be more reinforcing, he tended to spend less time out wandering about the neighborhood. Presumably, this in turn should also decrease the rate with which he set cars afire. There is an interesting conceptual problem posed by such low base rate events as "suicide," "homicide," and "fire-setting." As these events occur at such low rates, it is difficult to imagine the contingencies which one might arrange to alter their strength. For heuristic purposes the writers conceptualize such low base rate events as being the terminal member in a chain of responses. For example, following nonreinforcement, Sean would slip out of the house and wander about the neighborhood. On some occasions these wanderings would lead to fire-setting or stealing. Presumably the earlier components in the chain (nonreinforced interactions, leaving the home without permission, or wandering) all occurred at reasonably high rates which could be both counted and manipulated.

The second program was designed specifically to reduce the frequency with which he slipped away unannounced. The first step was to train the boy to talk to his parents, and at the same time, train the parents to reinforce him when he did so. Reprogramming the social environment usually involves the necessity of altering *several* aspects of the milieu *simultaneously*. For example, if Sean increased the frequency of his initiations to the family, but they failed to reinforce him, then his initiations would be short lived; therefore, the program must be designed to accelerate the rates for both events simultaneously. When the procedure was modelled in their home, it was a simple process to increase the rate of Sean's initiation. He was reinforced for initiating conversations, first with the experimenters and then with each of the other family members. Sean earned 10 M & M candies on each occasion that a portable signalling device activated by the experimenter emitted a "buzz;" a counter mounted in the device kept score. At the end of the session, the candies were divided among all of the children in the family. The children, including Sean, greeted this announcement with some enthusiasm.[11] The family greeted each of Sean's sallies with some interest and a great deal of support. The younger children avidly quizzed the experimenters to determine the current "score."

The first difficulty was encountered when it was the father's turn to function as reinforcer for Sean's talking. When E prompted Sean by asking him what he had done in school that day, Sean replied, "Played with a girl on the jungle gym." The father's immediate "reinforcer" was, "What did ja do ta her?" He then proceeded to grill Sean to determine whether he had molested the girl. The trials which followed a few minutes later produced reactions which were little better. The father's "reinforcers" varied from stony silence to awkward questioning. When engaged in discussions with members of his family, this man almost never functioned as a supportive-reinforcing person. When questioned about this, he said that he never used praise; observations of his behavior indicated that he seldom smiled or laughed.

A shaping procedure was introduced in which the father was reinforced by E for listening, and then for responding appropriately to Sean's talking. The details of a similar program are outlined in a report by Patterson and Brodsky (1966) in which a child was taught to reinforce his mother. Although an attempt was made to condition the father to use praise, approval, and other "high incentive" social reinforcers, this latter attempt was not very successful.

The parents were instructed to each spend 10 minutes a day in reinforcing Sean for his talking. They were to record a point for each social reinforcer; each point bought the mother 1 minute of driving instructor time; the latter was paid for out of the project funds.[12]

After several practice sessions in the home, the program was turned over to the parents and a telephone surveillance was maintained while the family practiced for several days. On 10/3, for example, the mother reported that Sean had talked to her 30 times and that she had reinforced him each time. However, she reported only sporadic cooperation from the father. In retrospect, it seems that we erred in not providing reinforcers for him. Working to obtain points for his wife's driving training was not an effective contingency for maintaining his participation. On 10/29, they recorded 70 events, 64 the next day and 18 the next. The observation data obtained in the home during this time indicated that there was little, or no, change in any of the important contingencies. It seemed as if the effect of the program was not generalizing beyond the practice sessions. It was also clear that for the parents, increases in the rate of a behavior such as "talking" were simply not reinforcing. Therefore, it was decided to introduce the second phase of the project in which they would obtain control over Sean's slipping away from home. This was a behavior of immediate concern to them. They were also told that the intervention program at school would not begin until they were successful in carrying out both the old and the new program.

In this new program, Sean was instructed to walk up to *E* and tell him that he was leaving the house for a few minutes. The report also included some information as to where he was going and when he would return. *E* reinforced him for each point of information with the "buzzer." Sean then practiced with his mother and father. The parents then both reinforced and recorded points as he practiced. The points which the parents recorded went toward Sean's earning a football (200 points).

On 10/17, the telephone follow-up showed that Sean had practiced 5 times that day, the next day 6 trials, and 7 the next. The program for reinforcing talking had been continued. He was now earning a steady 30-40 points each day. The mother was also obtaining a steady "income," and she went to her first driving lesson that same week.

On 10/24, she reported that there had been marked improvements in Sean's behavior. Our observations showed that members of the family seemed to be reinforcing him at a higher rate for *adaptive* social behaviors. However, the agent most responsible for the changes, the mother, was herself receiving only limited support from the family. It seemed probable that, following termination of the intervention program, there would be little that would maintain her recently acquired skills as a contingent reinforcer.

In a program to provide more support for the mother's behavior, the older children were first trained to use the wrist counter to record the general incidence of praise, approval, laughing or smiling. They were then trained to record these events as they observed each of the children in turn go up and "reinforce their mother." The first practice sessions were extremely awkward, having very much the quality of children's Easter recitations. The usual remark was of the kind, "Momma, your hair is pretty." The last child in this parade went up and gave his mother a kiss. Both *Es*, and the family, applauded this spontaneous interpretation of what was being asked. The mother blushed, but was obviously very pleased. The experimenters also gave additional suggestions of reinforcers appropriate for mother such as thanking her for a meal well cooked or clothing mended. Arrangements were made for regular counting sessions each day. All of the children worked for 100 points toward an ice cream orgy (to be paid for by the project). According to their data, the children earned a gallon of ice cream within the week. Periodic telephone follow-ups were made over the next 2 weeks checking on the three programs, then intervention was terminated.

Follow-up observations are now being carried out over a 6-month period. A month after termination, the mother reported her pleasure at the changes in Sean's behavior. He now talks to her and she to him; they both seem to get some real pleasure from being around each other. He also always asks for permission before leaving the house. She reported with pride that she received a call from her church group indicating their surprise at the changes in his behavior. At the time of this writing he had burned no cars.

Results of the program. The observation data in Figure 7.1 show the effect of the programs upon the occurrence of the following deviant behaviors: stomp, tease, dependence, noncompliance, cry, aggression, yelling, negativism, and destruction. The data in parentheses refer to the proportion of these behaviors which were positively reinforced by some members of the family. It was hypothesized that an adequate intervention program should produce a decrease in the overall rate of deviant behavior *and* decrease in the proportion of these behaviors which were positively reinforced.

Both sets of data are in keeping with the hypotheses. Sean had decreased the rate of his deviant behaviors in the home and the family was supplying less support for these behaviors.

The next requirement in determining whether the intervention program was effective for this family concerned the alteration in reciprocity patterns for the Sj family. Because of the massive increases in both

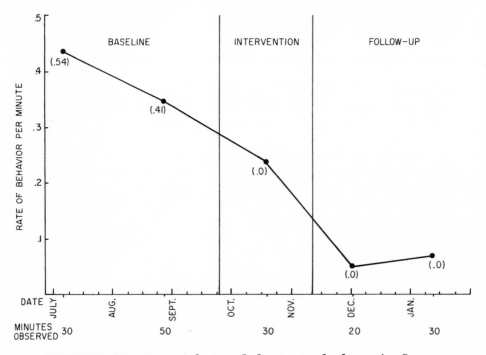

FIGURE 7.1 *Rate of deviant behavior in the home for Sean.*

social and nonsocial reinforcers dispensed to Sean one might expect, on the basis of a reciprocity notion, that he would increase the rate with which he reinforced other members of the family. His rate increased from .74 during baseline to 1.15 per minute during intervention. Presumably, these changes would also be accompanied by fewer coercive interchanges between Sean and other family members. The data in Table 7.4 summarize the analysis of variance of the matrix for the exchange of positive reinforcement during the intervention period.

TABLE 7.4 *Variance analysis of intervention data: Positive Reinforcement.*

Source	SS	df	MS	F
Scaling of giving capacity	251.05	7	35.86	1.79
Scaling of receiving capacity	159.05	7	22.72	1.14
Interaction	650.38	20	32.52	1.65
Asymmetry	110.50	7	15.79	.79
Error	420.00	21	20.00	

The overall analysis suggests that there had been rather marked changes occurring in the family structure. After intervention there were no major inequities among family members in the giving or receiving of social reinforcers; Sean and his mother were now dispensing the highest rate of social reinforcers. The nonsignificant interaction term also suggested that there tended to be fewer "unique distributions" of social reinforcers than was previously the case. These changes from baseline interaction showed that the intervention program accomplished more than "just" altering the rate of deviant behavior for Sean. The data suggests that the program may have had some effect upon family structure as well.

This last analysis was based upon only 30 minutes of observation data. The fact that aversive consequences were a low base rate event would mean that there were zero entries in the majority of the cells in the interaction matrix. For this reason, the data for aversive consequences were not analyzed.

Intervention in the school

The behavior of primary concern was "isolation." To the extent that Sean was not under the control of peer schedules of reinforcement, he was likely to become increasingly deviant. It was apparent from observing Sean there was little in his repertoire of skills that would serve to produce reinforcement from either boys or girls. Within the context of the reciprocity hypothesis, it was decided that the first step

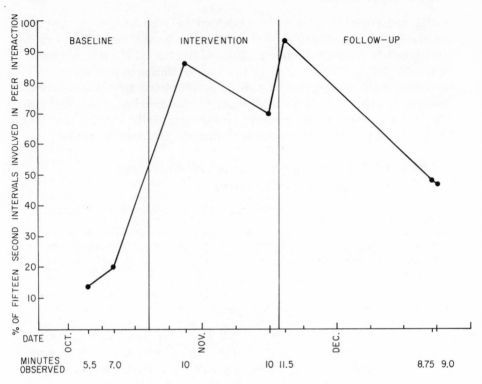

FIGURE 7.2 *Sean's peer interaction at recess.*

in the program would be that of strengthening a set of behaviors which would also be found high in the hierarchies of other children his own age. After considering the current playground activities of his peer group, it was decided to teach him to play football. Presumably, some skill in this area would produce increased reinforcement from peers.

A rapid survey of the teachers indicated that a young Negro boy named George was the best football player in the school. He readily agreed to be a coach for Sean. It was possible to train George in a few minutes to use reinforcement principles efficiently and to use shaping procedures in teaching "football." For example, he was instructed to use only praise and never criticism. Further, he first was shown how to toss the ball from a short distance (3 feet) to provide a reinforcer for a good catch; as Sean's skills increased, the distance was increased. The teacher and school counselor supervised the daily coaching sessions.

On the first day, *E* established that Sean's baseline performance for catching a ball at 20 feet was only 10 percent. It was agreed with the coach and the teacher that Sean would be reassessed each morning at recess, and on each day that the score improved, all of the children in the room would be let out 5 minutes early for recess. The word quickly spread and as *E* left the playground, George and Sean were surrounded by a throng of interested and *reinforcing* spectators. A member of the research team returned twice to supervise alterations in the program and obtain the data from the teacher. The data in Figure 7.2 show the effect of 5 hours of professional time spent in setting up, and carrying out, this program. The data were obtained by observers tabulating the frequency of interaction and isolation by 15-second intervals.

These data show dramatic changes in the rate of Sean's interaction with his peers. On a later occasion when one *E* returned to talk to the teacher, Sean was too busy interacting with his friends to pay much attention to the presence of his erstwhile friend. The teacher reported that Sean was now teaching other "less fortunate" children to play ball. It was clear that his behavior was under the control of peer reinforcement, and that the socialization process was once more well under way. Although the initial impact of the program was to produce a four or fivefold increase in interaction with peers, the follow-up data obtained a month later showed that this dramatic burst had decreased to approximately a threefold increase over baseline level. A similar drop during follow-up was obtained for an earlier report in which peers were "reprogrammed" to supply reinforcement for the behavior of another extremly deviant boy (Patterson & Brodsky, 1966). In that case, follow-up data over a 3-month period showed that the increases in interaction stablized to show about a "twofold" increase over baseline levels.

The data from both the school and from the home showed that there were significant alterations in the output of deviant behaviors in both settings and to some extent, significant changes in the reinforcement programs within the family. This, of course, is very gratifying, particularly in view of the difficulties involved. However, the writers would be less than candid if they did not indicate that both they and members of the clinical team have some reservations about what the follow-up data will show for this family. Any one of a number of events could reverse the positive outcome of the intervention. For example, further financial setbacks (which are quite likely) could again create a stress situation in which many persons within the family would be placed upon short-term deprivation (or extinction) schedules. Perhaps members of the family will gradually reduce the reinforcement programs which they used to support Sean and the mother; in this case, there could be a reciprocal reduction on their part which would, in turn, bring about changes within the family.

Poverty, itself, seems to have dimensions to it which the writers could sense in this family but only poorly describe. It is doubtful that 20 hours of professional time has altered the face of so overwhelming a phenomena as "poverty." Over the next 6 months, the data will tell its own story as to the success of this, our first effort; but in no sense do the writers believe that the present techniques represent anything more than a stoneage technology being applied to an overwhelmingly complex social problem.

CONCLUSION

This "position report" attempts to apply reinforcement principles to the problems involved in investigating dyadic interaction and family systems. The report stands as a preliminary statement about the "psychology of the dispenser." In discussing the problem of why it is that one person reinforces another, two rather obvious processes have been identified. The reinforcing behaviors of person A are maintained, on some occasions by the withdrawal of an aversive stimulus (coercion), and on other occasions by the presentation of a positive reinforcer (reciprocity). Presumably interactions characterized by marked deviations from parity or high frequencies of coercion are most likely to produce deviant behaviors.

The reciprocity and coercion constructs were used as a basis for speculating about the antecedents for some classes of deviant child behaviors. It was assumed that following the early training in responsiveness to social stimuli, the young child is particularly liable to be subjected to periodic deprivations for these reinforcers. Under conditions of deprivation, the child is likely to learn that deviant mands are an effective way of terminating deprivation states. Periodic deprivation of social reinforcers also increases the likelihood that the child will acquire self-stimulating behaviors. Under extended deprivation and in conditions where mand behaviors are not reinforced, the child may acquire withdrawal responses.

The general framework was also used as a basis for describing the family system. It was assumed that the family consists of mutually interdependent dyads and that the reciprocity data used to describe sets of dyads can be summarized to provide a meaningful description of a family. It was also assumed that in some families intervention programs must do more than simply reduce the output of deviant behaviors, in that the long term effects of such programs will be determined by other changes within the family system. For such families, changes in reciprocity, within dyads, will have predictive significance for the long-term effects of intervention programs.

The degree of investment made in a particular area of clinical research is generally a function of its apparent relevance to questions about pathology or behavior change. Undoubtedly, part of the attractiveness and impetus given the research in the area of "modelling" for example, has been due in part, to its relations to many clinically relevant variables (Bandura & Walters, 1963).[13] To a lesser extent, the reciprocity and coercion constructs display a similar kind of "relevance." From the viewpoint of the writers, these two constructs offer a wide array of hypotheses which are imminently testable by direct observation within families. Although the outcome of a few month's data collection cannot be considered as anything akin to confirmation, the results are of sufficient promise to merit serious consideration by other investigators.

NOTES

1. Perhaps it should not be necessary to apologize for making the tactical decision to restrict one's focus in carrying out an investigation. Although the present writers are aware of the potential importance of such determinants of interaction as motives, roles, norms, and expectancies, it seemed a more reasonable tactic to set these considerations aside and to proceed à la Procrustes and determine what, if any, contribution a singleminded application of reinforcement principles might make to an understanding of social interaction. In this sense we believe ourselves to be in the excellent company of other "naive tacticians" such as Hastorf (1965), Homans (1961), Lindsley (1963), Oakes, Droge, & August (1960), Oakes (1962), and Sidowski (1957), all of whom have used functional analysis as a basis for analyzing group process.

2. It is likely that many adult classes of deviant behaviors could also be viewed as deviant mands. For example, the hypochondriacal complaints of the elderly woman coerces the sympathetic attention of the well-socialized adult. For such a person, the greeting, "How are You" is an invitation to coercion. I. Goldiamond (Private communication, 1967) also suggests that for adults, stuttering may function as a coercive mand for the sustained attention of the audience.

   In social systems such as the family or a business, it is the writers' impression that many spouses or administrators function as "crisis generators." The effect of generating such a crisis is to control large segments of the time of members of the system. The termination of the crisis is of course reinforcing for the victim and certainly the massive increases in interaction during the crisis are reinforcing to the previously "forgotten" spouse or boss. In a sense, the crisis provided by such adults is akin to the temper tantrum of the child.

3. The research by investigators such as Berlyne (1965) suggests that stimuli which are characterized as novel are effective reinforcers. In the present context, this would suggest that the behavior of other persons which is novel would also be more likely to elicit attending behaviors.

4. It is also conceivable that there is yet another functional relation that automatically provides reinforcement for the listener. Conceptualizing the process within a Premack (1959) framework, one might also think of the low rate behaviors of the listener, i.e., this "Hmm-mm," as being reinforced by the high rate behaviors which he emits later in the conversation when it is "his turn to talk."

5. There are doubtless also more complex variations which better describe some types of interactions. One such variation, suggested by R. Weiss, assumes that reinforcing stimuli have an activating effect (autonomic or cortical). If one of the persons in the interaction provides a highly novel or interesting response, the effect is to activate the other person. The effect of this, in turn, is to alter the generalization gradient so that his next response is increasingly likely to be "novel." The novelty functions as a reinforcer and provides a further source of activation.

6. The families were informed that the procedures provided under the auspices of the University Psychology Clinic would definitely be experimental in nature. They were told that at the end of the baseline period a treatment plan would be outlined for them and they would be shown in their own home how to implement the plan. If the intervention program were not successful within 2 weeks (according to our observation data), they were told that the research project would then sponsor the family while they received traditional therapies by the clinic or physician of their choice. They were also told that data collected during the project would be published.

7. The writers owe a debt of gratitude to the observers who gave up their evenings to collect these data. In addition to being highly reliable, they collaborated in both analyzing the data and carrying out the intervention procedures with the families. These individuals were colleagues in the best sense of the word: Dana Schaeffer, Barbara Spence, David Shaw, Lynn Long, Kathleen Reid, and more recently, Elizabeth Gullion.

8. The writers wish to thank (1) Mrs. Petra Davenport, an undergraduate student, for her performance in carrying out this first pilot study, and (2) Linda Hoover and Harry Rinehart for the second pilot study in this series.

9. This general paradigm may be of some interest in that variables presumed to be significant in controlling behavior could be tested for their effectiveness by using observation data obtained *in situ*. For example, many of the laboratory studies investigating the effect of characteristics of child and social agent in determining responsiveness to social reinforcers could be replicated *in situ*. In addition, we could begin to investigate the reinforcing contingencies which actually maintain deviant and adaptive social behaviors. A recent investigation of this kind identified some of the reinforcing contingencies provided in the nursery school setting for assertive behaviors (Patterson et al., 1967).

10. This simplifying assumption is so obviously restrictive that perhaps there is little need to point out that the resulting perspective provides an incomplete picture of a family. For example, it is also possible to describe families in terms of the amount of negative reinforcement dispensed, the amount of interactions, or the number of initiations. For the time being, the problem of whether the information about the dyads should be combined in additive or in configural fashion to predict the output of deviant behavior is also being set aside. As the data are forthcoming, such questions will be amenable to empirical testing.

11. It is extremely important that the program be presented to the family in such a fashion that no one, including the identified deviant child, feels attacked. The family is told that the problem consists of a *general* situation in which all of them are doing something which makes others uncomfortable, and this is a situation which they can change. They are told that each of them will be given something to do in bringing about this change and that they will find it rewarding to participate. The subject of a program always receives massive social and nonsocial reinforcers for participating.

12. For many parents, the reinforcer appropriate for the support of their cooperating in a program of this kind is to be found in the reduction in rate of deviant behavior. While negative reinforcement might support the cooperative behavior of most parents, some parents such as the Sj's do not necessarily wish to have the behavior of their child altered; in fact, in many respects they might resent the necessity for cooperating at all. For such parents, it is necessary to find some "idiosyncratic psychological M & M" which will maintain their behavior. After discussing the matter with Mrs. Sj, it seemed that learning to drive a car (to get away from her unpleasant surroundings) was something of importance to her; therefore points for driving lessons seemed an appropriate reinforcer.

13. Modelling, per se, would seem to be a significant but limited determinant for deviant or adaptive social behaviors. The limitations are a function of the fact that the main relevance of modelling theory is in predicting which responses will be "tried." Modelling theory will eventually explicate the complex variables which will identify the conditions under which the child will observe, store, and perform modelled behaviors. However, as Bandura (1966) pointed out, in the present culture most children have ample opportunity to observe almost all relevant social behaviors. The variables which will determine which responses will be "tried" are probably *not* related directly to the problem of predicting which of the responses performed will eventually occupy a position of strength in the child's repertoire of social behaviors. It is obvious that trying out a response is of no great moment unless the behaviors are reinforced.

Within the framework of the reciprocity construct, it would be

assumed that the model would be most likely to reinforce those behaviors performed by the child which are also in the repertoire of the
model. Even though we may conceptualize socialization as a two-phase
process (modelling and reinforcement) information about one variable
(overlapping response repertoires) could account for variance in both
processes.

REFERENCES

Ackerman, N. W. *The psychodynamics of family life.* New York: Basic Books,
    Inc., 1958.
Adler, A. *Social interest: A challenge to mankind.* New York: Harcourt, 1927.
Allen, K. E., Hart, B. M., Buell, J. S., Harris, F. R., & Wolf, M. M. Effects of
    social reinforcement on isolate behavior of a nursery school child. *Child
    Development,* 1964, 35, 511-518.
Anderson, D. Application of a behavior modification technique to the control
    of an hyperactive child. Unpublished master's thesis, University of
    Oregon, 1964.
Azrin, N. H., & Lindsley, O. R. The reinforcement of cooperation between
    children. *Journal of Abnormal and Social Psychology,* 1956, 52, 100-102.
Balint, M. Individual differences of behavior in early infancy: An objective
    method for recording. *Journal of Genetic Psychology,* 1948, 73, 57-79.
Bandura, A. Social learning theory of identification process. In D. A. Goslin
    & D. C. Glass (Eds.), *Handbook of socialization theory and research.*
    New York: Rand McNally, 1966.
Bandura, A. & Walters, R. H. *Social learning and personality development.*
    New York: Holt, Rinehart & Winston, 1963.
Bayley, N. & Schaefer, E. S. Maternal behavior, child behavior and their in-
    tercorrelations from infancy through adolescence. *Monographs of the
    Society for Research in Child Development,* 1963, 28, No. 3.
Bechtel, G. G. The analysis of variance and pair-wise scaling. *Psychometrika,*
    1967, 32, 47-65.
Bechtel, G. G. A dual scaling analysis for paired compositions. *Oregon Re-
    search Institute Research Bulletin,* 1968, 8, No. 4, 1-41.
Bechtel, R. B. The study of man: Human movement and architecture. *Trans-
    actions,* May, 1967, 53-56.
Becker, W. C. The relationship of factors in parental ratings of self and each
    other to the behavior of kindergarten children as rated by mothers, fathers,
    and teachers. *Journal of Consulting Psychology,* 1960, 24, 507-527.
Becker, W. C., Madsen, C. H. Jr., Arnold, C. R., & Thomas, D. R. The contin-
    gent use of teacher attention and praise in reducing classroom behavior
    problems. *Journal of Special Education,* 1967, 1, 3, 287-307.
Bell, J. E. Family group therapy. *Public Health Monograph No. 64,* Depart-
    ment of Health, Education and Welfare, 1961.
Berlyne, D. E. *Structure and direction in thinking.* New York: Wiley, 1965.
Birnbauer, J. S., Bijou, S. W., Wolf, M. M., & Kidder, J. D. Programmed in-

struction in the classroom. In L. Ullmann & L. Krasner, (Eds.), *Case studies in behavior modification.* New York: Holt, Rinehart & Winston, 1965.

Buehler, R., Patterson, G. R., & Furness, J. The reinforcement of behavior in institutional settings. *Behavior Research and Therapy,* 1966, 4, 157-167.

Byrne, D., Griffett, W., & Stefaveak, D. Attraction and similarity of personality characteristics. *Journal of Personality and Social Psychology,* 1967, 5, 82-90.

Cairns, R. B. Attachment behavior of mammals. *Psychological Review,* 1966, 73, 409-426.

Charlesworth, R., & Hartup, W. W. Positive social reinforcement in the nursery school peer group. *Child Development,* 1967, 38, 1, 993-1002.

Cohen, D. J. & Lindsley, O. R. Catalysis of controlled leadership in cooperation by human stimulation. *Journal of Child Psychology and Psychiatry,* 1964, 5, 119-137.

Cromwell, R. L., Baumeister, A., & Hawkins, W. F. Research in activity level. In N. Ellis (Ed.), *Handbook of mental deficiency.* New York: McGraw-Hill, 1963.

Ebner, M. Observation of changes in reinforcement schedules as an outcome of successful behavior modification. Unpublished doctoral dissertation, University of Oregon, June 1967.

Fagot, B. The effect of sex of child upon social interaction and sex role behavior in a nursery school setting. Unpublished doctoral dissertation, University of Oregon, 1967.

Fisher, S., & Fisher, R. L. The complexity of spouse similarity and differences. In G. Zuk & I. Boszormenyi-Nagy (Eds.), *Family therapy and disturbed families.* Palo Alto, California: Science & Behavior Books, Inc., 1967.

Fontana, A. F. Familial etiology of schizophrenia: Is a scientific methodology possible? *Psychological Bulletin,* 1966, 66, 214-227.

Franks, G. H. The role of the family in the development of psychopathology. *Psychological Bulletin,* 1965, 64, 191-205.

Freedman, D. Hereditary control of early social behavior. In D. M. Foss (Ed.), *Determinants of infant behavior.* London: Methuen & Co., 1965.

Gewirtz, J. L. A learning analysis of the effects of normal stimulation, privation and deprivation on the acquisition of social motivation and attachment. In D. M. Foss (Ed.), *Determinants of infant behavior.* London: Methuen & Co., 1965.

Gewirtz, J. L., & Baer, D. M. Deprivation and satiation of social reinforcers as drive conditions. *Journal of Abnormal and Social Psychology,* 1958, 57, 165-172.

Grindee, K. T. Operant conditioning of "attending behaviors" in the classroom for two hyperactive Negro children. Unpublished paper, Department of Psychology, Reed College, 1964.

Hall, R. V., Lund, D., & Jackson, D. Effects of teacher attention on study behavior. *Journal of Applied Behavior Analysis,* 1968, 1, 1-12.

Hammerlynck, L. A., Donely, M., & Heller, D. Modification of high base rate verbal behavior by behavioral contracts. Unpublished manuscript, University of Oregon, 1967.

Hare, A. P. *Handbook of small group research.* Glencoe, Illinois: Free Press, 1962.

Haring, N. G., & Hayden, A. H. The program and facilities of the experimental education unit of the University of Washington Mental Retardation and Child Development Center. In M. U. Jones (Ed.), *Special education programs within the United States.* Springfield, Ill.: Charles C. Thomas, 1966.

Harlow, H. The nature of love. *The American Psychologist,* 1958, 13, 673-686.

Harris, A. M. Differences betwen severely retarded children and normal children in the frequencies of peer interaction, adult interactions and non-social behavior. Unpublished master's thesis, University of Oregon, 1966.

Harris, F. R., Johnston, M., Kelley, C. S., & Wolf, M. M. Effect of positive social reinforcement on regressed crawling of a nursery school child. *Journal of Educational Psychology,* 1964, 55, 35-41.

Hart, B. M., Allen, K. E., Buell, J. S., Harris, F. R., & Wolf, M. M. Effects of social reinforcement on operant crying. *Journal of Experimental Child Psychology,* 1964, 1, 145-153.

Hartup, W. W., Glazer, J. A., & Charlesworth, R. Peer reinforcement and sociometric status. *Child Development,* 1967, *38,* 1017-1024.

Hastorf, A. H. The reinforcement of individual actions in a group situation. In L. Krasner & L. Ullman (Eds.), *Research in behavior modification,* New York: Holt, Rinehart and Winston, 1965.

Hawkins, R. P., Peterson, R. F., Schweid, E., & Bijou, S. W. Behavior therapy in the home: Amelioration of problem parent-child relations with the parent in a therapeutic role. *Journal of Experimental Child Psychology,* 1966, 4, 99-107.

Homans, G. C. *Social behavior: Its elementary forms.* New York: Harcourt, Brace and World, Inc., 1961.

Honig, W. K. (Ed.). *Operant behavior: Areas of research and application.* New York: Appleton-Century-Crofts, 1966.

Hotchkiss, J. The modification of maladaptive behavior of a class of educationally handicapped children by operant conditioning techniques. Unpublished doctoral dissertation, University of Southern California, 1966.

Jenkins, R. L., & Glickman, S. Common syndromes in child psychiatry. *American Journal of Orthopsychiatry,* 1944, 2, 244-253.

Jennings, H. H. *Leadership and isolation.* (2nd Edition) London: Longmann's Green, 1950.

Jessor, S. G. The effects of reinforcement and of distribution of practice on psychological satiation. Unpublished doctoral dissertation, Ohio State University, 1951.

Kendon, A. Some functions of gaze direction in social interaction. Unpublished paper, Institute of Experimental Psychology, Oxford University, England, 1965.

Krumboltz, J. D., & Goodwin, D. L. Increasing task-oriented behavior: An experimental evaluation of training teachers in reinforcement techniques. School of Education, Stanford University, 1966, Final Report, Office of Education grant, 5-85-095.

Leary, T. *Interpersonal diagnosis of personality.* New York: Ronald Press, 1957.

Lindsley, O. R. Experimental analysis of social reinforcement. *American Journal of Orthopsychiatry,* 1963, 33, 624-633.

Lindsley, O. R. Training teachers to change environment. Presentation at University of Oregon Colloquia on Behavior Modification, Sponsored by School of Education, Eugene, Oregon, May, 1966.

Liverant, S. MMPI differences between parents of disturbed and non-disturbed children. *Journal of Consulting Psychology,* 1959, 23, 256-260.

Lott, A. J., & Lott, B. Group cohesiveness as interpersonal attraction: A review of relationships with antecedent and consequent variables. *Psychological Bulletin,* 1965, 64, 259-309.

Lovaas, O. I., Freitag, G., Gold, V. J., & Kassorla, I. C. Experimental studies in childhood schizophrenia: Analysis of self-destructive behavior. *Journal of Experimental Child Psychology,* 1965, 2, 67-84.

Macfarlane, J. W., Allen, L., & Honzik, M. P. *A developmental study of the behavior problems of normal children between 2 months and 14 years.* Los Angeles: University of California, Los Angeles Press, 1962.

Newcomb, T. *The acquaintance process.* New York: Holt, Rinehart & Winston, 1961.

Oakes, W. F. Reinforcement of Bales' categories in group discussion. *Psychological Reports,* 1962, 11, 427-435.

Oakes, W. F., Droge, A. E., & August, B. Reinforcement effects on participation in group discussion. *Psychological Reports,* 1960, 7, 503-514.

O'Leary, K. D., O'Leary, S., & Becker, W. C. Modification of a deviant sibling interaction pattern in the home. *Behavior Research and Therapy,* 1967, 55, (2), 113-120.

Patterson, G. R. An empirical approach to the classification of disturbed children. *Journal of Clinical Psychology,* 1964, 20, 326-337.

Patterson, G. R. Behavioral techniques based upon social learning: An additional base for developing behavior modification technologies. In C. M. Franks (Ed.), *Behavior therapy: Appraisal and status.* New York: McGraw-Hill, 1969.

Patterson, G. R., & Brodsky, G. D. A behaviour modification programme for a child with multiple problem behaviours. *Journal of Child Psychology and Psychiatry,* 1966, 7, 277-295.

Patterson, G. R., & Fagot, B. Selective responsiveness to social reinforcers and deviant behavior in children. *Psychological Record,* 1967, 17, 369-378.

Patterson, G. R., & Gullion, M. E. *Living with children: New methods for parents and teachers.* Champaign, Illinois: Research Press, 1968.

Patterson, G. R., & Harris, A. Some methodological considerations for observation procedures. Paper presented at the meeting of the American Psychological Association, San Francisco, September 1968.

Patterson, G. R., McNeal, S., Hawkins, N., & Phelps, R. Reprogramming the social environment. *Journal of Child Psychology and Psychiatry,* 1967, 8, 181-195.

Patterson, G. R., Littman, R., & Bricker, W. Assertive behavior in children:

A step toward a theory of aggression. *Monographs of the Society for Research in Child Development,* 1967, 32, No. 5, (Serial No. 113).

Peterson, D. R. Behavior problems of middle childhood. *Journal of Consulting Psychology,* 1961, 25, 205-209.

Precker, J. A. Similarity in valuings as a factor in the selection of peers and near authority figures. *Journal of Abnormal and Social Psychology,* 1952, 47, 406-414.

Premack, D. Toward empirical behavior laws: I. Positive reinforcement. *Psychological Review,* 1959, 66, 219-223.

Prugh, D. G., Staub, E., Sands, H., Kirschbaum, R., & Lenchan, E. A study of the emotional reactions of children and families to hospitalization and illness. *American Journal of Orthopsychiatry,* 1953, 23, 70-100.

Quay, H. C. Personality dimensions in delinquent males as inferred from the factor analysis of behavior ratings. *Journal of Research in Crime and Delinquency,* 1964, 1, 33-37.

Quay, H. C., & Quay, L. C. Behavior problems in early adolescence. *Child Development,* 1965, 36, 215-220.

Quay, H. C., Sprague, R. L., Werry, J. S., & McQueen, M. M. Conditioning visual orientation of conduct problem children in the classroom. *Journal of Experimental Child Psychology,* 1967, 5, 512-517.

Ray, R. S. The training of mothers of atypical children in the use of behavior modification techniques. Unpublished master's thesis, University of Oregon, 1965.

Reid, J. B. Reciprocity and family interaction. Unpublished doctoral dissertation, University of Oregon, 1967.

Rheingold, H. L. The modification of social responsiveness in institutional babies. *Monographs of the Society for Research in Child Development,* 1956, 21, No. 2.

Rosenfeld, H. M. Approval-seeking and approval-inducing functions of verbal and nonverbal responses in the dyad. *Journal of Personality and Social Psychology,* 1966, 4, 597-605.

Rosenfeld, H. M. Nonverbal reciprocation of approval: An experimental analysis. *Journal of Experimental Social Psychology,* 1967, 3, 102-111.

Schaeffer, H. R., & Emerson, P. The development of social attachments in infancy. *Monographs of the Society for Research in Child Development,* 1964, 29, No. 3.

Shah, S. Training and utilizing mother as the therapist for her child. Unpublished manuscript, National Institute of Mental Health, Chevy Chase, Md., 1967.

Sheppard, W. Operant control of infant vocal and motor behavior. *Journal of Experimental Child Psychology,* 1969, 7, No. 1, 36-51.

Shirley, M. A behavior syndrome characterizing prematurely born children. *Child Development,* 1939, 10, 115-129.

Skinner, B. F. *Verbal behavior.* New York: Appleton-Century-Crofts, 1957.

Sidowski, J. B. Reward and punishment in a minimal social situation. *Journal of Experimental Psychology,* 1957, 54, 318-326.

Straughan, J. H. Treatment with child and mother in the playroom. *Behavior Research and Therapy,* 1964, 2, 37-41.

Szasz, T. S. *The myths of mental illness: Foundation of a therapy of personal conduct.* New York: Hoeber & Harper, 1961.

Tharp, R. Psychological patterning in marriage. *Psychological Bulletin,* 1963, 60, 97-117.

Thibaut, J. W., & Kelley, H. H. *The social psychology of groups.* New York: John Wiley & Sons, 1959.

Thorne, G. L., Tharp, R. G., & Wetzel, R. Behavior modification techniques: New tools for probation officers. *Federal Probation,* 1967, 31, 21-26.

Verhave, T. *The experimental analysis of behavior.* New York: Appleton-Century-Crofts, 1966.

Wahler, R. G., Winkel, G. H., Peterson, R. F., & Morrison, D. C. Mothers as behavior therapists for their own children. *Behavior Research and Therapy,* 1965, 3, 113-124.

Walters, R. H., & Parke, R. D. Social motivation, dependency, and susceptibility to social influence. In L. Berkowitz (Ed.), *Advances in experimental social psychology.* Vol. 1. New York: Academic Press, 1964.

Weiss, R. L. Studies in emitted reinforcing behavior. Paper presented at the meeting of the Western Psychological Association, Honolulu, Hawaii, 1965.

Wolf, M. M., Mees, H. L., & Risley, T. Application of operant conditioning procedures to the behavior problems of an autistic child. *Behavior Research and Therapy,* 1964, 1, 305-312.

Wolking, W., Quast, W., & Lawton, J. MMPI profiles of the parents of behaviorally disturbed and nondisturbed children. Paper presented at the meeting of the American Psychological Association, Los Angeles, 1964.

Zimmerman, E. & Zimmerman, J. The alteration of behavior in a special classroom situation. *Journal of the Experimental Analysis of Behavior,* 1962, 5, 59-60.

8: Self-Regulation: Research, Issues, and Speculations

FREDERICK H. KANFER

The capacity of the human organism to develop means for regulating his own behavior in the absence of immediate consequences in the physical or social environment has long been an intriguing topic for speculation and theorizing. Many basic personal relationships and social organizations depend upon the individual's capacity for adequate self-regulation since social rules are generally not enforced by continuing and immediate reinforcement of each response chain in the vast and complex range of human activities. Thus, the simple social demand for self-control of many behaviors is tantamount to a prerequisite for participation in the social community.

Personality theorists have postulated a variety of conceptual structures, such as the moral instincts, the superego, or the conscience as hypothetical self-regulatory mechanisms in human affairs. These directing systems are presumed to govern such divergent behaviors as conformity to social rules, postponement of immediate satisfactions, self-evaluation and self-correction of one's own behavior in relation to social norms, inhibition of acts which are harmful to other organisms, and many others. The acquisition of self-regulatory mechanisms necessary for the socialization of the child has often been postulated either in terms of

This paper was written for presentation at the 1967 Institute on Behavior Modification in Clinical Psychology at the University of Kansas. Since its delivery, rapid strides have been made in the use of self-control procedures in the clinic; and recently completed research has aided in the clarification of the underlying mechanisms. The essential points in this paper have not required revision of our views, however. On the contrary, the most recent data have tended to support the general view of the amenability of self-regulation mechanisms to a behavioral analysis.

The paper was completed in conjunction with research supported in part by Research Grants MH 06921-05 and MH 06921-06 from the National Institute of Mental Health, U.S. Public Health Service. The author's studies on self-reinforcement which are reviewed here have been conducted with support from NIMH, under the same or prior research grants.

human predispositions toward behavior consistent with societal rules by some "inner moral agent," or by the assumption that a fully developed complex of behavioral rules is "internalized" early in the child's development as a product of intimate child-parent relationships and conflicts.

Recently, there has been increasing interest in analyzing these complex behaviors from a behavioristic viewpoint. Skinner (1953) has defined the *self* as "simply a device for representing *a functionally unified system of responses*" (p. 285). The behaviors associated with self-regulation can be considered as one important subsystem of personality. From this point of view, the area of self-control is amenable to investigation, in principle, by the same methods as other response systems, and the origins of particular self-regulatory behaviors are traced to learned experiences. However, behavioristic formulations are not without difficulties because the critical antecedent conditions and even the behavioral components in a self-controlled sequence may lie entirely in the domain of private experience. Further, self-control implies that the same person is cast in the role of subject and object of the behavior. At the same time that the person is purveyor of the independent variables which affect his behavior, he also responds to these variables as he carries out the behavior under their control. Since these self-regulatory responses are often inaccessible, there arises the additional problem of accounting for some reinforcing process by which these responses are selectively strengthened.

Perhaps it is this entanglement with methodological and conceptual difficulties which has slowed research in the area of self-control in the behavioristic camp until recently. The rapid expansion of behavior modification techniques has highlighted the urgent need for consideration of this problem area. Even during the early stages of the development of behavioral engineering techniques, it has become apparent that principles of modification based only on the use of continuous environmental control are insufficient for the treatment of most psychiatric problems, for long-range modification of social attitudes, or for improvement of educational techniques. In almost all instances the behavioral engineer, by whatever other name the therapist may be called, finds himself forced to rely on the actions of his subject to maintain behavior changes, even when they have been initially obtained by direct environmental manipulations.[1]

In this paper no attempt will be made to cover the numerous theoretical constructions which have attempted to account for human self-regulation, nor will we cover the many experiments which have relevance to the topic. In keeping with the goals of the presentations at this Institute, the central portion of this paper will report the author's investigations and the problems and implications associated with this area of research. After a review of selected experiments germane to the problem of defining the area of self-control, we will turn to a series of studies on self-reinforcement. This section will attempt to summarize empirical findings about one essential ingredient for the behavioristic conceptualization of self-control, i.e., the motivational component by which S can maintain, or change, his own actions. The subsequent section will deal briefly with the relevance of these investigations for behavior modification approaches. In the following section we will discuss some methodological and theoretical problems posed by the characteristics of the behavior encompassed in self-regulatory events and the limitations of current philosophical and methodolgical approaches to the study of "subjective" segments of human behavior. A final section will offer some theoretical speculations which might serve as the foundation for further refinement of research methods and practical applications in the study of self-control. Inherent in the consideration of the issues in this paper is the quest for a clearer definition of self-control, one which is more consistent with experimental findings, even though it does not overlap with the popular conception of self-control as a constant personality trait.

SELF-CONTROL AS A SPECIAL RELATIONSHIP BETWEEN RESPONSES

Skinner (1953) has defined the process of self-control as one in which an "organism may make the punished response less probable by altering the variables of which it is a function. Any behavior which succeeds in doing this will automatically be reinforced. We call such behavior self-control." (p. 230). Skinner illustrates a number of methods for exercise of self-control, all of which involve the manipulation of *controlling responses* in such a way that the contingent *controlled response* becomes either impossible or less probable. Of eight techniques which Skinner uses to illustrate the process of self-control all but two accomplish the reduction of the probability of the controlled response by prior manipulation of the subject's social, physical, or physiological environment. The applications of self-reinforcement and self-punishment in self-control are considered more difficult. In both cases the question arises whether these are simply special cases under which a chain of responses is interrupted because an alternative (a controlling response) is followed by greater positive reinforcement than the original sequences, or whether the administration of self-punishment provides escape from even more aversive conditions (e.g., guilt) associated with the chained behavior.

In this discussion of self-control Skinner appears to deal primarily with the process by which a controlled response is reduced in frequency, or is inhibited. A broader definition would include cases in which a response is facilitated despite its noxious effects. Thus, at least two separate cases of self-control can be distinguished: (1) the case in which a highly valued event or reinforcing stimuli is available *ad lib.* and the subject *fails* to execute a behavior, and (2) the case in which a behavior is *executed* despite its known aversive consequences. In most human situations, commonly considered to lie in the domain of self-control, the response under question has conflicting consequences. It is only when the controlled behavior has immediate positive reinforcing value and long-range aversive consequences (e.g., drinking or smoking), or it has immediate aversive consequences but long-range positive effects (e.g., heroic acts, tolerance of pain) that any question at all arises whether the person is exercising self-control.

In both cases, strengthening of the "resistance to temptation" or increasing tolerance of aversive stimuli usually involves the provision of supplemental controlling variables to counteract the effects of the precurrent reinforcer. In neither case can the behavior be changed in the absence of such strong variables nor can it be expected to endure when parameter values of these variables change to reinstate the earlier balance.

Ferster (1965) distinguishes three forms of self-control. The most widely encountered form concerns performances that alter the relation between the individual's behavior and his environment so that ultimately aversive consequences to the person are reduced. The control of eating behavior in an obese person is an example of this first form. A second form of self-control involves the performance of behaviors which increase a person's long-range effectiveness, even when the consequences are long delayed. Engaging in such educational activities as piano practice or study illustrates this form of self-control. A third form involves the alteration of the physical environment rather than the person's behavior. Ferster's analysis suggests the importance of examining the consequences of all self-control in optimizing the individual's relationship to his social and physical environment for the eventual obtainment of reinforcers available in the given cultural and physical setting.

Aronfreed (1964) postulates a somewhat different process underlying the various forms of self-control. He emphasizes the importance of self-critical behaviors which inhibit socially punished responses because of their anxiety-reducing properties, acquired as components of earlier punishment in the child.

> Once a child has had some contact with punishment for transgression, it will experience anticipatory anxiety in the intervals which occur between subsequent transgressions and the occurence of punish-

ment. Certain of the stimulus components of punishment can therefore acquire value as signals for the attenuation of the child's anticipatory anxiety, since they mark the end of the interval of anticipation. . . . When the punitive behavior of socializing agents includes the verbalization of labels or standards, a criticism can accordingly attain, like any other component of punishment, some anxiety reducing significance for the child. The child can then provide itself with anxiety reducing cues following a transgression even in the subsequent absence of a socializing agent, by reproducing the criticism (Aronfreed, 1966, pp. 108-109).

Stress on the role of anxiety in self-control tends to put the burden of self-regulatory behaviors mainly on inhibitory mechanisms.

In a series of experiments investigating variables affecting the delay of gratification (Mischel & Gilligan, 1964; Mischel & Metzner, 1962; Mischel & Staub, 1965), Mischel has examined the case of self-control in which the reward is present and S fails to take it. Self-control was defined by the investigators as the ability to postpone gratification in choosing a delayed but larger reward over an immediate smaller one. Such variables as a person's generalized expectancies for the reinforcement consequences of either choice, the subject's reinforcement history, situational manipulations, the reward value of the choice item, and the duration of the temporal delay were among those which determined the experimental outcomes. These findings point to the utility of widely practiced methods of altering the probability of immediate reward consummation by training, promises or modifying the desirability of the reward. The paradigm is useful in illustrating the *relative* nature of self-control. In these studies E retains control over the future delivery of rewards even though the child's choices are generally honored. The situation resembles other practical situations in which individuals postpone reward consumption for the sake of natural long-range consequences not completely under their control. A classic example is that of the highly disciplined spendthrift who foregoes immediate pleasures for the sake of later ones. The possibilities of currency devaluation, depression, robbery or similar external interventions tend to weaken such "self-controlling" behaviors as long as the ultimate consequences remain uncertain.

Bandura and Walters (1963) have discussed several behavior manifestations of self-control. Among these are considered: (1) situations in which a social reward is delayed or withheld, and the degree of self-control is assessed by the individual's capacity to tolerate such delay; (2) situations in which a desired object is inaccessible or not readily obtainable. Self-control may be maintained by devaluating the goal object, especially if the person can select a reference group whose members mutually reinforce devaluating behaviors; (3) situations in which there is temptation to engage in deviant behaviors. Resistance to such temptation represents a manifestation of self-control; and (4) situations in which self-control is manifested when a person sets explicit standards for his own performance and makes self-rewards contingent on achievement of such performance.

Early manifestations of self-control are usually encouraged during childhood training. Regardless of their conceptual framework, most authors call attention to the frequent and continuing reinforcement of self-regulatory behaviors, especially the *nonexecution* of response during the child's early socialization training. For example, in early toilet training or in training a child not to handle fragile objects, the consequences of inhibiting such behavior often consist of the adult's administration of large measures of approval, material rewards, or other reinforcement associated by words and action to the child's controlling behavior.

The critical requirement for a definition of self-control in the tolerance of noxious stimulation is the availability of responses to S which are incompatible with at least some elements in the behavioral chain leading either to receipt of the aversive stimulation or the response to it. Since the cues for these antagonistic responses can be self-administered, the observer is often moved to conclude that the person's actions represent disciplined voluntary acts which defy natural behavioral principles, when, in fact, such a conclusion is based on an incomplete analysis of the controlling variables. In a demonstration of the effects of simple controlling responses on the tolerance of painful ice water immersion of the hand, Kanfer and Goldfoot (1966) provided either verbal responses or external distractions to different groups of female students. Tolerance time was significantly affected by the availability of these controlling responses and greater tolerance was observed in Ss for whom external stimulation was provided. The study illustrates, in principle, the modifiability of "self-controlling" behavior by the mechanisms suggested in a behavioral analysis of this process. The dearth of knowledge of the particular variables and training conditions needed for application of these principles to common human problems or in clinical treatment indicates not so much a lack of power of the behavioristic analysis but the inadequacy of previous formulations of self-control as voluntary, characterologically fixed behavior.

The sufferance of noxious stimulation, and especially the apparent "voluntary" procurement of pain stimuli has often been characterized as an illustration of abnormal behavior in clear contradiction of common motivational principles. There are many examples in the literature of situations in which both rats and men seem to seek out noxious stimulation. For example, D'Amato and Gumenik (1960) present data to suggest that humans prefer immediate over randomly delayed shock.

The relevance of such studies for an understanding of self-control lies in their demonstration that time-limited observation of behaviors cannot serve as the sole basis for a behavioral analysis. Sandler (1964) has reviewed a series of experiments in which characteristic responses to pain in animals were modified by experimental operations. Both Sandler (1964) and Brown (1965) conclude from their analyses of masochism that the disregard of other relevant variables, e.g., change in the biological state of the organism, or the presence of some other contingencies in the organism's history, often leads to deceptively narrow definitions. In such situations it is probable that the momentary observation reflects only a fragment of a behavioral episode in which conflicting avoidant and approach responses have intricately related histories determining their respective dominance at any point in time. Appeal to such concepts as the "breakdown of self-control" for these behaviors serves to obscure rather than explain the process under observation.

In this section we have reviewed some definitions of self-control and illustrated by examples the nebulous boundaries and incomplete analyses of behavioral situations included under the term "self-control." A common feature of the class of events discussed under this term appears to be an organism's execution of responses which are regarded, from the observer's perspective, as inconsistent with a simplistic hedonistic principle or a correspondingly oversimplified drive-reduction or reinforcement principle. It further appears that at the time of observation, the observer cannot describe a particular compelling set of concurrent controlling stimuli in the environment whose operation would account for the behavioral outcome. When dealing with complex and multiply determined human behavior, the observations are the more baffling because the determinants of the observed behavior may be related to highly idiosyncratic antecedent factors of which the observer has little knowledge. The demonstrations that the unusual outcomes of natural situations can be replicated by selection of particular antecedents in controlled laboratory studies may be sufficient at this stage to suggest that the ultimate origin of self-regulatory behavior lies in the social and biological environment of a person, as it does in E's operations during an experiment. Such a view does not eliminate the distinction of a class of behaviors which fall under the rubric of self-regulation. It does suggest that this class only presents a special case which can be handled within an environmentalistic learning theory framework, albeit with much additional work needed in explicating the specific process by which such control is acquired by the individual. It also makes it imperative to work toward a definition of self-control which yields more fruitful experimental paradigms than is possible with surplus meanings of self-control as a case of exception to behavioral principles.

MECHANISMS FOR SELF-REGULATION

The success of self-regulatory behaviors requires that the person be able to initiate some behavior which, in turn, influences the probability that he will execute a specific class of subsequent responses. We will consider here three possible areas for study of self-regulatory behaviors. Perhaps the most difficult area for experimental analysis lies in ascertaining the contributions of autonomic responses (respondents) in self-regulation. The problems are connected both to the relative inaccessibility of these behaviors to observation and their presumed immutability under training. Nevertheless, the respondent control of operants remains one important channel for self-regulation. A second source of self-regulation lies in verbal responses. The flexibility and economy of verbal behavior and its frequent inaccessibility to observation represent many advantages for its use in self-regulation. Verbal control of other verbal or of motor behaviors is so commonly required that its absence would totally incapacitate a person for all social interactions. Yet, only few studies have dealt with the acquisition of such control and the parameters under which it breaks down. A third area deals with the motivational aspects of self-regulation. When behavior is maintained without external reinforcement, the individual may supply some parallel motivating operation in the form of self-reinforcement as a substitute for the environmentally supplied consequences. The exploration of this area aims to disclose the behavioral mechanisms which have enabled humans to persist in or to change their actions with relatively less dependence on their environment than infra-human organisms.

The Role of Respondents

The manner in which information is utilized when arising from "internal" cues such as those provided by autonomic responses has long been of interest. In one form or another, the problem has been posed as early as the days of the James-Lange theory. The early questions revolved about the relative contributions of physiologic and verbal operant responses to emotional behavior and the temporal or "causal" sequence of their occurrence. The major questions of interest here concern the capacity of the human organism (a) to utilize internal biologic events as discriminative stimuli for operants, and (b) to control in turn the frequency or intensity of such respondents by operants.

Research by Schachter and his coworkers (Schachter & Singer, 1962; Schachter & Wheeler, 1962) has demonstrated the importance of verbal labeling responses as determinants of S's self-report about his physiological activity. Labeling of the internal state as a given emotion appears to vary as a function of S's capacity to identify the conditions in which the autonomic arousal takes place. It follows that self-descriptive or self-evaluative statements need not be related to the particular physiological state which is a component of actual current functioning. The behavior which follows the "emotion" therefore depends on numerous psychological variables rather than solely on the biologic state. Nisbett and Schachter (1966) provide an example of the extent to which the behavioral consequences of an objectively invariant pain stimulus can be varied by verbal directions. In different groups the usual physical side effects of shock were attributed either to a placebo or to the shock, and S's level of fear was manipulated by instructions leading to high or low expectations of discomfort due to shock. Reported pain was lower and shock tolerance was greater when shock-produced autonomic symptoms were attributed to the placebo pill than when attributed to shock. It would also be expected that divergent self-regulatory mechanisms may be called into play under conditions which elicit highly similar respondents, associated with the history of the person in regard to labeling these cues and to appropriate actions to be taken. The behavioral episode illustrates an operant-respondent overlapping chain of responses, the connections of which have been gradually shaped and differentially developed in the person's individual history.

The hypothesis of differential labeling and use of information provided by respondents finds support in the many studies on emotions. In the clinical area, correlations between questionnaire scores on statements about frequency of somatic symptoms and neurotic self-descriptions (Korchin & Heath, 1961) also suggest the wide range of individual differences in attending to body function cues and in their use as cues for further actions.

Direct experimental evidence of the effects of information about autonomic feedback on subsequent behavior has been provided by Valins (1966, 1967). In one experiment, male students viewed slides of seminude females. Experimental groups were led to believe that they were hearing an amplified version of their heartbeat while watching the slides. In control groups the identical sounds were offered but they were not associated with S's heartbeats. On selected slides some students heard their alleged heart rate increase markedly while others heard a marked decrease. In comparison with the slides on which no change occurred, Ss rated slides to which they heard a marked change, either increase or decrease, as significantly more attractive and significantly more desirable as remuneration for their participation in the study. In contrast, control Ss to whom the sounds were not interpreted as their own heartbeats, showed no differences in their ratings of the slides as a function of sound increase or decrease. Further, Valins found that feedback of alleged heart rate increases had a greater effect than the feedback of alleged decrease. In a subsequent study Valins (1967) used a similar procedure with subjects who had been rated as emotional or unemotional in prior testing. He found somewhat greater effects of the bogus heart rate changes on attractiveness ratings in Ss who had psychometrically been classified as emotional. The greater susceptibility of emotional persons to such autonomic cues, real or fancied, is consistent with frequently reported clinical observations. It also suggests the possibility that self-regulatory behaviors would occur under a wider range of conditions in neurotics than in normals. These examples of recent research in the field of emotions seems to leave little doubt that operants associated with descriptions of internal states, whatever their content validity may be, function as critical determinants of subsequent behavior.

A second question about the role of respondents in self-regulation concerns the capacity of humans to utilize respondent behaviors in ways which would permit their enhancement of self-control, by serving as controlling responses for other behaviors. For instance, one method of self-control would consist either in manipulation of autonomic responses so that later links in a chain of contingent undesirable behaviors would no longer occur (illustrated by the clinical practice of anxiety-reduction therapy), or in the relabeling of presumably unchanged autonomic behaviors so that new behaviors can be substituted in the chain (as practiced in some persuasion therapies).

Lang (1968) has reported several studies in which Ss achieved control over their visually monitored cardiac rate. The experimental Ss were able to decrease variability of their heart rate so that its corresponding visual indicator was maintained within a predesignated area. Further research by Lang, Sroufe and Hastings (1967) indicated that such control was effective when the Ss were given accurate feedback and were told the true purpose of the task, but not for Ss to whom the display was presented as a tracking task, or who were misinformed. These findings confirm earlier reports from Shearn (1962) who has reported that respondent behavior can be brought under operant control. Demonstrations of the modifiability of respondent behavior in humans suggest one of the means by which men may regulate their own behavior.

Kimble (1961) summarizes several other studies reporting "voluntary" control over respondents and suggests that operant responses might serve as intermediaries because the so-called involuntary or respondent behaviors can be elicited indirectly as byproducts of other operant behaviors. For example, Kimble suggests that operant control of vasomotor responses, GSR, and similar respondents might only require "that the subject become a little tense to acquire voluntary control over the involuntary process" (1961, p. 102). This suggestion helps to save the distinction between the operant and respondent effects of conditioning. Taken together with experimental evidence of the modifiability of respondent behaviors by operant control, it expands the domain in which self-regulation can be exercised.

Verbal-motor Control

While the possibility of the effective control of respondents by verbal responses presents an interesting area of investigation, the verbal control over social or motor behavior has been questioned less often. The natural environment provides ample and continuing evidence of the fact that verbal responses can control the behavior of another person or of oneself under most circumstances. Therefore, it is not demonstration of its feasibility but explanation of the verbal controlling mechanism which is wanting. Possibly related to the widely held assumption of the unusual power of verbal behavior, few systematic investigations have been reported on the parameters which modify the degree of verbal control. For our purpose it will suffice to illustrate briefly the problems in this area by citing some research on the impact of instructions on performance, and on the generalization of verbal learning to specific motor responses.

The facilitation of discrimination learning and concept formation by use of verbal labels has been studied extensively. However, the generalization of training from verbal to content-related nonverbal behaviors has not been subjected to systematic investigation. For example, parameters affecting the degree of verbal control, induced by learning or by instructions, are not well known; the conditions required for self-regulation by verbal control are similarly uncharted; and the range of stimulus functions across verbal and nonverbal modalities has remained relatively unexplored. The role of verbal responses in controlling other motor behaviors in the same organism seems of central importance in the study of self-regulation, since frequent instances are encountered in which a person "knows" or verbally describes a behavioral episode but is unable to execute the behaviors. In such instances the verbal and motor repertoires appear to be uncorrelated. Since such poor association between motor and verbal behavior is infrequent and often of serious social consequence, "dissociation" has attracted more interest among psychopathologists than among students of human learning.

Luria (1961) reports a series of observations in Russian laboratories which focus on the development of the regulatory role of language in children, and on its disruption following cerebral pathology. These experiments trace the self-regulatory function of verbal responses in the young child from the early dependence on cues provided by the environment or by feedback from the child's own motor responses, through stages of partial control of initiating and inhibitory responses by gradual substitution of sensory cues by verbal responses, to the final stages of inner speech for the active control of the environment and for behavioral adaptation. Regardless of their theoretical matrix the experiments reported by Luria demonstrate that 3- to 4-year-olds typically cannot respond to verbal instructions requiring control over their motor response in absence of external stimuli.

One of Luria's experiments has been replicated by S. L. Bem (1967). She found that 3-year-olds were unable to press a lever corresponding to the number of lights previously exposed on a display. To distinguish between a maturational and learning hypothesis, Bem established a training procedure in which the children were first trained to respond correctly in the presence of external feedback. Control of the response was then shifted from external to self-control (verbal self-instruction) by a fading procedure. Successful training demonstrated the useful role of learning in the development of verbal self-control. These experiments do not fully describe the necessary preconditions for the growth of self-regulatory mechanisms, verbal or nonverbal, but they do represent significant support for the hypothesis that self-control evolves out of the social learning context in which extensive external monitoring of behavior is gradually shifted to self-monitoring through continuous guidance and reinforcement from the child-rearing environment.

The relationship between verbal and motor behaviors has been described in simplified reciprocal terms, as if either behavioral response mode could deplete a common reservoir or response-bank (e.g., the cathartic hypothesis in psychotherapy, the need-reduction hypothesis of fantasy). The complexity of these interrelationships has been pointed out repeatedly but only a few studies have examined the actual effects of modifying verbal responses on the occurrence of related motor behaviors. Lovaas (1961) reported that conditioning of aggressive verbal responses increased subsequent nonverbal aggressive behavior in children. In a second study, (Lovaas, 1964) reinforcement of the naming of selected foods during a conditioning session resulted in an increase of actual consumption of those foods. However, these results were not obtained for all Ss and decreased intakes were observed on successive days of conditioning. These studies are suggestive of an experimental method for systematic evaluation of verbal-motor controlling relationships, but their results by no means yield clear evidence of the simple conditioning of motor behavior via verbal control.

Brodsky (1966) investigated the relationship between verbal and nonverbal behavior change in a behavior modification study with two retarded females. One S was reinforced for statements concerning social behavior. A verbal conditioning effect was obtained but not a corresponding increase in observed social behaviors. A second S was reinforced for social behaviors in a controlled setting. Increased social behavior generalized to a natural setting and to verbal interview behavior about social interactions.

These isolated studies point to the feasibility of systematic research on the conditions which are favorable for extension of control from verbal to motor responses but they also raise doubts that general statements about verbal-motor relationships hold over a wide range of parameter values.

Self-reinforcement

Among the techniques described for self-control by Skinner (1953) and by Ferster (1965) are classes of behavior which alter the consequences of a person's behavior to maximize the reinforcement potential of the environment. Self-reinforcement of operant behaviors represents a special type of self-initiated behaviors which can have far reaching consequences in maintaining or modifying almost any behavior in a man's repertoire.

But the act of self-reinforcement is not one that can be easily related to the variables controlling it. Skinner has defined one property of positive self-reinforcement (SR) by stating that it "presupposes that the individual has it in his power to obtain reinforcement but does not do so until a particular response has been emitted" (1953, pp. 237-238). While this supposition emphasizes the contingency of SR on particular discriminative stimuli, it does not provide a full definition of the class of behaviors to be discussed here. Self-administered reinforcing stimuli can be of the positive (SR+) or of the aversive (SR−) kind. Their administration is often contingent not on external events but on the incidence of any of a wide range of previously established responses by the person. For example, self-reward may be predicated on achievement of a given performance level, or on the feeling of fatigue after an exercise. Self-castigation (SR−) may follow a disturbing thought or a disapproved social act.

The research in this area needs to account not only for the variables controlling incidence of SR, but also for the conditions under which a person refrains from continuous *ad lib.* administration of available SR+, and for the conditions under which he withholds administration of SR−, even when it would set the occasion for escape from or avoidance of more painful externally delivered aversive stimuli. To provide firmer grounds for the analogy between reinforcing properties of social or physical stimuli and self-administered stimuli, it is also necessary to demonstrate that the operations designated for SR share some of the motivational, discriminative and maintaining properties claimed for other reinforcing stimuli.

The empirical support for the SR concept provides increasing evidence for a mechanism which has the special function of controlling the person's behavior, independent of momentary environmental circumstances, thereby fostering the autonomy of human organisms.

CURRENT RESEARCH ON SELF-REINFORCEMENT

The bulk of studies of the self-reinforcement process in the laboratory have followed three major paradigms:

The Directed Learning Paradigm

In this procedure, reported by Kanfer and his coworkers (Kanfer, 1965; Kanfer, Bradley, & Marston, 1962; Kanfer & Duerfeldt, 1967a, 1968a, 1968b; Kanfer & Marston, 1963a, 1963b) a reinforcing stimulus is administered by S subsequent to his performance of a task response. The S is instructed to make SR contingent on his judgment that he has made a correct (or incorrect) response. In this procedure the instructions link the SR closely to S's evaluation of his performance. The S is usually exposed first to a learning task on which external reinforcement is provided until a low level of learning is achieved. Such external reinforcement may be contingent or noncontingent on S's performance. After acquisition, S is generally given control over the reinforcing stimulus. He is asked to take over E's function and instructed to continue administration of the reinforcing stimulus when he believes that he has responded correctly. This paradigm has been used to investigate variables controlling the incidence of SRs, the motivational properties of SR and the relationship between SR behavior and other dependent variables commonly investigated in learning tasks. Since the task response continues, its accuracy or latency can be recorded and related to SR. The procedure also permits a distinction between accurate and inaccurate SRs, since correct responses can be defined during acquisition if a contingent reinforcement method of learning is used.

The Vicarious Learning Paradigm

Bandura and his coworkers (Bandura, Grusec, & Menlove, 1966; Bandura & Kupers, 1964; Bandura & Perloff, 1967) have studied the incidence of SR in children as a function of previous observation of modelled SR. The child is first exposed to a model playing a miniature bowling game. Upon attainment of a prearranged score, the model can take self-rewards in the form of candy or tokens from a freely available supply. The score-contingency and criteria for SR are made explicit by the model's verbal comments about the contingencies, self-evaluative statements, and accompanying self-praise or self-criticism. Following the observations, S is asked to play the same game and obtains scores similar to those of the model according to a predetermined program. The dependent variable is generally the number of SRs or trials on which rewards are taken. The design permits control over the child's apparent performance level on the game of skill by manipulation of the scores. It is especially suited for exploration of the effects of parameters of model characteristics and child-model relationships on the transmission of SR behaviors.

The Temptation Paradigm

Several variations of this paradigm have been reported, with varying focus on the relevance of the data to the area of SR. The common elements consist in the provision of *ad lib.* rewards administered at S's discretion, a set of explicit rules describing the proper standards for SR, and apparent lack of control by E to enforce or even to observe S's adherence to the stated contingencies. The E's knowledge of S's actual performance, by observation or constraints built into the task, permits tabulation of S's administration of undeserved or inappropriate SRs. When desirable rewards are made available, the procedure is one which invites behavior commonly known as cheating or dishonesty. Mischel and Gilligan (1964) used a procedure first reported by Grinder (1961) in which children play a shooting-gallery game. The object of the game is to obtain a high score, ostensibly by skillful marksmanship. However, a moving target and rigged score indicator permitted manipulation of scores which were noncontingent on S's skill. The S is asked to keep score himself and prizes are promised for attaining a given level of performance. When E is out of the room, S can cheat on his score-keeping, thus obtaining undeserved prizes. The inflation of point scores represents the inappropriate SRs.

Kanfer (Kanfer, 1966; Kanfer & Duerfeldt, 1968b) used a class procedure in which children were asked to think of a number on each trial, prior to E's drawing a slip from the lottery box. The children were instructed to reward themselves with a point recorded in their scoring booklet, whenever the number drawn by E coincided with their anticipated guess. Since the probability of anticipating E's number (from 0 to 99) more than once in a series of trials is negligible, nearly all points which a child credited to himself constitute underserved SRs.

Other examples of the temptation paradigm have not been directly concerned with evaluation of self-reinforcing behavior within the same conceptual framework as is presented here. Therefore these studies will not be reviewed here. Nevertheless, it is obvious that any procedure in which the administration of rewards is left to S and no apparent aversive consequences are present to hold S to strict conformity to the standards for self-reward, provides data on the variables which modify the dispensation of SR. The procedures in this paradigm are useful for investigation of the effects of population or individual difference variables, of instruction and incentive magnitude variables on the appropriation of underserved SRs.

The experiments following the three paradigms have yielded results which bear differing relationships to the SR concept. Since our own research has mainly used the first paradigm, it will be discussed in detail in this section.

Research with the Directed Learning Paradigm

Using the procedures described above, studies have been conducted which investigated the effects of prior learning, motivation variables, subject characteristics, response form, instructions and other situational variables on the rate of SR. Some data have also been reported on the relationship between SR and other responses. These studies are beginning to form an empirical network from which should emerge an understanding of the antecedent conditions needed for the formation of SR patterns, and of the wide consequences which these patterns may have on other facets of a person's behavior.

Task-competence and Self-reward. When a person performs a well-practiced task with skill and without errors, there are few occasions on which he would stop to evaluate his performance. It is even more unlikely that he would reward or criticize his achievements following his self-assessment, unless his performance on the task were unusually good or bad. While continuous self-monitoring may be common in creative work or during acquisition of a new skill, the smooth execution of simple and habitual operants would be impossible under constant self-surveillance. In fact, effective performance of a response sequence would appear to represent the limiting case in which maintenance of the response chain may occur by feedback from the smooth linkage to following response, provided only when early responses are properly executed. One can only speculate whether SR blends into natural proprioceptive feedback serving to maintain the behavior without specific reinforcing events (cf. Guthrie), or whether the successful termination of the sequence serves the reinforcing function (cf. Skinner). In any event, the monitoring function of self-appraisal and SR appears to play a prominent role mainly when S has low skills, or inadequate criteria for judging his own performance. Under laboratory conditions requirements for over self-monitoring should disclose increased accuracy and frequence of SR+ with higher competence on the experimental task.

Kanfer, Bradley and Marston (1962) investigated the effect of the degree of learning on the subject's ability to administer correct SRs in a concept formation task. Two groups had 25 or 50 acquisition trials and then were instructed to administer self-rewards following correct responses. The results confirmed the hypothesis about the relationship between correct SRs and degree of learning. Thus, the frequency of SRs appeared related to the amount of training on the task for which self-evaluations were required. In a verbal discrimination task, Kanfer and Marston (1963a) obtained similar results when subjects were trained to an accuracy criterion of 0.5, 0.7, and 0.9, respectively. The findings also yielded a striking relationship between the frequency of reinforced correct responses (CR) at the end of the acquisition and the frequency of SRs over a series of test trials. Subjects who had the lowest learning criterion showed a greater excess of SRs over CRs during the test phase than those who were trained to a higher criterion. In addition, poorly trained Ss also yielded higher mean proportions of incorrect SRs than Ss with longer training. These findings support the conclusions that SRs are directly related to S's competence on the monitored task, and that they increase both in frequency and accuracy with longer acquisition training.

Perhaps these findings simply underline the commonplace statement that higher competence on a difficult task results in more frequent self-rewarding behavior which, in turn, maintains accurate performance even when external feedback is no longer available. The regularity of the relationship between rate of external reinforcement during acquisition on one hand and SR rate and the distribution of correct and incorrect SRs on the other hand does suggest that empirical functions between the values of various parameters can be obtained. It also increases our confidence that self-reinforcing responses are subject to control in the same manner as other learned behavior, although they may often be inaccessible to direct observation in everyday behavior.

Once external feedback is shut off, Ss in the experimental procedure tend to maintain a stable rate of SR over long series of trial blocks (Kanfer & Duerfeldt, 1968a; Kanfer & Marston, 1963a; Marston & Kanfer, 1963). The effect of training conditions seems to be mainly in establishing an overall SR rate early during the SR test procedure. This stability has been found in college students (Kanfer & Marston, 1963a), school children (Kanfer, 1966) and retarded children (Kanfer, 1965), and across different experimental conditions. Two exceptions are worthy of note. When the stimulus list in a verbal discrimination list was changed slightly (Kanfer & Marston, 1963a), the mean frequency of SR was initially very low but gradually increased until it approached the rate at which external reinforcement had been given in the final acquisition block. In a study in which S had to make self-critical evaluations (SR—), there was a significant quadratic trend over trial blocks, reflecting an increase from an initially low level of self-critical responses, and a later decrease (Kanfer & Duerfeldt, 1968a). While the effects of cumulative SR— may influence a person's rate of subsequent self-reinforcement, no similar effects have been observed in studies on self-reward (SR+).

The match of SR rate to rate of prior external reinforcement seems to obtain only when the criteria for judging the adequacy of the response are ambiguous. Whether *S*'s matching represents his decision to adopt *E*'s criterion for reward-taking in the absence of any other information, or whether it represents learning of the payoff schedule appropriate for the particular experimental situation is not clear at this time. On post-experimental questionnaires Ss have been found to show distorted estimates of the number of reinforcements delivered by *E* as a function of specific experimental conditions. These results suggest that the matching is neither a verbally mediated nor a deliberate strategy by *S*.

That self-regulation can be more efficient when a person has sufficient familiarity with the task to provide himself with accurate feedback comes as no great surprise. However, the problem of self-regulation is usually crucial in everyday situations only when relative incompetence exists. The cited studies strongly suggest that ignorance on a task, poor performance, and inaccurate feedback may go hand in hand, and that poor performance is, in turn, made worse by these consequences.

Tolerance Limits for SR. The basis for self-evaluation can be shifted by explicit definition of the tolerance range for accurate performance. This variable is expected to modify further the incidence of SRs. Whether a person rewards his own behavior is not only a function of his ability to judge the adequacy of his response but also of the stringency or leniency which he defines for the congruence between his own performance and the designated standards. To test the effects of variation in the tolerance of deviation of a person's own performance from set standards, Kanfer and Marston (1963a) varied instructions for Ss. Three experimental groups received instructions which were intended to facilitate, inhibit, or remain neutral with regard to *S*'s criterion of administering an SR. While the facilitation group was told that the task was a very difficult one, the inhibition group was told to be cautious and to be sure that they were right before taking a reward. These instructions resulted in the predicted differences in SR rates for the groups. A control group closely approximated the terminal rate of external reinforcement during acquisition. The facilitating instructions resulted in almost twice the number of SRs over the number given by Ss in the inhibited group. Further, facilitating instructions yielded increased proportions of incorrect SRs in comparison with the two other groups.

The Role of Incentives in SR. Variation in frequency of SRs can be obtained not only by operations which modify the performance upon which an SR is contingent or by instructional specifications which establish stringent or liberal criteria for administration of SR, but also by changing the immediate consequence of the stimulus employed as an SR. It would seem obvious that increase of the magnitude of the reinforcing stimulus available for self-administration should increase the probability of self-reward, or at least the temptation toward SR. However, in college students participating in a psychological experiment, linear relationships between magnitude of the reinforcer (SR) and frequency of its *ad lib.* administration may not be the rule. In fact, it could be argued that lifelong training prepares the adult subject for more conscientious attitudes and more cautious behavior when the stakes are high. Variation in incentives was carried out in a study by Marston and Kanfer (1963), in which SR consisted of a green light, of poker chips, or of poker chips which could be exchanged for prize packages at the end of the session. An SR phase was introduced after training on a verbal discrimination task to a criterion of 60 percent. It was found that the incentive conditions did not affect the total number of correct responses during the SR test. Further, there were no significant effects of the incentive level among the three groups However, the incentive groups differed significantly in mean proportions of incorrect SRs. Students who were under the high incentive conditions gave fewer SRs following incorrect responses than those in the low incentive conditions. Subjects under medium incentive conditions gave the highest number of SRs following incorrect responses.

In numerous studies we have noted that despite the *ad lib.* availability of points, prizes, or small cash awards, college students did not disregard the task, nor did they procure many reinforcers by continued administration of SR. Instructions required Ss to proceed in orderly fashion through a three link chain, consisting of (a) a correct response, (b) an evaluation of the accuracy of that response, and (c) an SR if appropriate for the given conditions of (a) and (b). Since reinforcement was continuously available, Ss could bypass these instructions and take reinforcers in large numbers. However, a breakdown in the contingency of SR behavior on the instructed response sequence was obtained only when the experimental paradigm was slightly varied. In a study by Kanfer (1964) Ss were trained on a fixed ratio schedule of FR10, FR25, and FR50 for lever pulling. Reinforcement consisted of the dispensation of a penny at the prescribed schedule. When Ss were shifted to SR and asked to administer pennies whenever they felt they deserved them, 6 of the 15 Ss on FR10, 4 of the 15 Ss on FR25, and I of the 15 Ss on FR50 eventually stopped lever pulling at their previous rate and operated the penny dispenser continuously; several additional Ss gave themselves pennies at a high rate with only few interspersed trials. Prior to this breakdown of the procedure, Ss gave themselves SRs at a stable rate, roughly at ratios of half to one third of the values established by *E* during acquisition training. In contrast to the breakdown on this operant task not a single subject behaved in this way among the many hundred subjects run on SR studies with prior learning of a more meaningful task.

With only these exploratory data available one can do no more than hypothesize that the limits of orderly SR performance, contingent on performance of a preceding response, may be reached when the task is not considered meaningful by *S*, when *S*'s interest lags, or when other experimental conditions permit *S* to break through the constraints of the instructions and to maximize his gains by disregarding conventional rules. These observations suggest interesting tentative extrapolations from this analogue to the clinical problems of "loss of self-control" and therefore seem to merit further investigation. Training for restraint in SR behavior, so that it occurs only under socially acceptable (or experimenter-instructed) conditions may be feasible only when there is a favorable balance between the subject's concern with social approval (or experimenter acceptance) and his approach tendency to the available reward. While it is strategically useful to limit incentive conditions intentionally within a modest range of reinforcer magnitudes in order to study effects of other variables on SR behavior, analysis of this dimension in its own right certainly appears necessary.

SR as a Conditioned Reinforcer. In accounts of the genesis of self-reinforcement it is often presumed that such verbal comments as "I did well" or "I was wrong" are at first contemporaneous with the occurrence of external reinforcement. As the child has increasing experiences with language these self-initiated observations also serve as discriminative stimuli in whose presence external reinforcement has a high probability of occurrence. Eventually the self-administered stimuli acquire secondary or conditioned reinforcing properties. It is probable that large sets of responses in an individual's repertoire constitute equivalent classes of verbal self-rewards. Once their occurrence becomes covert, it is difficult to collect observations about their relationships to other publicly displayed reinforcing stimuli. It is also hard to modify their contingency on external events, their magnitude and their reinforcing effects. Once the reinforcer has been made overt in the laboratory, it is possible to change its physical dimensions or the relationship between the external and overly self-administered reinforcing stimulus. Still, no control can be obtained over the subject's simultaneous and covert verbal self-rewards during the acquisition training or during open performance of the SR operation.

In most of the studies which follow the present paradigm, the physical reinforcing event for SR was identical to the one previously used by *E*, differentiated only by the shift of the control to *S*. Operationally, the manipulandum for activating a signal, previously used to report external reinforcement, was handed to S, or he was instructed to take *ad lib.* candy or tokens from the same container out of which E dispensed reinforcement. This procedure has the virtue of providing a manipulandum for SR whose reinforcing properties are established by a similar history for all Ss during training. It also literally turns over administration of reinforcement to S.

The relative contribution of the physical similarity of the SR manipulandum to the external reinforcing stimulus is of interest. Is it necessary that an actual overt, pretrained, and clearly discriminable signal function as a SR? Kanfer and Marston (1963a) compared two groups who differed in the physical characteristic of the reinforcing stimulus. Both groups were given a switch which E had used to turn on a green reinforcing light during previous training. However, in one group the green light was disconnected for the SR procedure. The presence or absence of the light signal had no significant overall effect on the frequency of SRs, or on correct responses. However, these groups were elements in a factorial design and some interesting interactions were observed. When the task was made more difficult by changing the original list of stimulus words at the same time, the light enhanced correct responding with the changed list, suggesting its possible additional utility as a discriminative stimulus. The frequency of SRs was not affected, but the proportion of incorrect responses was reduced in the presence of the light when the original training list was changed. The experimental control for conditioned reinforcing effect in SR work with humans becomes difficult because E cannot ascertain whether some verbal response by the subject might not be contiguous with external reinforcement and continued during SR. However, there is probably sufficient communality among people's experiences to warrant combined treatment of many conditioned reinforcers, verbal or physical, which could function alternately in self-regulation.

Further evidence to support the suggestion that the particular physical characteristics of the reinforcing stimulus may not be essential for its effectiveness was obtained by Marston (1964). Five different tasks were used in a self-reinforcement design, and SR consisted in procuring a green light, or a poker chip, or in making a confidence rating. It was found that there were significant effects due to the form of the SR manipulandum on only two of the tasks. In these two tasks the rating method yielded a slightly higher incidence of SR than chip-taking or light-pressing responses.

While the particular instruments for obtaining rewards or indicating self-criticism may be interchangeable under many conditions, there is apparently as little comparability between self-rewards and self-criticisms as there is between externally administered positive and negative reinforcing stimuli. Kanfer and Duerfeldt (1968a) studied the relative effects of training on an ambiguous task either by 50 percent positive or 50 percent negative noncontingent reinforcement by E on a frequency of either self-rewarding (SR+) or self-critical (SR—) responses during training. Additional groups received both positive and negative reinforcement in training and either SR+ or SR— on testing. If S transposes without bias the information obtained from positive and negative external reinforcement during training, both self-rewards and self-criticisms should occur at a complementary rate. Therefore, under a 50 percent training schedule the rates of SR+ and SR— should be comparable. These predictions assume that the particular mode in which S expresses his self-evaluations has little bearing on his judgment in a two-choice task whether he was correct or not. But the data clearly show that self-criticisms (SR—) were made significantly less often than self-rewards, regardless of the reinforcing mode used in training. In this study, Ss who could administer self-rewards matched closely the 50 percent rate of reinforcement obtained during training. However, groups who could make only self-critical responses ("I was wrong") showed a lower frequency of SR—, ranging from 28 percent to 40 percent. In a later study Kanfer, Duerfeldt, and LePage (1969) found a significant relationship between rates of self-reward in two different experiments using the same Ss. No significant correlation was obtained between self-reward and self-criticism when groups of Ss were shifted to SR— in the second experiment, and SR— rates were significantly below the 50 percent level of prior external reinforcement during training. These findings clearly indicate that the frequency of SRs is determined not only by task performance and other variables affecting S's self-evaluation but also by variables which have direct effects on the basal frequency of the type of SR administered.

If such differing existing base rates are associated with self-rewarding and self-critical responses, the prior history of individual Ss with regard to these behaviors becomes an important factor to be considered. In clinical populations, any discrepancy between such base rates for self-critical and self-rewarding behaviors would have further implications for the constancy with which (externally) nonreinforced behaviors are maintained. For example, persons with a tendency to give many self-critical responses should show greater variability of behaviors which are externally not reinforced. Responses which are under a low intermittent schedule, or for which there is no external feedback at all, would tend to persist longer in Ss whose rate of self-rewards is high than in Ss whose rate of self-criticism is high. If self-reinforcement has any reinforcing properties at all, such divergency should increase individual differences not only in laboratory learning studies but also in the maintenance of everyday behaviors which are acquired under tutelage until they reach an asymptotic level and then mainly under the person's own control.

Motivational Properties of SR. The most significant function of self-rewards and self-criticisms has been the assumed potentiality of these responses to affect preceding behaviors. In verbal learning studies workers have repeatedly observed that Ss develop consistency of performance even in the absence of external feedback. Such response "fixation" during extinction on laboratory tasks has been attributed to self-reinforcement for contingent matchings of S's current response against a remembered past response. In supporting of this suggestion Butler and Peterson (1965) demonstrated the tendency of Ss to repeat the same overt responses during extinction, whether a correct response or error.

In the SR paradigm, Marston and Kanfer (1963) found that the preceding critical task response (CR) is maintained at the same strength over a long series of blocks on which external SR was available, in contrast to a decline in an extinction group and an increase in a continued acquisition group under similar experimental conditions. The effects of SR on the preceding CR have been reported only incidentally in several studies which were designed to evaluate mainly the effects of different variables on SR frequency. For example, Kanfer and Marston (1963a) found that Ss decreased in response accuracy when SRs were given indiscriminately, thereby providing self-reinforcement following many incorrect responses. Bandura and Perloff (1967) compared the relative efficacy of self-monitored and external reinforcement and found that external and self-reinforcement sustained substantially more manual work responses in children than either noncontingent reward or no reward.

Verbal learning tasks do not lend themselves readily to a test of the motivational effects of SR because a verbal response does not decline rapidly in strength once it is learned. In a study by Kanfer and Duerfeldt (1967b) the motivational effects of SR were examined in a perceptual task. Noncontingent reinforcement was administered for matching a tachistoscopically presented sample from four response choices (geometric figures). Since each sample item was presented only once, changes in S's report accuracy could be attributed to nonassociative effects of the reinforcing stimulus. When the residual effects of external noncontingent reinforcement and SR were compared during subsequent extinction, Ss in the SR group gave significantly more accurate recognitions than in other groups. The results demonstrate the nonassociative facilitative (motivational) effects of SR training and suggest that withdrawal of external feedback is of less consequence after SR training.

Individual Difference Variables and SR. The base rate of self-criticisms and self-rewards is often viewed as an important personality parameter. If motivational properties are associated with such base rates, it could be hypothesized that differential self-learning and self-maintenance of social behaviors may constitute one of the mechanisms by which diversity of personal behaviors is facilitated. Several studies have pointed to the probable difference in SR rates associated with personality test scores or membership in special populations. Marston (1964), using an SR procedure, reported that Ss who had high faith in their ability to control the environment (measured by Rotter's Internal-External scale) showed significant increases in SR over trials, while "external control" Ss decreased over trials. In the same study, highly task-oriented Ss (measured by Bass' Orientation Inventory) increased in SR over trials while interaction and self-oriented Ss did not change. Kanfer, Duerfeldt and LePage (1969) permitted Ss to administer *ad lib.* SRs on a time-estimation task. In an ostensibly unrelated word-association task the same Ss were instructed to self-administer either SR+ or SR— after training under noncontingent 50 percent reinforcement by E. The two tasks were given in different laboratories and by different Es, and postexperimental questionnaires demonstrated that the Ss perceived the tasks as unrelated. Those Ss who gave themselves many SR+ on the first task also did so on the second task ($r = 0.68$). The Ss were divided into high and low self-rewarders on the basis of their performance on the time-estimation task. High self-rewarders exceeded low self-rewarders on the word-association task in the SR+ frequency. However, rates of SR+ responses on the time-estimation task and SR— responses on the word-association task were not correlated ($r = -0.07$). These findings suggest that SR+ patterns may represent cross-situational individual personality characteristics of some stability, whereas SR+ and SR— patterns are relatively independent behaviors.

Kanfer (1966) found that third and fourth grade boys in an SR procedure differed in frequency of incorrect SRs as a function of their assignment by their teacher to the upper or lower half of their class in general class performance. Low performers showed no differences in partial learning of the visual discrimination task but they gave significantly more incorrect SRs than children rated to be in the upper half of their class. In the same study, these children also tended to show lower resistance to temptation and their performance in the two experimental conditions showed a moderate significant correlation of $r = .45$. In a later study (Kanfer & Duerfeldt, 1968b) the relationship between resistance to temptation and teachers' ratings were again found in children from second to fifth grade. The frequency of undeserved SRs decreased significantly with increasing age. When visual-motor cues were added to enhance commitment by the child and to provide clearer criteria for SR, inappropriate self-rewards also decreased. With self-criticism (SR—) as the dependent variable, Marston and Cohen (1966) found that Ss who scored high or low on intropunitiveness (scored from a modified Rosenzweig P-F test scale) administered significantly fewer SR— than Ss in the medium range of scores. In this study Ss who were frustrated by exposure to difficult problems for which insufficient time was allowed, also gave themselves more SR— than Ss who were not frustrated.

Additional research on self-regulatory behaviors in patient populations would be of great interest because individual self-reinforcing patterns may, in fact, constitute the basis for the diagnostic description of deviant behaviors. For example, the failure to provide sufficient self-initiated feedback may retard behavioral output, as in depressions; while indiscriminate self-reinforcement of the self-critical type might be expected in the neurotic and of the self-rewarding type in the grandiose personality. These conjectures are currently not supported by research but appear worthy of pursuit. One study on mental retardates has been reported (Kanfer, 1965) which used the directed learning SR paradigm. Adolescents with IQs ranging from 43 to 77 showed maintenance of an SR rate close to the rate of previous external reinforcement, similar to normal controls. However, unlike the normal Ss, the retarded Ss did not decrease in correct responses, nor in frequency of SRs, when an extinction phase was interpolated between acquisition and test for SR.

The Relationship of SR to Self-Evaluation, and Conditioning of SR

Realistic self-appraisal has often been suggested as the logical basis on which a person judges his own behavior, when no external consequences are present to permit an objective assessment of the effectiveness of one's behavior. This presumed relationship is of special interest to psychotherapists because on it rests the hypothesis that more accurate self-knowledge (insight) brings about desirable changes in other daily behaviors which depend on the person's accurate self-perceptions. Therefore, changes in the self-concept would result in further self-induced behavioral changes, in congruence with newly established criteria for SR that are closer to those of the social community. Cautela (1965) and Aiken, Dicken and Grossberg (1965) have reported evidence that changes in verbal self-evaluation do not necessarily modify other instrumental behaviors. Kanfer and Duerfeldt (1967a) used the SR paradigm to test the effects of experimental manipulations of self-evaluative statements on later self-evaluations and on the frequency of self-criticisms (SR—). It was found that favorable and unfavorable evaluations of S's performance by E during training significantly influenced later self-evaluations. However, changes in S's statements about his own performance were not accompanied by corresponding changes in the rate of self-critical responses. The latter (SR—) responses matched approximately the rate at which the negative reinforcer had been dispensed by E during training.

The rate of SR itself can also be affected either by direct reinforcement for its emission (Kanfer & Marston, 1963b), or by models whose SR rates are imitated (Bandura & Kupers, 1964). Since the latter case involves use of a different paradigm it will be discussed later. However, the findings of these and previously mentioned studies suggest that it is possible to modify separately a person's verbal reports about himself, his actual criterial performance, and the rate at which he rewards or punishes himself for his behavior. Continuing inconsistencies between these three classes of behaviors in an individual can result in reduced effectiveness in interpersonal relationships, clinically viewed as behavior pathology, because they tend to produce inconsistent consequences from the social environment. The separate origins of these behaviors in the history of psychiatric patients is therefore often of great interest to the clinician. The further implications of these research findings suggest that separate modification of each of these behaviors may be necessary in therapy, and corresponding changes in a person's self-evaluations, self-reinforcing behaviors and instrumental behaviors cannot always be taken for granted.

Self-criticism and Self-reward. The use of negative self-reinforcement in the directed learning paradigm has suggested that the rate of SR— may be subject to change by similar variables as SR+ but that SR— rates are generally lower than the rates of external negative reinforcement in training (Kanfer & Duerfeldt, 1968a; Marston & Cohen, 1966). If information from the environment were processed on a logical basis and if it were used without bias about the mode in which the self-originated feedback is delivered, self-rewards and self-criticisms should have equivalent effects in monitoring one's own behavior. The studies by Kanfer and Duerfeldt (1968a) and Kanfer, Duerfeldt and LePage (1969), cited above, suggest that there may be different response systems associated with self-rewards and self-criticisms, even though both sets of response classes may share some common properties. Further comparions of SR+ and SR— behaviors would be of special interest with regard to the comparability of the consequences of these different SR modes in their impact on other behaviors, their respective resistance to change by new information, the width and slope of generalization gradients, etc. In fact, many of the questions raised in discussion of the relative effects of positive and negative external reinforcement appear pertinent in the study of SR+ and SR— effects.

Research with the Vicarious Learning Paradigm

Among a series of studies investigating the influence of modelling or vicarious learning in children, Bandura and his coworkers have reported the modification of self-reinforcement by prior exposure to models who execute self-reinforcing behaviors. The most potent variables shown to affect SR behavior were the characteristics of the model, his relationship to S, the standards set for SR and the discrepancy between model and S standards. Since reviews of many of these studies can be found in summaries of research on vicarious learning (Bandura, 1965a; 1965b) only a brief review is given here.

With the bowling game as a vehicle, Bandura and Kupers (1964) found that children who observed adult models tended to match closely the SR patterns exhibited by their models, with regard to the criterion for which they rewarded themselves with freely available candy. In addition, self-approving and self-critical verbalizations given by models were imitated by the children. Peer models were not as effective as adult models in setting standards for nonreinforcement of low-level performance. Further, a higher percentage of the children who had observed peer models exceeded the magnitude of candy rewards taken by the model on each occasion than those who had seen adult models. In an attempt to separate the effects of apparent model competence from the rate at which SR is taken by the model, Marston (1965) examined the effects of observation of SR administration in college Ss on a word association task. In addition, Marston also used groups who alternated with the model. Some Ss could give SRs during the observation trials, while others could only respond. During the observation trials, the presence of a model tended to decrease S's SR rate, regardless of the model's rate of SR. However, on postobservation trials the model's rate of SR resulted in group differences. The Ss who heard a higher SR rate by the models took significantly more SRs than the low model groups.

The adoption of criteria for SR by model observation has an interesting consequence not only on S's self-evaluation but also on his own evaluation of others. Marston (1965) found that Ss also reinforced another person at a higher rate after observation of a high-SR model than a low-SR model. These findings are similar to those of Mischel and Liebert (1966) who used the bowling game procedure with children and found that the criteria S imposed on another child tended to be identical with those imposed on himself.

The adoption of criteria for self-reward depends not only on the model's performance but also on the model's imposition of standards on S. Mischel and Liebert (1966) reported that this interaction effect resulted in more lenient criteria-adoption for children whose criteria were different from those manifested by the model. The role of demonstrator for other children was more consistent with the observed model-role when the demonstration occurred prior to rather than following the child's own performance.

The adoption of high criteria for SR is not a direct function of observation of a model alone. Bandura and Whalen (1966) used the bowling game procedure after the children had undergone success or failure experiences on games appearing to measure physical strength, problem solving ability and psychomotor dexterity. Groups of children saw models play the bowling game who set high, moderately high or low criteria for SR. The results showed that different effects of treatments were found for varying performance levels in the expected direction. The prior experience of success or failure did not influence SR rates at this level. At a low level of performance, however, children who had a failure experience rewarded themselves less often after observation of inferior models, while children in the success condition took more SRs than those who observed equally competent superior models. The results point to the complex interaction between modelling cues, prior history, and performance as joint determinants of SR administration.

The effects of combinations of prior nurturant interaction with an adult model, observation of reinforcement to the model, and additional observation of a peer model with low criteria for SR were examined by Bandura, Grusec and Menlove (1966). The authors expected model nurturance and vicarious reinforcement to increase and peer modelling to reduce imitation of stringent criteria for SR. It was found that observation of model reinforcement resulted in adoption of more stringent criteria, while model nurturance and exposure to lenient peer models led Ss to adopt more lenient criteria for SR. The studies by Bandura and his coworkers suggest that the acquisition of SR patterns during childhood is governed by exposure to numerous situations which serve to provide conditional determinants guiding behavior in later tasks. Among these, the child's familiarity with and skill on the task, his experience with adults with whom he can identify on the task, the expectations set for his performance by adults have now been demonstrated to be effective variables. It is probable that not only additional environmental determinants but also self-originated stimuli, e.g., self-competition (Swingle, Coady & Moors, 1966) and feedback from past performance in a wide variety of related behaviors will be noted to influence acquisition of SR patterns for specific performances.

The review of work on SR to date has begun to define some characteristic properties of this response class which can briefly be summarized by the following general statements, applicable when the task is ambiguous.[2]

SR behavior:

(1) can be modified by social reinforcement.

(2) is affected by S's competence on the task for which it is given.

(3) tends to match or exceed slightly the rate of prior external reinforcement (for self-reward).

(4) tends to remain below the rate of prior external reinforcement (for self-criticism).

(5) tends to remain stable over many trials.

(6) maintains the preceding response better than extinction.

(7) can be generalized to another task.

(8) tends to show correlations in individuals across dissimilar tasks, and with such related behavior as cheating.

(9) is related to some personality variables.

(10) can be transmitted by modelling.

(11) can be maintained independent of self-evaluative statements.

(12) is affected by the response mode (SR+ or SR−), and these modes are not reciprocal.

(13) can be modified by instructions about the stringency of criteria to be adopted for SR.

(14) is influenced by the magnitude of the reward obtainable by the SR response.

(15) is related to the reinforcement schedule under which the evaluated response is acquired.

(16) depends on the specific instrumental response selected (e.g., verbal or motor) for representation of SR only in conjunction with other variables.

(17) shows some small long range effects in modifying the accuracy level of a preceding response, especially if the SR− mode is used.

(18) tends to affect S's judgment of the performance of another person on the same task.

These early findings suggest that continued exploration of the role of SR in human self-regulation may be fruitful in describing the conditions under which self-regulatory processes develop and function in social behavior. The potential utility of the SR paradigm is also shown by the consistency of results under many different conditions and their relative independence of the specific laboratory operations used for measure of the response.

CLINICAL IMPLICATIONS

A major criticism of early learning approaches to psychiatric problems has been the superficiality of any technique aimed exclusively at behavior change. It has been argued by dynamic therapists that only reorganization of the personality, removal of unconscious blocks, or exposure of unconscious wishes can bring about lasting changes. Symptom removal or learning of more effective behaviors has been viewed solely as incidental by-products of change in more fundamental psychological processes. The criticism appeared especially cogent because early instances of behavioral approaches concentrated on symptoms which consisted of overt motoric responses and were easily controlled by direct environmental manipulations. These therapeutic approaches have been most dramatic in use with institutionalized psychotics and children. Due to the extensive control available with these populations, consequences of symptomatic behaviors can be relatively easily changed and a wide range of reinforcers can be used in acquisition and maintenance of new behaviors. In adult neurotics, the greater independence of the problematic behaviors from the controlling social environment has posed problems in definition of the target behavior, in arranging more favorable response-reinforcement contingencies, and in providing effective reinforcers (Kanfer & Saslow, 1965). These problems seemed especially difficult with patients whose symptomatic behaviors consisted mainly of private responses which are usually covert, unshared, often inaccessible, and not under direct environmental control. Furthermore, these behaviors constitute what have been called "mental events" and, on methodological and philosophical grounds, they were excluded from the early behavioristic systems.

The challenge to a behavioristic approach in clinical psychology lies in demanding that a good theory of human behavior provide engineering principles which cover *all* human functions, or handle the full range of problematic behaviors which have been tackled by traditional psychotherapies. The clinician recognizes in his daily contact with patients that a person's habitual patterns of response to his own past experiences, to his biological functions, to the variables controlling his behavior, and to his potential for dealing with his environment and himself are powerful determinants of his actions. Knowledge of the relationships governing the genesis and operations of these classes of "self-responses" is an essential requirement, if clinical practice is ultimately to be based on a science of psychology. While technological advances can be made on an essentially pragmatic basis, a science of human behavior and its derived engineering principles cannot ignore or exclude the domain of behaviors which govern the individual's actions in relation to himself and are only initiated or distantly maintained by his social and physical environment.

The importance of self-reinforcement in psychotherapy has been noted even in the earliest learning formulations of the therapeutic process (e.g., Shaw, 1946; Shoben, 1949). For these authors, the lifting of repression and subsequent insight pave the way for constructive planning which is regulated by the patient's self-reinforcement. Recent developments in behavior therapy give evidence of the growing awareness of the necessity for inclusion of "self-reactions" in the treatment of behavior problems. Homme (1965) has proposed the term "coverant" for a class of operant responses whose main distinguishing characteristic is their relative inaccessibility to observation. These response cover events commonly described as thinking, imagining, fantasying, etc. Homme (1966) suggests their amenability to control by the same general principles as hold for other operants. The use of self-controlling procedures in the treatment of behavior problems has been discussed by Goldiamond (1965) which illustrates the feasibility of applying similar methods in the modification of one's own behavior as in the modification of the behavior of another. In extending aversion therapy procedures, Cautela (1966) has substituted covert CS and US presentations with obese and alcoholic patients. Davison (1968) has reported use of self-controlled counterconditioning sessions in the treatment of a sexual problem. Techniques in which the patient assumes some part of the therapist's role are not an innovation of behavior therapy. The importance of self-regulation in achieving happiness has been stressed by ancient philosophers and moralists and is encountered in many religions. Behavior therapists differ not in applications of these general techniques but in their efforts to incorporate them into a theoretically consistent model of behavior modification and to provide the patient with supplementary behaviors which make self-regulation easier. Kanfer and Phillips (1966) have described a group of procedures, under the term *instigation therapy*, which have in common the general method of helping the patient to exercise control over his own environment and to modify his own behavior. The usual steps in these techniques involve training the patient in self-observation, in evaluating and categorizing his behavior, in planning to rearrange his environment or his own acts on the basis of learning procedures, and in providing self-reinforcement for maintaining improvements. The many advantages of these techniques are described elsewhere (Kanfer & Phillips, 1966).

Ultimately, most patients leave therapeutic supervision. It is apparent that training in self-control can help not only to shorten the therapeutic process but also to maintain and extend the changes initiated in therapy. Training in self-reinforcement for appropriate new behaviors has been used by the author in the context of clinical interviews as well as in systematically programmed training by eliciting self-evaluative responses to the patient's taped report of social interactions, followed by reinforcement from the therapist. The procedure has been found useful for adult patients and for children who live in an unfriendly or solitary environment and who cannot rely on external feedback for evaluation of their own behavior. It has also been used to supplement efforts at self-control of symptomatic behaviors, and to maintain planned programs in patients with serious behavior deficits.

The introduction of instigation therapy techniques among behavior therapies proceeds toward closer integration of interviewing and conditioning methods and expands the scope of learning-theory derived methods. The systematic use of training in self-control for "autotherapy" may be easier when data accumulate about the characteristics of people who can benefit most from such procedures, and about specific techniques which can provide more economical training for patients than is provided in the experimental efforts reported so far.

An experimental analysis of self-control also helps to foster interest in the study of specific techniques by which a person can learn to arrange his own behavior to maximize the attainment of socially sanctioned reinforcers. The contemporary cultural attitude implies that self-control is an active, conscious and unitary process, and that its function is to inhibit socially undesirable behavior. In literature and in religious writings it is often regarded as man's noblest character trait and the explicit assumption is made of man's dual nature, the good and evil. When "loss" of self-control is pictured as the person's submission to ever-present irrational and evil urges, then it is reasonable to emphasize treatment methods which aim mainly at reestablishment of control, inhibition over desires and impulses, and training in the tolerance of hardships and deprivations. Such "control-restoration" methods may sacrifice more effective treatments.

It is likely that the same view also serves to maintain many pathological behaviors. A patient who justifies his deviant behaviors repeatedly by saying: "I cannot control myself," or "I do not know what makes me do it," is often viewed as mentally ill, deviant or at least temporarily incapacitated in controlling his actions. The practical consequences of these attitudes is that many of the patient's previously punished deviant behaviors are now tolerated with sympathy. Social expectations of the patient are modified and responsibility for his actions may be assumed by social agents. The most common examples encountered in the clinic are of the juvenile delinquent who verbalizes his lack of control for the purpose of self-justification and avoidance of punishment, or the neurotic whose demands for support and special treatment are based on his plea that he cannot control his fears, his hypochondriacal concerns, or his depressive thoughts. The views expressed here suggest a therapeutic strategy which includes rejection of the patient's statements about his inability to control himself as an explanation of his problems, and incorporation of training in specific self-controlling and appropriate self- reinforcing behaviors, or use of environmental intervention as part of the treatment program.

Another potential use of the self-reinforcement and self-control procedures described in the preceding section, lies in their adaptability for diagnostic purposes. Patterson[3] has used the SR procedure with patients to obtain data on their rate of SR as a pre- and posttherapy measure. With a standardized procedure SR+ and SR— frequencies, the discrepancies between those rates, their resistance to change under controlled procedures and the extent of their generalization to related standardized tasks may yield useful samples of patients' self-attitudes. While the experimental methods reported above are crude procedures, they do suggest the possibility of a battery of tests for assessing self-responses which hold greater promise for standardization and quantification than current projective tests covering a similar range of behaviors.

SOME ISSUES AND SPECULATIONS

The crucial problems of observing and changing the psychological processes involved in the control of human behavior when they proceed in the same individual upon whom control is to be exerted involve many philosophical, methodological and substantive questions. An underlying philosophical issue which has been extensively debated since the advent of behaviorism concerns the separation of behaviorism as a philosophical doctrine, closely related to the physicalism of Carnap and the Vienna circle, and behaviorism as a set of rules for scientific methodology. The rich inheritance of our cultural past and the constant contrast between a model of human functioning based strictly on a behavioristic philosophy and the commonsense dualistic models encountered in our daily lives make it difficult for the clinician and the researcher to operate professionally in one framework and to discard this framework in all other roles in daily living as parents, citizens, lovers, friends, and so on. Consequently, the multiple impacts of patients, competent nonpsychological professionals and institutional or agency policies, as well as the coarse experiences and descriptions which the patient presents to the clinician make it even harder to maintain an "artificial" appearing behavioral orientation (and language) in the clinic than in the laboratory.

A further dilemma of the behavioral scientist and engineer lies in the fact that the objects of his observations are organisms whose behavior is somewhat known to him by his own experiences. Chemists or physicists are not likely to succumb to the temptation of placing themselves in the position of their subject matter, since intentions, goals or fears are rarely assigned to chemical or physical objects under study. The interchangeability of E and S would appear to give the psychologist enormous advantages over his fellow scientists. The assumption that "After all, we are all pretty much alike" (Bakan, 1956) has apparently not served as a catalyst but rather as a diversion along the path toward a theory of human behavior. Perhaps, the advantage of E's capacity for anticipating S behaviors needs to be more clearly confined to the domain of hypothesis-formulation (the "context of discovery") and more rigorously excluded from data collection and data processing activities (the "context of verification").

The errors of introspectionism and phenomenology have been to assume a) verbal reports are based on observation of existing inner mental events, and b) that these events are faithfully depicted by the reports. Behaviorism attempts to tackle the same phenomena by observations of behavior and by assuming that the genesis and change of behaviors which constitute "consciousness" are ultimately determined by the social community. The specific content of covert responses is traced back to originally overt responses and corresponding experiences of the individual, eventually leading to self-observations. These self-observations are given the status of data language similar to that of responses observed in another person. This position has been widely criticized. The clearest basis for the objections has been presented by Malcolm (1964), who calls the treatment of first-person-present tense sentences the Achilles' heel of behaviorism. Malcolm asserts that statements about one's feelings, plan, or other *self-testimony* are not based on self-observations, nor are they verifiable against physical events or circumstances other than the person's own testimony. Consequently, "self-testimony is largely *autonomous,* not replaceable even in principle by observations of functional relations between physical variables." (Malcolm, 1964, p. 154). Behaviorism is found lacking because it regards man as *"solely an object."*

Chomsky and his group attack behaviorism on somewhat similar grounds for its failure to grant some preprogrammed proclivity for ordering language and thoughts. A nativistic assumption fits better some of the remarkable capacity of the child to acquire competence not in speaking specific sets of utterances but a well-articulated language, by transformation of abstract rules for speech-part relationships (Chomsky, 1965; Katz, 1966). Recent information processing and computer-simulation models also propose that complex "structural" characteristics of psychological functions can explain universalities in covert processes in a way which differs radically from the simplistic S-R view that "subjectivity" and the content of covert responses can be accounted for by a combination of learning and social variables, acting within the limits of the biologically given universality of capacity for various behaviors.

These problems in agreement on the degree to which human thought processes and other covert behaviors are genetically determined present major obstacles to research in self-regulation.

Firmly established views about the nature of voluntary behaviors, free will, conscious awareness and similarly complex and partly covert intraindividual processes have bolstered the historical bias for acceptance of a different model for human behavior than for that of infrahuman organisms, not on a basis of greater complexity but on the assumption of emergent phenomena mainly associated with man's use of language. There are many current efforts to extend the behavioristic formulation to areas of problem-solving (e.g., Goldiamond, 1966; Skinner, 1966), to self-perception (D. J. Bem, 1965, 1967), verbal conditioning (Kanfer, 1968; Krasner, 1962; Verplanck, 1962), awareness (Maltzman, 1966) and other areas. Nevertheless, the role and mechanisms of covert behaviors and the general problem of handling events in which the same person is actor and object of action in momentarily shifting roles have not yet been resolved in a satisfactory way. It would seem to be the burden of those who urge the behavioristic model to continue their efforts to encompass these phenomena and to demonstrate their ultimate origin in the social-verbal environment, molded by the particular structural and functional characteristics of the human biological organism. They must show that environmental influences can, and do, originate and modify subjective experiences. Without incorporation of these phenomena into the behavioristic model it is quite probable that the days of even a methodological behaviorism are numbered. It is the author's belief that the study and understanding of self-regulatory processes occupy a central position in this area of controversy.

The clinical utility of behavioristic models may be limited to pragmatics. Current behavior modification clinicians appear to operate at two levels. New methods for observation of behaviors and for modifying specific target behaviors seem to derive well from learning methods and principles. In creating new procedures for treatment (and for diagnosis) an expanded store of techniques is becoming available for application to increasingly diverse problems. However, in decisions about selecting the target for therapy, in predictions of the probable effectiveness of procedures and in hundreds of momentary judgments about the patient and his response to various methods, clinicians of all persuasions shift to the commonsense model, drawn from their personal histories and other nonpsychological resources. While this compromise does retain the "human element" in treatment, it is important to recognize it as a compromise. Perhaps this facet of clinical work represents the art component encountered in any applied science. Even if the therapist's basis for application of his techniques is not fully understood, knowledge of the patient's capacity for self-regulation and of means by which it can be modified would still contribute toward more effective and economic procedures for behavior modification.

The specific task in the study of self-regulation concerns demonstration of the processes by which a person can modify his own behavior, with accounts of conditions which initiate the modification efforts, of the methods and mechanisms used for the modification, and of the cessation of modifying efforts.

If such terms as self-regulation or self-control are used, it is necessary to specify the limits of the types of behaviors which would fall into these categories. This requirement raises first the question about the continuous vs. temporary nature of self-regulatory processes. Reflection suggests that the simple definition of self-control as either (1) the omission of behavior which would lead to attainment of rewards or avoidance of punishment, or (2) the commission of acts which have known aversive consequences, appears to be inadequate because it would cover thousands of easily observed examples in daily life in which behavior seems to be under such control without any apparent intentional or special intervention by the person himself. Further, there appears to be a cultural definition inherent in the use of the term "self-control." In many instances occurrence or nonoccurrence of the same response will consensually not be accepted as examples of self-control, depending upon the circumstances. For example, it is trivial to consider as an instance of self-control a healthy adult's failure to wet his pants. But the same behavior in a 3-year-old child might be used as such an example. Thus, the *nonoccurrence* of many behaviors which may have had earlier functions in procuring reinforcing events is not sufficient evidence for self-regulation.

It appears that the process of self-regulation must have at its origin strong motivational components which are related to the physical or social environment of the person. In continuous daily adult behavior, there are points at which self-regulatory processes begin, and the cues for the onset of such processes need to be examined. On a speculative basis it is proposed that self-regulatory processes begin when self-monitoring of behavior reveals a departure from a band or range of consensually acceptable behaviors in a situation which may have ultimate aversive consequences. To explain the nature of this self-monitoring process one can take recourse to early learning when a mother, teacher or other adult functions as monitor for young children by interfering only when a particular behavioral sequence shows some properties which are either excessive or deficient with regard to the band of behaviors appropriate for that situation. Such training in self-monitoring is facilitated when the trainer labels the cues for detecting deviations and assists in rectification of the behavior by direct training or by permitting the child to observe corrections. To some extent, a useful model may be one that is similar to the feedback circuitry involved in quality control analysis. At first the feedback loop affects only the mother of a child and brings into play corrective behaviors by the mother. Eventually direct feedback to the child is established and the necessity for mother's labelling and corrective responses no longer exists. Such a hypothesis would propose that self-regulation is *not* a continuous process, but is invoked as a self-correcting procedure only when discrepancies, cues of impending danger, or conflicting motivational states activate the monitoring system.

The implication of this approach is to deny the existence of a unitary and continuously acting inhibitory mechanism. Rather, it is suggested that the onset of self-controlling responses depends on the individual's learning history and on situational cues. The notion is also rejected that self-control is an internalized personality trait which affects the person's pattern of moral behaviors, guilt, shame or other secondary social controlling techniques. The latter may be conceptualized as related but independent of self-controlling processes, based on separate developmental histories. Our line of thought suggests that self-regulatory behaviors are not always socially effective or desirable. Only if the person has had experiences under conditions similar to the current one and is familiar with the cultural expectations for the range of appropriate behaviors will his self-controlling behavior be adequate. A simple example is that of a foreigner who makes a faux pas, recognizes its deviational quality because of social signals from spectators, proceeds to modify his own behavior but often does so only to aggravate the situation because of his lack of socially prescribed standards for it. Similarly, self-control by administration of aversive stimuli may have only detrimental social effects.

We propose then that learning to monitor one's behavior is an essential prerequisite for the proper application of self-regulation and self-control. As a corollary, it would be expected that adequate self-control is encountered to a greater extent in individuals who have had better training in self-observation and self-monitoring, and who can activate the self-regulatory process when called for. The deviations from the culturally determined and commonly agreed behavioral band may be in terms of physical response characteristics, functional consequences, rate of the behavior, or any other characteristic.

Our view of self-regulation leads us to consider self-control as a special case of self-regulation. While self-regulatory behaviors generally result in some modification of one's own behavior or of the environmental setting, self-control is characterized as a special case in which there is some underlying motive for *nonexecution* of a response sequence which, under other circumstances, would be predicted to have a high probability of occurrence. Self-control always involves a situation in which there is potentiality of execution of highly probable behaviors, but instead a response of lower probability occurs. The interest is in the variables which effect the reduction of the occurrence of the probabilities of such behaviors. Self-regulation also includes instances in which simple adjustments occur, shifting the relative probabilities of a set of behaviors. These changes may follow self-monitoring or any event which leads the person to change his behavior toward greater effectiveness. For example, poor results from use of a paint brush may result in use of a different brush, washing it, or abandonment of the project. Such a behavioral episode involves self-regulation as defined here, but not self-control.

A number of cues for the onset of self-monitoring behaviors seem to be available. Among these are: (1) Intervention by others, e.g., the threat of punishment, or focus on one's own behavior by an external event. A mother's critical comment or a boss's low performance rating for a specific job are examples in this class. (2) The presence of extreme activation levels, either excessively high or low may serve as cues for self-monitoring. For instance, physiological feedback of hyperactivity, excitement, emotional states, boredom, depressed behavior, may serve such cue functions for self-monitoring. (3) The failure of predicted consequences to occur as the result of one's own behavior may occasion self-monitoring. Such cues are illustrated by a person's failure to achieve anticipated physical consequences, e.g., operation of an unfamiliar car does not lead to starting the engine, telling a joke in a social setting does not lead to laughter, a verbal response fails to exert control over a physical or social stimulus object. (4) The availability of several different roles or response sets, as encountered in most "choice" behaviors, can trigger self-monitoring.

A separate and somewhat subordinate question concerns the particular mechanisms which are available to the individual in a culture for control over problematic behaviors, once these behaviors are recognized and labeled as problematic by the individual. The description of these mechanisms constitute the main content of research in self-control. Demonstrations of the regulation of behaviors by "conscience," "guilt," or other devices for establishing self-control represent technical descriptions of methods for achieving the desired end, i.e., for modifying the probability of occurrence of a highly probable response without use of direct external contingency relationships between the response and its immediate social consequences. It is also in this area that some motivational constructs, such as self-reward and self-punishment mechanisms, are required in order to invoke learning principles applying to motivated behaviors. Controls initiated by the person may involve the utilization of secondary positive *or* negative reinforcers. They may involve manipulation of the environment or of other response probabilities in the person's repertoire, or the utilization of verbal behaviors for the purpose of rearranging contingencies under his own control. It is this area in which expanded knowledge may bring both improved conceptual models of human functioning and more effective methods for behavior modification.

NOTES

1. The current applications of behavioral analysis and modification techniques to social institutions, ranging in size from family units to entire school systems, raise the interesting question whether social engineering can eventually produce environments which neither develop nor maintain socially undesirable behaviors. But even in Skinner's utopia (Walden Two), self-control requires extensive and early training. By its very nature of inaccessibility to constant social monitoring, self-regulation may remain refractory to complete social control, to the relief of champions of free democratic societies and advocates of social systems permitting change and nonconforming variations.

2. Task-ambiguity in the laboratory situation represents an analogue to the natural conditions under which SR is most likely to occur, i.e., when a response chain is not smoothly operating to produce the (expected) habitual effects on the social or natural environment. This point is discussed in the last section.

3. Personal communication, 1966.

REFERENCES

Aiken, E. G., Dicken, C. F., & Grossberg, J. M. Self-concept conditioning and rehabilitation. *Research Report*. Proj. RD-892. Western Behavioral Sciences Institute, 1965.

Aronfreed, J. The origin of self criticism. *Psychological Review*, 1964, 71, 193-218.

Aronfreed, J. Conduct and conscience: The socialization of internalized control over behavior. Unpublished Manuscript (1966).

Bakan, D. Clinical psychology and logic. *American Psychologist*, 1956, 11, 655-662.

Bandura, A. Behavioral modification through modeling procedures. In L. Krasner & L. P. Ullmann (Eds.), *Research in behavior modification*. New York: Holt, Rinehart & Winston, 1965. (a)

Bandura, A. Vicarious processes: A case of no-trial learning. In L. Berkowitz (Ed.), *Advances in experimental social psychology.* New York: Academic Press, 1965. (b)

Bandura, A., Grusec, J. E., & Menlove, F. L. Observational learning as a function of symbolization and incentive set. *Child Development,* 1966, 37, 499-506.

Bandura, A. & Kupers, C. K. Transmission of patterns of self-reinforcement through modeling. *Journal of Abnormal and Social Psychology,* 1964, 69, 1-9.

Bandura, A. & Perloff, B. Relative efficacy of self-monitored and externally imposed reinforcement systems. *Journal of Personality and Social Psychology,* 1967, 7, 111-116.

Bandura, A. & Walters, R. H. *Social learning and personality development.* New York: Holt, Rinehart & Winston, 1963.

Bandura, A. & Whalen, C. K. The influence of antecedent reinforcement and divergent modeling cues on patterns of self reward. *Journal of Personality and Social Psychology,* 1966, 3, 373-382.

Bem, D. J. An experimental analysis of self-persuasion. *Journal of Experimental and Social Psychology,* 1965, 1, 199-218.

Bem, D. J. Self-perception: An alternative interpretation of cognitive dissonance phenomena. *Psychological Review,* 1967, 74, 183-200.

Bem, S. L. Verbal self-control: The establishment of effective self-instruction. *Journal of Experimental Psychology,* 1967, 74, 485-491.

Brodsky, G. D. The relation between verbal and nonverbal behavior change. MA thesis, University of Oregon, 1966.

Brown, J. S. A behavioral analysis of masochism. *Journal of Experimental Research in Personality,* 1965, 1, 65-70.

Butler, D. C. & Peterson, D. E. Learning during "Extinction" with paired associates. *Journal of Verbal Learning and Verbal Behavior,* 1965, 4, 103-106.

Cautela, J. H. Desensitization and insight. *Behavior Research and Therapy,* 1965, 3, 59-64.

Cautela, J. H. Treatment of compulsive behavior by covert sensitization. *Psychological Record,* 1966, 16, 33-41.

Chomsky, N. *Aspects of the theory of syntax.* Cambridge, Mass.: MIT Press, 1965.

D'Amato, M. R. & Gumenik, W. E. Some effects of immediate versus randomly delayed shock on an instrumental response and cognitive processes. *Journal of Abnormal and Social Psychology,* 1960, 60, 64-67.

Davison, G. C. The elimination of a sadistic fantasy by a client-controlled counterconditioning technique: A case study. *Journal of Abnormal Psychology,* 1968, 73, 84-90.

Ferster, C. B. Classification of behavioral pathology. In L. Krasner & L. P. Ullman (Eds.), *Research in behavior modification.* New York: Holt, Rinehart & Winston, 1965.

Goldiamond, I. Self-control procedures in personal behavioral problems. *Psychological Reports,* 1965, 17, 851-868.

Goldiamond, I. Perception, language, and conceptualization rules. In B. Kleinmutz (Ed.), *Problem solving: Research, method and theory*. New York: John Wiley & Sons, 1966.

Grinder, R. E. New techniques for research in children's temptation behavior. *Child Development*, 1961, 32, 679-688.

Homme, L. E. Perspectives in psychology—XXIV. Control of coverants, the operants of the mind. *Psychological Record*, 1965, 15, 501-511.

Homme, L. E. Contiguity theory and contingency management. *Psychological Record*, 1966, 16, 233-241.

Kanfer, F. H. Self-reinforcement following operant lever pressing. Unpublished study, 1964.

Kanfer, F. H. Self-reinforcement in retardates. Research report to Oregon State Board of Control, 1965.

Kanfer, F. H. The influence of age and incentive conditions on children's self-rewards. *Psychological Reports*, 1966, 19, 263-274.

Kanfer, F. H. Verbal conditioning: A review of its current status. In T. R. Dixon & D. L. Horton (Eds.), *Verbal behavior and its relation to general S-R theory*. Englewood Cliffs, New Jersey, Prentice-Hall, 1968.

Kanfer, F. H., Bradley, M. M., & Marston, A. R. Self-reinforcement as a function of degree of learning. *Psychological Reports*, 1962, 10, 885-886.

Kanfer, F. H. & Duerfeldt, P. H. The effects of pretraining on self-evaluation and self-reinforcement. *Journal of Personality and Social Psychology*, 1967, 7, 164-167 (a).

Kanfer, F. H. & Duerfeldt, P. H. Motivational properties of self-reinforcement. *Perceptual and Motor Skills*, 1967, 25, 237-246. (b).

Kanfer, F. H. & Duerfeldt, P. H. A comparison of self-reward and self-criticism as a function of types of prior external reinforcement. *Journal of Personality and Social Psychology*, 1968, 8, 261-268 (a).

Kanfer, F. H. & Duerfeldt, P. H. Age, Class-standing and commitment as determinants of cheating in children. *Child Development*, 1968, 39, 545-557 (b).

Kanfer, F. H., Duerfeldt, P. H., & LePage, A. L. Stability of patterns of self-reinforcement. Psychological Reports, 1969, 24, 663-670.

Kanfer, F. H. & Goldfoot, D. A. Self-control and tolerance of noxious stimulation. *Psychological Reports*, 1966, 18, 79-85.

Kanfer, F. H. & Marston, A. R. Determinants of self-reinforcement in human learning. *Journal of Experimental Psychology*, 1963, 66, 245-254 (a).

Kanfer, F. H. & Marston, A. R. Conditioning of self-reinforcing responses: An analogue to self-confidence training. *Psychological Reports*, 1963, 13, 63-70. (b)

Kanfer, F. H. & Phillips, J. S. Behavior therapy: A panacea for all ills or a passing fancy? *Archives of General Psychiatry*, 1965, 15, 114-128.

Kanfer, F. H. & Saslow, G. Behavioral analysis. An alternative to diagnostic classification. *Archives of General Psychiatry*, 1966, 12, 529-538.

Katz, J. A. *Philosophy of language*. New York: Harper & Row, 1966.

Kimble, G. A. *Hilgard and Marquis' Conditioning and learning*. New York: Appleton-Century-Crofts, Inc., 1961.

Korchin, S. J. & Heath, H. A. Somatic experience in the anxiety state: Some sex and personality correlates of "Autonomic Feedback." *Journal of Consulting Psychology,* 1961, 25, 398-404.

Krasner, L. The therapist as a social reinforcement machine. In H. H. Strupp & L. Luborsky (Eds.), *Research in psychotherapy,* Vol. 2, Washington, D.C.: American Psychological Association, 1962.

Lang, P. J. Fear reduction and fear behavior: Problems in treating a construct. In J. M. Schlien (Ed.), *Research in Psychotherapy,* Vol. 3. Washington, D.C.: American Psychological Association, 1968.

Lang, P. J., Sroufe, L. A., & Hastings, J. E. Effects of feedback and instructional set on the control of cardiac-rate variability. *Journal of Experimental Psychology,* 1967, 75, 425-431.

Lovaas, O. I. Interaction between verbal and nonverbal behavior. *Child Development,* 1961, 32, 329-336.

Lovaas, O. I. Control of food intake in children by reinforcement of relevant verbal behavior. *Journal of Abnormal and Social Psychology,* 1964, 68, 672-678.

Luria, A. R. *The role of speech in the regulation of normal and abnormal behavior.* New York: Pergamon Press, 1961.

Malcolm, N. Behaviorism as a philosophy of psychology. In T. W. Wann (Ed.), *Behaviorism and phenomenology.* Chicago: University of Chicago Press, 1964.

Maltzman, I. Awareness: Cognitive psychology vs. behaviorism. *Journal of Experimental Research in Personality,* 1966, 1, 161-165.

Marston, A. R. Personality variables related to self-reinforcement. *Journal of Psychology,* 1964, 58, 169-175.

Marston, A. R. Imitation, self-reinforcement and reinforcement of another person. *Journal of Personality and Social Psychology,* 1965, 2, 255-261.

Marston, A. R. & Cohen, N. J. The relationship of negative self-reinforcement to frustration and intropunitiveness. *Journal of General Psychology,* 1966, 74, 237-243.

Marston, A. R. & Kanfer, F. H. Human reinforcement: Experimenter and subject controlled. *Journal of Experimental Psychology,* 1963, 66, 91-94.

Mischel, W. & Gilligan, C. Delay of gratification, motivation for the prohibited gratification, and responses to temptation. *Journal of Abnormal and Social Psychology,* 1964, 69, 411-417.

Mischel, W. & Liebert, R. M. Effects of discrepancies between observed and imposed reward criteria on their acquisition and transmission. *Journal of Personality and Social Psychology,* 1966, 3, 45-53.

Mischel, W. & Metzner, R. Preference for delayed reward as a function of age, intelligence and length of delay interval. *Journal of Abnormal and Social Psychology,* 1962, 64, 425-431.

Mischel, W. & Staub, E. Effects of expectancy on working and waiting for larger rewards. *Journal of Personality and Social Psychology,* 1965, 2, 625-633.

Nisbett, R. E. & Schachter, S. Cognitive manipulation of pain. *Journal of Experimental and Social Psychology,* 1966, 2, 227-236.

Sandler, J. Masochism: An empirical analysis. *Psychological Bulletin,* 1964, 62, 197-204.

Schachter, S. & Singer, J. E. Cognitive, social and physiological determinants of emotional state. *Psychological Review*, 1962, 69, 379-399.

Schachter, S. & Wheeler, L. Epinephrine, cholorpromazine, and amusement. *Journal of Abnormal and Social Psychology*, 1962, 65, 121-128.

Shaw, F. A stimulus-response analysis of repression and insight in psychotherapy. *Psychological Review*, 1946, 53, 36-42.

Shearn, D. W. Operant conditioning of heart rate. *Science*, 1962, 137, 530-531.

Shoben, E. J., Jr. Psychotherapy as a problem in learning theory. *Psychological Bulletin*, 1949, 46, 366-392.

Skinner, B. F. *Science and human behavior*. New York: Macmillan, Co., 1953.

Skinner, B. F. An operant analysis of problem solving. In B. Kleinmutz (Ed.), *Problem solving: Research method and theory*. New York: John Wiley & Sons, 1966.

Swingle, P., Coady, H., & Moors, D. The effects of performance feedback, social and monetary incentive upon human lever pressing rate. *Psychonomic Science*, 1966, 4, 209-210.

Valins, S. Cognitive effects of false heart rate feedback. *Journal of Personality and Social Psychology*, 1966, 24, 400-408.

Valins, S. Emotionality and information concerning internal reactions. *Journal of Personality and Social Psychology*, 1967, 6, 458-463.

Verplanck, W. Unaware of where's awareness: Some verbal operants—notates, nonents, and notants. In E. E. Jones (Ed.), *Behavior and awareness*, Durham, N. C.: Duke University Press, 1962.

9: Procedures in Common Described by a Common Language

OGDEN R. LINDSLEY

Those readers who know me, know that I believe the "eternally true" statement of the wise man of Ancient Egypt, that "this too shall come to pass."[1] This includes almost everything presented at the Institute upon which this volume is based. The important thing is: How will this change come about? How will the current approaches to behavior modification pass away? Will it require a totally new discipline? Is our legacy no more than 50 years of superstition? Will some bright, young kids, of a decade hence, find us wrong and have to attack and destroy us to bring about change?

I believe that the most important thing about science is that it can modify its own behavior. The more precisely a discipline does this, the more scientific it is. If we in behavior modification can build systems for improving our own performance, then we shall not pass away. Rather we shall constantly improve—the grandfathers who presented information in this volume will all have prolific and successful grandchildren. On the other hand, if we start repeating over and over again some catechism—"stimulus, response, reinforcing stimulus, schedules of reinforcement," ad infinitum, we will change nothing. Then we would end up just as superstitiously redundant and data-poor as the present day Freudians.

Two things are making it difficult for us to change. One is our ex-

This research was supported by Training Grant NB-05362-01, National Institute of Neurological Diseases and Blindness, and Research Grant HD-00870-01. National Institute of Child Health and Human Development from the U.S. Public Health Service, Department of Health, Education, and Welfare to the Bureau of Child Research, University of Kansas.

I extend my gratitude to the other speakers at the Symposium for stimulating and contributing to this summary and to Eric Haughton for his help in recording the rates.

treme popularity. The second is our reliance on verbal stimulation. There are few experienced operant conditioners in the country. The current speaking demand is so great, that the free-operant conditioners are spread extremely thin. For example, you can ask yourself: What new thing has come to free-operant conditioning or to behavior modification in the last 5 years? Most of us are so busy talking that we seldom look and hence more rarely do we discover.

SYMPOSIUM SUMMARY

I was asked to summarize the Institute. My summary will be an experiment. I will use the methods of Behavior Modification to summarize a Behavior Modification Symposium. I will practice what I preach. This is the way to stay relevant. As I struggle downhill from 40 to 60 to 80 to the grave, I will do all I can to keep operant conditioning modifying itself and applying its own principles to itself. For the time being, let us not be content with improving the behavior of an

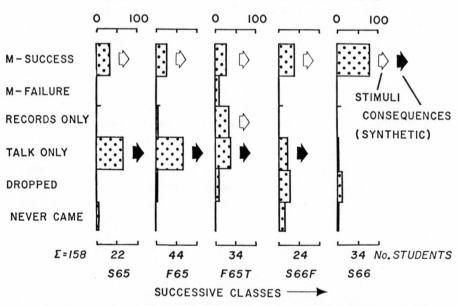

FIGURE 9.1   *Successful modifications increased 228 percent when required for a passing grade in a university course (Education 115). "I" was given for incomplete modification and "F" for falsified data.*

autistic child, when we have one superstitious free-operant conditioner loose at the full professor level.

Figure 9.1 proves that I can take some of my own medicine. This figure indicates my failure for four semesters as a university professor. I spent time spraying words on students, begging teachers to do more than beg their children. I tried to stimulate people into using consequences, and got a 30 percent payoff. Only 30 percent of my class successfully modified a child's behavior when I begged them to do it. These are what I call the "stimulus responders." The rest of them only talked good Behavior Modification—they didn't do any. These glib failures—the "talkers" included my own doctoral candidates; they gave me beautiful excuses in operant terminology of why the child was still wetting the bed at the end of the semester. Obviously, they didn't have a conditioned reinforcer to make the mother do something—but the bed was still wet in the morning. Three or 4 weeks through the Spring semester, it dawned on me that I wasn't taking my own medicine. I wasn't using any consequences. My successful students weren't being treated any differently from the glib failures.

Then I announced, "Kids, the world has changed. I have caught myself making a terrible error. You can drop the course if you want to; but from now on, if you fail to improve a child's behavior beyond the .001 level of confidence, you will receive a grade of 'incomplete,' for 'incomplete modification.' The grade 'F' will be used for 'falsified data'."

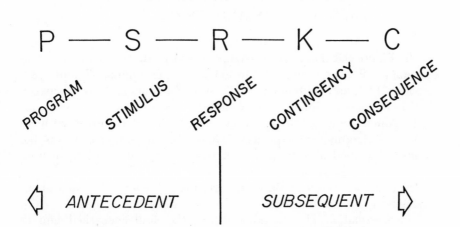

FIGURE 9.2 *Operant Equation used to summarize the content of each presentation of the symposium.*

This procedural change brought about fantastic results: 228 percent successful modification projects because 54 percent of the students turned in more than two projects. I had required only one. With that success, I later increased the requirement to three cases a semester. Already halfway through the semester most have completed their projects. The next requirement will be eight projects—who knows what the upper limit might be. There is only one way to find out!

In Figure 9.2, the basic operant equation is diagrammed. The five basic components of the equation are the program (P)—stimulus (S)— response (R)—contingency (K)—consequence (C). Ferster and Skinner (1957) did almost all their classic research on contingencies. This is really what we were in the later 1950s—world's experts on contingencies. We held responses (pigeon pecking or rat pawing) constant. We held consequences (pigeon grain or rat pellets) constant. We varied only the contingencies to study their effects.

This operant equation was used to analyze the behavior of our symposiasts. I asked one of my most hard working graduate students, Eric Haughton, to sit in the audience and record the comments made by each participant. He used the following categories: (1) the speaker mentioned something about a program (P); (2) he spoke about the stimulus (S); (3) he mentioned something about responses (R); (4) he referred to the contingency (K); or (5) he spoke about the consequences (C). Eric also separately recorded the rates of mentioning accelerating consequences (AC), decelerating consequences (DC) and withdrawing consequences or inconsequation (I).

SUMMARY OF CONTENT OF EACH PRESENTATION AND ITS DISCUSSION

In Figure 9.3, Don Baer's lecture is analyzed. He mentioned programming (P) very seldom—only .06 times per minute. Stimuli (S), responses (R), and contingencies (K) were mentioned at rates between .7 and .8 times per minute. Accelerating consequences (AC) were his most frequent topic; referred to over once a minute! He made no mention of decelerating consequences (DC). Inconsequation (I) was the method, described at a frequency of twice every 10 minutes, he used to eliminate undesirable behavior.

In their discussion of Baer's lecture, the audience asked him about responses (R), contingencies (K), accelerating consequences (AC), and inconsequation (I). In other words, the audience asked him to discuss the traditional free-operant procedures and components—whereas Baer had gone beyond that limited frame of reference in his lecture.

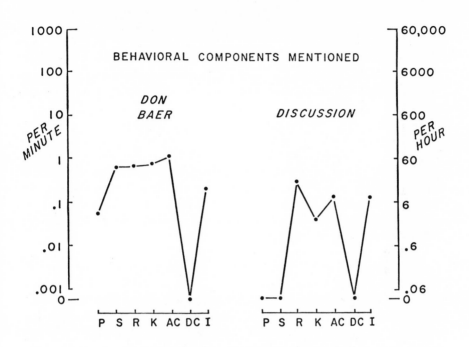

FIGURE 9.3 *Baer's lecture is low on programming and totally avoids decelerating consequences. The discussion tries to narrow him further by ignoring his references to stimuli.*

He received no question about the stimuli that he mentioned as often as he did responses!

If such discussions function as accelerating consequences to Baer, he could become a mere caricature of his former self as the audience shapes his lectures to fit their mold!

Figure 9.4 presents Ivar Lovaas's lecture rates. It is a pretty even profile actually, more so than Baer's because Lovaas is not afraid to mention decelerating consequences. He was a little low on his references to contingencies. However, much of his work involves shaping, and shaping is almost always a one-to-one fixed ratio contingency. In Lovaas' discussion the audience only wanted to hear about punishment—responses, contingencies, and decelerating consequences! It appears that the audience asked the speakers about what they had heard about them prior to the lecture. Lovaas is gossiped about as an expert on decelerating consequences. They didn't ask him about what he said in his lecture. They didn't ask him about programs, stimuli, accelerating consequences, or inconsequation—all of which he referred to. They asked him only

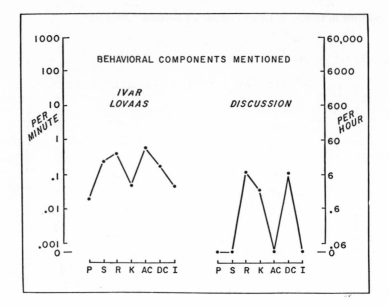

FIGURE 9.4 *Lovaas mentioned responses and accelerating con-sequences most frequently, but the discussion did not reflect this. The audience caricatured him as "Mr. Punishment."*

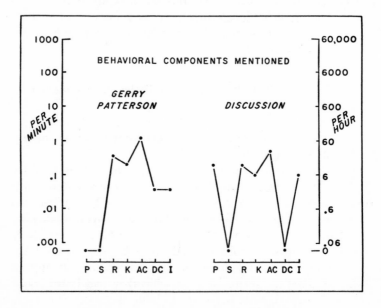

FIGURE 9.5 *Patterson mentioned decelerating consequences as often as inconsequation, but the audience ignored this.*

about decelerating consequences which he had mentioned only .2 times per minute. They failed to ask him about accelerating consequences which he mentioned over .6 times per minute—three times as often as decelerating consequences! In such ways are caricatures maintained and straw-men built! Ivar, please ignore them and go your own way!

Figure 9.5 analyzes Gerry Patterson's lecture. On the lecture chart Gerry holds his own. He is very good at this new form of publication, oral presentation.[2] He talked mostly about responses, contingencies, and consequences, all at rates above .2 per minute. He did not mention programming or stimuli. He was more or less traditionally free-operant in his point of view except for mentioning decelerating consequences as often as inconsequation. The traditional free-operant man would not mention decelerating consequences.

Patterson's audience ignored his reference to decelerating consequences and curiously queried him about programs which he did not mention at all.

Israel Goldiamond's presentation was next. I thought Goldiamond made one of the best presentations. Figure 9.6 reveals that he delivered

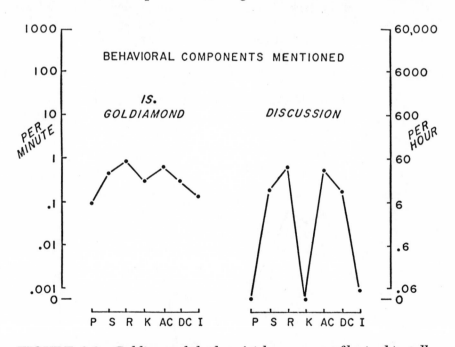

FIGURE 9.6 *Goldiamond had a fairly even profile in his talk, However, the discussion concentrated on stimuli (S), responses (R), accelerating (AC), and decelerating (DC) consequences. The discussion ignored programs (P), contingencies (K), and inconsequation (I).*

about the most even or complete operant profile of all the speakers. He mentioned programs about once every 10 minutes and responses about once a minute. However, the reactions to Goldiamond involved no questions on programming, none on contingencies, and none on inconsequation. So here again, the audience narrows and caricatures an even and complete free-operant presentation.

Figure 9.7 represents Ted Ayllon's speech and its discussion. He mentioned all five components but referred to the traditional free-operant trinity of response (R), contingency (K) and accelerating consequence (AC) from 10 to 100 times as often as the other components. His discussion was representative of this profile, though depressed in rate.

Figure 9.8 shows Jack Michael's speech and discussion rates of mentioning free-operant components. Jack mentioned all components except programs at high rates between 0.1 and 1.0 per minute. Michael's discussion was somewhat aborted because the session lasted a little too long. When Michael and Goldiamond started a private discussion, the audience began to leave. The moment they turned to talk to each other, 10 people stood up. Jack Michael noticed them leaving and terminated before he was completely finished. This indicates that both the speaker and the audience each had control over the other.

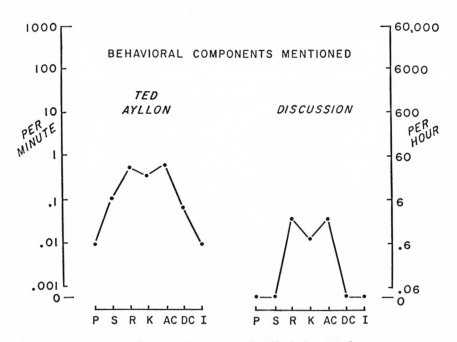

FIGURE 9.7   *Ayllon's talk covered all behavioral components, but the discussion caricatured him as a traditional R-K-AC mid-'50s type of operant conditioner.*

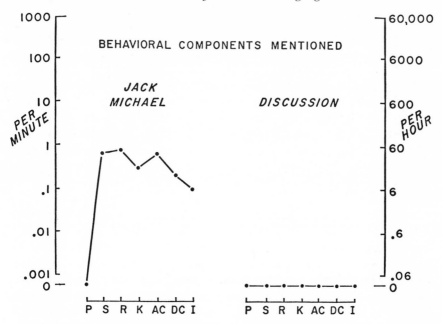

FIGURE 9.8   *Michael's talk was fairly even except for no programming references, but the discussion was interrupted by a private conversation.*

Figure 9.9 contains the component mentioned rates for Roger
Ulrich's presentation. Roger discussed all free-operant components from
.04 to over 2.0 per minute. He mentioned stimuli more often than contingencies which is certainly not following the traditional "R-K-C" party
line! The audience was remarkably faithful to his presentation in its
discussion as it questioned at a somewhat lower component rate, but
along a very similar profile.

Figure 9.10 presents Fred Kanfer's lecture profile. This again shows
a remarkably eclectic profile for a free-operant type. However, his highest mentioning rates were for responses and accelerating consequences.
His discussion faithfully follows his lecture profile but is exaggerated as
the audience fails to mention contingencies (K) or inconsequation (I).

In figure 9.11 the component mentioning rate profiles for Malcolm
Kushner's lecture and its discussion are presented. Here again we see
an exaggeration of the lecture in its discussion except for one slight
change where the discussion covers decelerating consequences at a
higher rate than did the lecture. It looks like they are trying to make
him into a "punishment man" along with Lovaas.

In Figure 9.12, I have presented my own component rates for this
presentation and its subsequent discussion. This obviously was inserted

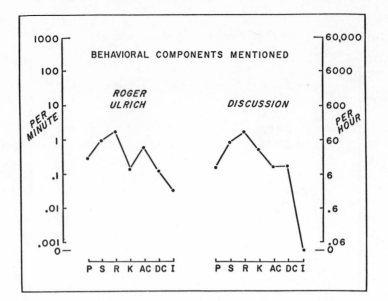

FIGURE 9.9   *Ulrich's presentation was fairly well balanced with more stress on stimuli and responses than the other components. The discussion ignored his references to inconsequation.*

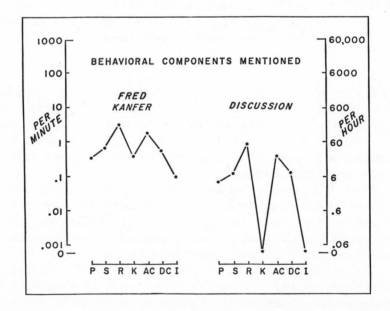

FIGURE 9.10   *Kanfer presented a well balanced lecture, but the audience again exaggerated his small rate differences into a caricature with no references to contingencies or inconsequation.*

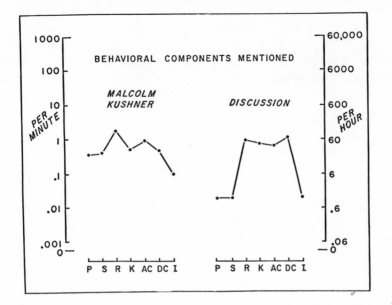

FIGURE 9.11　*Kushner's lecture and its discussion were both fairly well balanced presentations of all behavioral components. Again, though, the audience exaggerated the small rate differences in the presentation.*

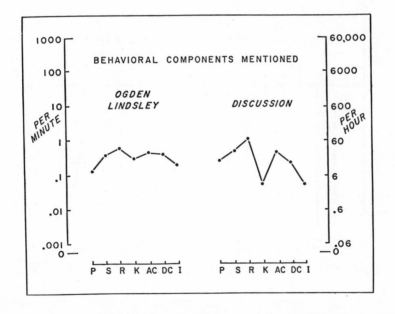

FIGURE 9.12　*Lindsley's presentation and its discussion covered all behavioral components at moderately high rates, but the audience's tendency to exaggerate small differences is still seen in the discussion profile.*

after the talk and was not part of the original audio-tape recording. Here again all components are mentioned at rates between .1 and .6 per minute and the discussion is an exaggeration or caricature of the lecture profile.

SUMMARY OF COMPONENTS COVERED BY ENTIRE SYMPOSIUM

Figure 9.13 is a summary of all ten presentations in the symposium. The median mentioning rates for each component are connected to reveal a "symposium profile." The ranges are drawn in as vertical lines. In a way, the generalists, the historians, and the textbook writers are right. We are, as a group, strong on statements about responses (.7 per minute), contingencies (.3 per minute), and accelerating consequences (.7 per minute). However, we mentioned stimuli at a higher rate (.4 per minute) than we did contingencies. This is quite remarkable when

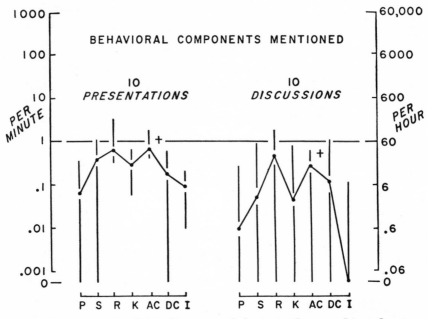

FIGURE 9.13   *Medians (connected dots on the graph) and ranges (the vertical lines) of the mentioning rates for all seven behavioral components by the ten symposiasts. The tendency for the audience to exaggerate the small rate differences from the presentations in their discussion questions shows up here even in the grouped (medians) rates.*

you consider our claim to fame is that we are world's experts on contingencies—yet we talk about stimuli just as often!

It seems clear to me that Behavior Modification and free-operant conditioning will stay strong as long as most of us continue to pay attention to all components of the operant reflex. I feel that the strongest and most creative behavior modifiers are those whose lecture profiles include all operant behavioral components.

RANKING OF DELIVERY AND CONTENT

Since I had become involved in analyzing part of these results after the actual presentation of this paper in order to include my own performance rates, we thought it best to have members of the audience rank each participant in both quality of delivery and quality of content. Ten members of the audience representing three university departments did the ranking. None of those ranking had been involved in recording the performance rates, nor were they being advised by either Baer or Lindsley, the two University of Kansas members of the symposium. The delivery rankings and the content rankings are highly correlated with a correlation coefficient of $+.80$ and a probability that this would happen by chance of less than .00004. The median rankings for each participant on both delivery and content are almost exactly the same except for one inversion. Figure 9.14 presents the median rankings of each participant for both delivery and content.

COMPARISON OF DELIVERY RATE
AND STYLE WITH RANKING

In addition to recording the rates of mentioning the different behavioral components, other graduate students recorded the rate of laughs produced in the audience, the rate of presenting slides and other visual aids, and the total frequency of mentioning major points for each participant. It was hoped that the rate of mentioning major points would indicate the speed of covering content or "pacing" of each lecture. The audience laugh rate should indicate how humorous or "entertaining" the lecturer was. The slide presentation rate would record the use of visuals.

Figure 9.15 presents these three movement rates for each participant. The participants are ranked on the basis of the overall rank of the lecture taken from Figure 9.14.[3] It is clear that the highest ranked presentation tended to cover major points at the lowest rates. The poorer ranked lecturers tried to cover close to ten points per minute! Whereas, the more highly ranked speakers didn't cover more than two points per minute.

The more highly ranked lecturers produced higher laugh rates in the audience. The laugh rates varied from one every hundred minutes to one a minute—a frequency range of over 100 times. Note that the top four ranked participants, ranked top in both delivery and content, produced the highest audience laugh rates—all above .5 per minute! Although this may seem a very high rate of laughter, it is from 4 to 10 times slower than the laughter produced by professional entertainers. Harold Ensley, a local Kansas City sports fisherman, and Johnny Carson of the "Tonight Show" and national TV fame both regularly produce around 4.0 laughs per minute in their monologues. Interestingly enough, both are outproduced by Joan Rivers, a professional gag writer turned entertainer, who guffaws an audience at the rate of 8 laughs per minute! No one knows what the ideal or maximum laugh rate is for a professor, but we are now in a position to find out with precise recording of rates.

The slide presentation rates show that it is not necessary to use visual aids to deliver a highly ranked lecture, nor to get high laugh rates (neither Baer nor Patterson used any). However, it does appear that, if slides are used, the more highly ranked lecturers use them at higher rates than do the lower ranked lecturers.

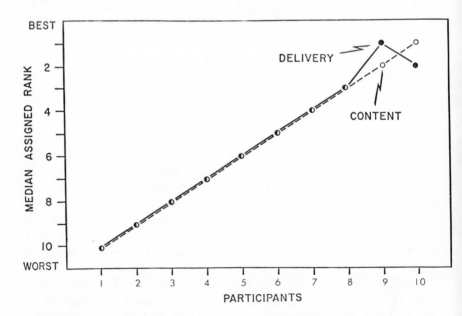

FIGURE 9.14   *Median ranks assigned for both delivery and content are identical except for one inversion.*

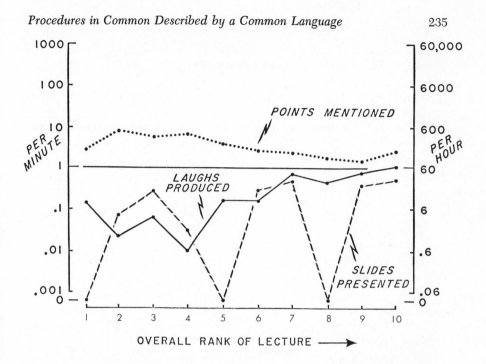

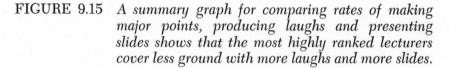

FIGURE 9.15 *A summary graph for comparing rates of making major points, producing laughs and presenting slides shows that the most highly ranked lecturers cover less ground with more laughs and more slides.*

In summary then, if one rates the rates of rate specialists presenting their rates, the most highly rated make two points, a half a slide, and a laugh per minute!

NOTES

1. Wiseman, A. E. Personal Communication, Cairo, July, 1944.
2. If lectures are oral, what are printed publications?
3. This concluded my experimental summary of the symposium. The remainder of the time allotted to me at the symposium was spent in reporting twelve sample modification projects. These projects have been reported elsewhere on film and in print, and things are moving so fast that I am sure most readers will have conducted modification projects of their own every bit as good. So, why add bulk to an article that has already made its point? (See Lindsley, 1968.)

REFERENCES

Ferster, C. B., & Skinner, B. F. *Schedules of reinforcement*. New York: Appleton-Century-Crofts, 1957.

Lindsley, O. R. Training parents and teachers to precisely manage children's behavior. In *Special education* colloquium. Flint, Mich.: C. S. Mott Foundation, 1968.

10: The Institute: Some Missing Papers and a Dominant Theme

JACK C. MICHAEL

The collection of papers that comprises this book is the outgrowth of the University of Kansas Ninth Annual Institute for Research in Clinical Psychology. There were several reports made at the Institute however that are not represented by the papers that appear in this volume. Three of the Institute's consultants did not contribute papers because they had just completed or were preparing reviews summarizing their work which were already committed to other publication sources. In what follows there is a brief description of the contributions of these three men and also the suggestion of an important theme which seemed to permeate much of the Institute's proceedings.

Dr. Teodoro Ayllon described several examples of his work with the chronic psychotic adult patient. His presentation at the Institute included reference to some of the work done at Saskatchewan State Hospital in Canada and also some of the more recent work at Anna State Hospital in Illinois. Ayllon began his behavior modification career in 1959 at Saskatchewan State Hospital where he took an approach which seems to have been a highly significant one. By the middle 1950s a number of clinical and experimental psychologists, with an operant conditioning orientation, had begun to extend their laboratory concepts and procedures to applied areas. The general behavioristic optimism regarding man's (even schizophrenic man's) modifiability was a part of the behavioral literature of that period. With respect to the psychotic patient this approach consists in the view that such patients differ from the normal individual only in the specifics of their behavioral repertoire. All that is needed to make them more normal is to strengthen the effective aspects of their repertoire and to eliminate those behaviors that cause difficulty. This general notion is straightforward but the necessary technology was certainly lacking in 1959. The chronic psychotic patient, often having been hospitalized for many years, had a repertoire that was defective in many ways. It was hard to know where to begin. Which good behavior should one reinforce first, and which bad behavior should be eliminated? Another difficulty concerned the means of recording one's progress. Still another problem was the fact that often the behavioral difficulty, which led to the patient's hospitalization, only occurs outside of the hospital environment. From the viewpoint of the variables controlling the behavior modifier's behavior, this area was not seen to be very reinforcing. Work with a grossly defective repertoire is not likely to lead to the ultimate release of the patient for years, if ever, and since this was the usual criterion of successful treatment it was hard to be enthusiastic about any changes that one might bring about.

However, in addition to being grossly ineffective in many ways, the hospitalized chronic psychotic patient often shows behavior problems which originated within the hospital setting. These ward behavior problems, of concern only to the staff responsible for the daily care of the patients (usually nurses and aides), are interpreted by psychologists and psychiatrists as simply another manifestation of the individual's psychosis, but of minor significance. An example of a ward behavior problem is the patient who requires a great deal of help and encouragement to eat his daily meals. Another is the patient who "hides out" somewhere in the ward (e.g., in a bathroom) and does not generally participate in any ward activities. Another is the patient who persistently pesters the nurses with requests or questions. These are behaviors which are often known to be of hospital origin and relatively unrelated to the causes of hospitalization. Before Ayllon's work these behaviors were of little interest to anyone since it was obvious that even when such behaviors were altered the patient would still be psychotic and would still have to remain in the hospital.

From Ayllon's point of view, however, these ward behavior problems were especially interesting since they could often be characterized in behaviorally objective terms and, since their frequency of occurrence was sufficiently high, could be counted or quantified in some way. Ayllon's interest in these problems was also related to the view that the more socially significant behavior problems leading to the patient's hospitalization were not basically different from the behaviors that one sees on a chronic ward setting (i.e., Ayllon did not share the belief of many clinical psychologists that the person's psychotic behavior was the result of a underlying psychological disease process, and he did not share the view that in order to "cure" the patient one had to make contact with this disease process). He further felt that the psychosis of the patient was simply the concatenation of many behavior problems whose making and un-making one could observe in a ward setting. If he could develop a technique for observing and altering the ward behavior problem of the psychotic patient, it would constitute an effective demonstration of the susceptibility of such patients to behavioral control, and would constitute a beginning of a technology of prevention and cure. If the patient who "hides-out" in the bathroom can be easily induced, with the procedures of reinforcement, extinction, or punishment, to participate in more therapeutic ward activities then the same methods can be used to alter other aspects of the patient's behavior and his "defectiveness" can be overcome piece by piece.

Ayllon set about to collect examples of ward behavior problems and to develop techniques for recording and modifying such behaviors within the hospital setting. Many of these problem behaviors proved to be relatively easily modified, and the methodology became increasingly sophisticated and effective. Eventually it became clear, although perhaps he knew this all along, that whatever target behavior one chose, all that was needed to alter it was that it be objectively defined, recordable in some way, and that some behavioral consequence be systematically related to it. It eventually becomes obvious, however, that the piecemeal rebuilding of the defective repertoire of chronic psychotic patients was a very time-consuming procedure requiring considerable manpower. Ayllon, therefore, began to develop techniques that could be applied in a more wholesale manner and also automatically. He began to alter the entire ward in such a way that a small number of staff could maintain an environment that was in many respects "therapeutic." The main characteristic that such an environment must have is that the various reinforcers for the patients should be available only for approximations to a more appropriate behavior (again, a theoretically straightforward notion, but one whose details represent a considerable problem). The working out of these details constituted the next phase of this approach which he and his colleague, Nathan Azrin, accomplished at Anna State Hospital. This project has been recently described (1968) in detail and is of the greatest significance both for understanding and for altering the behavior of the psychotic patient as well as that of other institutionalized patients. In addition it is of great significance in the design of behaviorally effective environments whether they be with respect to psychotic, mentally retarded, criminal or other populations.

Ayllon's contribution to date, therefore, consists in the recognition of the ward behavior problem as a relatively easily studied prototype of maladjustment, the development of a technology for the analysis and modification of such behavior problems, and with his colleague, Azrin, the further development of environmental settings with behavioral features such as to alter the behavior of a large number of patients. Although all of this work has been carried out in the setting of the chronic psychotic ward, it has relevance for most institutional settings and has constituted a source of encouragement and guidance for many other psychologists.

Dr. Ivar Lovaas presented a somewhat historical survey of his work with autistic and schrizophrenic children. The autistic child differs from the normal child in lacking many important kinds of human behavior (e.g., effective communication skills), in having some very strong behaviors that prevent him from being dealt with normally by adults (e.g., self-injurious behavior), and also strong avoidence behaviors with respect to all forms of social contact. However, from Lovaas' behavioral point of view, confirmed by prolonged and careful studies of such children, they were clearly normal in several significant respects. In particular, their behavior could be strengthened by reinforcement and weakened by punishment. It could also be brought under control of complex patterns of stimuli by some form of discrimination training and some of these stimuli could function as acquired reinforcers. So there seemed to be no reason for not trying to train them to do some of the things that normal children do and thus help them toward normalcy. Again, all that was lacking was the technology, which Lovaas set about to develop.

It was obvious that the only effective initial reinforcers and punishers for most of such children were the unconditioned reinforcers and punishers (i.e., food, water, painful stimulation, etc.). When behavior was so strong that it interfered with educational efforts Lovaas arranged for such behavior to be followed by some form of painful stimulation, including electric shock delivered to the body surface. He found that he could reduce or completely eliminate self-injurious behavior by punishing it. More normal social behaviors could then be developed by shaping them with the use of a strong reinforcer. The reinforcer that was most useful, at least during early training of such children, was food after moderate food deprivation. In other words, Lovaas found and made effective use of strong punishing stimuli and strong reinforcers to develop new behavior repertoires in autistic children—a direct and straightforward application of behavior principles.

In his work with the intricacies of building speech his approach is correspondingly more complex and is best understood by contact with his own written description of his work (Lovaas, 1967). It seems that his direct application of behavioral principles to the control and training of the autistic child represents a very important contribution to the development of the behavior modification movement. When considered in the context of both the prevailing psychodynamic attempts to understand this most intransigent of child behavior disorders, and of the many failures to alter such disorders, Lovaas' approach is highly significant. His accomplishments certainly function as a powerful form of encouragement to behavior modifiers, and therefore maintain the optimism level associated with the behavioral approach to human problems. Behavior, no matter how bizarre, is behavior that can be explained, predicted, and controlled by the manipulation of environmental variables.

Israel Goldiamond described his early research with fluency and stuttering (1965) and some recent developments in the treatment of stutterers. Again this approach illustrates a direct application of behavioral procedures, particularly those involving the consequences of behavior, to a problem which has been the subject of much interpretation but has remained relatively resistant to treatment. Goldiamond's early work showed that fluency and stuttering were affected by reinforcement and punishment as are other forms of operant behavior, and could be manipulated by the use of such consequences. His subsequent use of delayed auditory feedback as a form of consequence and his manipulation of this variable to help develop normal speech patterns in stutterers, like Lovaas's work with speech, is quite complex in its details and is best described by Goldiamond himself (1965). But, again, his direct approach to a form of undesirable behavior, consisting in the manipulation of consequences to reduce this behavior represents a very significant contribution to behavior modification. It is especially important since it deals with adults who, with the exception of their speech defect, are normal and highly verbal. Some skeptics may be willing to grant the relevance of reinforcers and punishers to the behavior of autistic children, chronic hospitalized psychotics and other humans who seem "subhuman" in so many ways. The normal, often well educated adult stutterer, however, differs from other humans only in the possession of a very bothersome and inconvenient speech pattern. If this behavior can be controlled by such straightforward and direct applications of behavioral procedures then the domain of applicability of this technique seems to be very extensive.

It is this direct approach illustrated so well in the work of Ayllon, Lovaas and Goldiamond, which seems to be an essential feature of the modern behavior modification movement. The approach is based on an enthusiasm for the literal and direct application of behavior principles and procedures to the modification of any form of human behavior. It disregards the use of "learning theory" as a means of explaining various forms of abnormal behavior, as was quite popular in the 1940s and 1950s. This theme seemed to be very much a part of the Institute discussions and formal presentations.

REFERENCES

Ayllon, T. Azrin, N. H. *The token economy: A motivating system for therapy and rehabilitation.* New York: Appleton-Century-Crofts, 1968.

Goldiamond, I. Stuttering and fluency as manipulatable operant response classes. In L. Krasner & L. P. Ullmann, (Eds.), *Research in behavior modification*. New York: Holt, Rinehart and Winston, 1965.

Lovaas, O. I. A behavior therapy approach to the treatment of childhood schizophrenia. In J. Hill (Ed.), *Minnesota symposium on child psychology*, Minneapolis: University of Minnesota Press, 1967.

Appendix

A Case for the
Selective Reinforcement
of Punishment

DONALD M. BAER

Dr. Kushner has presented us with some intriguing examples of a relatively new technique applicable to clinical problems. He has been able to show good results with this technique. He has also cited similar recent work by other researchers in the field, much of which showed similar results. He has pointed to an extensive area of earlier research with animals using analogous techniques, out of which this human application was derived. Finally, he has been able to show that both the animal experiments and the recent human applications can be related to a common body of theory concerning the behavior of organisms in general.

By the usual standards of science, there ought to be delight and applause throughout the relevant clinical and research communities. Consider: a problem area of human suffering has been attacked, by bringing new ideas to it from what might be a closely related area of knowledge. The attack has proceeded in a responsible manner, first by repeated and intensive experimentation with laboratory animals; then, following promising results in that effort, by cautious applications to human cases typically not responding well to standard methods of treatment. The human applications have often been made in hospital settings under the scrutiny of concerned professionals, and when necessary have sacrificed good experimental design to the interests of the patient's best welfare. All of that, I suggest, is the essence of good and responsible science devoted to man's benefit. Had the technique in question been a vaccination to immunize us from cancer, there would indeed have been delight and applause. The delight would have been tempered by our standard scientific uneasiness about using a technique not yet completely understood, but that would simply have led to further research efforts in all relevant directions, and the applause, I think, would have been undiminished.

In this particular case, I wonder whether there will be that sort of celebration throughout the relevant communities, or whether uneasiness will be the prepotent response. Preliminary sorts of observations over the last few years suggest the latter to me. This case is different because the name of the technique is not *vaccination* but *punishment*.

Punishment is something that we may think we know a lot about, and none of it good. My own field of specialization is child development. In that field, I am repeatedly jarred by statements of the form, "We know that punishing a child is worse than ineffective . . ." We know? My students are being taught that we *know* what we can demonstrate. They are probably happy with Dr. Kushner's report, because it is full of demonstrations and references to demonstrations with rather good consistency in what they show. I hope that my students are also uneasy about not possessing a complete understanding of punishment and its total effect on human behavior. However, their squirming should mean only that they wish I would be quiet soon so that they can politely return to the lab and try to answer some of the unanswered questions by demonstrations of their own. I mean to humor them in this ambition; I have only a few points to make here, and they are essentially moralistic rather than scientific points. Moralistic points are typically brief, perhaps because they require no experimental design.

I have suggested that we know what we can demonstrate. I have also suggested that we *think* we know that punishment is inherently a bad technique for accomplishing desirable behavioral changes. But Dr. Kushner's demonstrations and the others that he cites suggest the opposite: Punishment may be a very desirable technique indeed for accomplishing certain behavioral changes. If there is a moral point here, it is the one familiar to all scientists and practitioners alike: we had better get what we know in line with what we can demonstrate. That leads in a very straightforward way to a deduction: We had better continue a careful and extensive study of the punishment of human behavior. But if I read the feeling of the field correctly, there will be objections to continuing these demonstrations, as there have been objections in the past, and are today. It will be a shame if, consequently, the demonstrations are not pursued as extensively as our current curiosity and ignorance press us to do.

It will be even more of a shame if objections to such research on punishment are intrinsically confused in their own moral stance. Suppose, for example, that I show you a child, institutionalized as a retardate, who has over the years developed a very successful attention-compelling behavior—self-destruction. Suppose that in this case, the child pulls persistently at his ear and has finally come to the point where, if he is unrestrained, he will in fact literally rip it from his head. He has, let us say, half succeeded in this venture already. As a result, he wears a straightjacket throughout the hours of his existence, and he is so heavily tranquilized that he lies in a semi-stupor gazing vacantly at the ceiling. I suggest that he was taught this performance. He was reinforced for ear-tugging rather than for other, more desirable behaviors, because his caretakers were busy and could ignore acceptable behavior more easily than self-destructive behavior. Successively in their busy lives, they became used to his current self-destructive behavior, so that only when it was more self-destructive than usual would they consider that they must do something. Thereby, they reinforced intense self-destruction rather than mild self-destruction. Had they designed a shaping program to instruct the child in his own destruction, they could hardly have proceeded better. Note the systematic care with which they taught him to endure greater and greater pain in return for a few seconds of their attention. Note that they used some of the cheapest reinforcers available to them: a little glancing at the child, a modest amount of vocal noise, and some brief laying on of hands. A moral onlooker to this process, if he understood it as such, might understandably display anger and indignation. Do we institutionalize our retarded children so that they may be taught, as cheaply as possible, to approach their own self-destruction; and do we then frustrate them on the brink of accomplishment in favor of the living death of 24-hour-per-day restraints or the half-living death of 24-hour-per-day stupor?

Certainly not by design. Yet it is strange how often it works to the same outcome, design or no design. No doubt we may escape the onlooker's moral indignation by pointing out that we meant well, and that we had no idea that response differentiation could be accomplished that easily with so simple a stimulus as human attentiveness, even in settings where attentiveness is rare. We may even point out that the whole indictment is, after all, only a hypothesis. (This last point is in fact a strong one, because the hypothesis is unlikely ever to be proven directly. I am unaware of any behavior therapist who would shape a child to pull his ear off his head, just to prove how easily it could be done by social influence in an institutional setting.)

However, we may not so easily escape the next moral trap. That is the one which becomes possible when our behavior therapist colleagues appear, apparatus in hand. They note the existence of self-destroyers in our institution, and wonder if they might not end that horror with some carefully applied aversive faradic controls. Some of us will be very interested until we discover that they mean electric shock. If we refuse *because* they mean electric shock, then I suggest that we have fallen thoroughly into the moral trap. In our professional wisdom, we have assigned people to institutional life, allowed them to be taught their own self-destruction, and confined them to a small hell in consequence. Can we now refuse that they endure a small number of painful episodes over a short span of sessions, hopefully designed to let them live the rest of their lives awake and untied?

My example is extreme. However, the behavior therapist is knocking at doors other than those of the institutions, and he is asking about behaviors other than those that are clearly self-destructive. Nevertheless, the moral formula (as best I can discern with training only in psychology) is much the same in any case. Is not a small number of brief painful experiences a reasonable exchange for escape from a life indefinitely distorted by durable maladjustment? It seems to me that this question changes only a little in its meaning, even when the form of maladjustment varies from the grave problems of self-destruction, drug addiction, and alcoholism to such quirks as excessive blinking. As many as twenty shocks over a few sessions may be greatly preferred to a lifetime of social handicap brought about by the fact that people think you look absurd blinking away like that—especially when they find themselves beginning to blink, too, and decide to keep away from you.

Am I arguing that a better life is an end which justifies a means to that end even as immoral as punishment? Clinical practice is too complicated, I believe, to allow even that simple formula to apply. *Not to rescue a person from an unhappy organization of his behavior is to punish him, in that it leaves him in a state of recurrent punishment.* The punishment may not be faradic, but apparently it hurts nonetheless. When the seventy-seventh girl that you have met starts edging away, staring strangely as you blink furiously on to new achievements in rate, then I think that in your misery you may ask your therapist some pressing questions. Among these should be the following:

1. Why won't you shock those blinks out of me? People hurt me when I blink at them; they do it every day and have done so for years; and either I turn into a hermit or they will keep hurting me the rest of my life.

2. All right, you're going to do it with positive methods instead. How long will it take?

3. All right, you're going after the real dynamics, not just the symptoms. How long will it take?

That question, *How long will it take?* is the morally critical question, in my opinion. For as time goes by while the therapist tries his hopefully more benevolent or more basic methods, the patient still undergoes punishment while he waits for a good outcome. In effect, the therapist has assigned the patient to a punishment condition from which he might have long since removed him. This robs that therapist of any *moral* superiority over another therapist who will assign the patient to shock punishment so that he may escape from social punishment. The basic questions would seem to be, which punishment is tougher, and which lasts longer? We have merely a bookkeeping problem here, not a moral one.

Is it really true that the therapist might have removed the patient from a socially punishing condition, by shocking his blinks out of him in a few brief sessions? Dr. Kushner's studies, and those of others, suggest that it may very well be true, at least sometimes. If we object to the study of punishment in humans, however, we will not find out much more about it. In particular, we will not find out when it is likely to work well and when it is not, and consequently we will be unable to do our bookkeeping. That is tantamount to saying that we will not find out when the process of therapy could be less punishing than it often is, because we object to research on punishment. More specifically, we would be saying that we will not find out how to make therapy less *socially* punishing than it often is, because we object to research on *shock* punishment.

One of the delights of moralistic argument, I am discovering, is the ease with which it can be extended in all direction. Let me now warn us all *against* punishment.

Punishment works, I submit. There is too much affirmative, careful demonstration to resist that conclusion. Consequently, punishers should succeed often in eliminating the behavior they mean to eliminate. That may reinforce them, which is to say, their rate of using punishment in the future, and in more diverse situations, will rise. Contributing to that tendency is the extreme simplicity of punishment technique and technology. Anyone with a hand to swing is equipped with a punishing device. The Sears-Roebuck farm catalog lists a number of inexpensive and reliable cattle prods. Furthermore, the punishment contingency is the essence of simplicity, compared to which positive reinforcement and its allied art of shaping looms as a formidable mystery indeed. Thus, it is possible that punishment could become the first and, woefully, the exclusive behavioral technique some carelessly trained persons might use. That would indeed be a tragic outcome. For one thing, punishment is painful, and the essence of my argument (and of everyone else's) is that we should have as little pain as we can. Thus, we want to use as little punishment as we can, not as much. To find out how to use one form of punishment so as to minimize other forms of punishment, and what the exchange relationships can be, we will have to study punishment; to study, we will have to use it. But to use punishment successfully is to subject oneself to an environmental event which may press one to use it again, and more than necessary. That, we shall have to watch with great care.

Furthermore, to apply punishment to another is to become discriminative for that punishment, very likely. Stimuli which are discriminative for punishment but for nothing else can acquire a punishing function themselves. If the person who applies punishment becomes himself a punishing stimulus for another, he should expect all the relevant behaviors: escape, avoidance, and removal with respect to that stimulus. One way to remove a social stimulus is to murder it. Clearly, anyone using punishment should look to his total stimulus function with great care. This care is very apparent in Kushner's studies, and even more apparent in those of Ivar Lovaas. Very limited punishment is combined with extensive positive reinforcement of other behaviors. In Lovaas' work particularly, positive reinforcement programs surpass "extensive" and approach "monumental." Probably, it is difficult to err in that direction.

Finally, it should be remembered that punishment is most effective as a behavior-removing technique. Some of the problems of clinical practice are exactly that, but they are typically combined with more extensive problems of behavior building (if a good and thorough outcome is to be achieved). Punishment is not an efficient technique of behavior building. In principle, it can be used. One can specify a behavior to be acquired, and punish all response other than that. The behavior may indeed by built up, but very often it will be acquired slowly, while the subject learns that whoever is programming the punishment would be a good stimulus to be rid of.

The fact that behavior which escapes punishment will increase is important to the design of punishment studies. If the therapist places himself in the position of programming punishment for the patient until the patient reports improvement, then the therapist should always consider that he may have conducted verbal conditioning rather than a therapeutic change in the patient's more critical behaviors. As long as the patient can avoid further punishment sessions simply by remarking that he no longer is impotent, or afraid of crowds, or depressed, or smoking, it remains possible that he will do just that—and only that. A considerable number of therapy studies seem to rely upon the patient's verbal report of his condition as the sole measurement of that condition. Verbal behavior responds to reinforcement, punishment, and extinction contingencies just as do other operant behaviors. The fact that the content of that verbal behavior appears to be a description of other behaviors does not remove it from sensitivity to such contingencies. This truism applies to any therapeutic technique, of course, but it may well have special urgency in punishment techniques.

In summary, then, it must be clear that I have not recommended punishment either as a way of life or as a way of psychotherapy. It is a technique of sharply limited applicability in the processes of behavioral change, but, as Kushner, Lovaas, and others show us, its applicability is well above zero, and its benefits may be great. To find out more thoroughly the extent to which this is true, we shall have to use punishment experimentally and carefully—but we shall have to use it. For it may be the case that we are now forcing some patients to endure much greater punishment than necessary, simply by declining to apply a smaller amount of punishment to them systematically and therapeutically.

Name Index

Numbers appearing after each entry in the name index refer to the person being mentioned in the text and references. Where the person referred to in an entry is the author of one or more chapters in this volume, the inclusive page numbers appear.

Subject Index